"Poetry, literature, visual art and deep theological thinking collide here! What better way to think about what it means to be made in God's image, and what it means to bear God's image, to a world beset with so many false images? Students, pastors and theologians alike will find here a meaty conversation and, better yet, an invitation to bear God's image well."

Jana M. Bennett, University of Dayton

"This is a fecund collection of essays on theological anthropology. In it one can find treatments of the image of God from biblical, systematic and constructive theology, but one can also find essays that reflect on the imaging of God in the arts: in poetry and in literary criticism. Here too there is reflection on our witness to the divine image in a culture of commodification and a world where the color of one's skin has displaced the divine image in which we are all created. These explorations of the doctrine of the image of God offer readers a rich and satisfying smorgasbord of essays and art that repay careful reading and reflection."

Oliver D. Crisp, Fuller Theological Seminary

"Bringing together art, literature and theology, these essays are a prism of Christian reflection on what is perhaps the most urgent question of our time: What does it mean to be a human being created in the image of God?"

Timothy George, Beeson Divinity School, general editor of the Reformation Commentary on Scripture

THE IMAGE OF GOD IN AN IMAGE DRIVEN AGE

EXPLORATIONS IN THEOLOGICAL ANTHROPOLOGY

EDITED BY BETH FELKER JONES
AND JEFFREY W. BARBEAU

An imprint of InterVarsity Press
Downers Grove, Illinois

InterVarsity Press
P.O. Box 1400, Downers Grove, IL 60515-1426
ivpress.com
email@ivpress.com

InterVarsity Press® is the book-publishing division of InterVarsity Christian Fellowship/USA®, a movement of students and faculty active on campus at hundreds of universities, colleges and schools of nursing in the United States of America, and a member movement of the International Fellowship of Evangelical Students. For information about local and regional activities, visit intervarsity.org.

Cover design: Cindy Kiple
Interior design: Beth McGill
Images: Cover sculpture and photo by David J. P. Hooker

ISBN 978-0-8308-5120-1 (print)
ISBN 978-0-8308-9960-9 (digital)

Printed in the United States of America ∞

Library of Congress Cataloging-in-Publication Data
Names: Jones, Beth Felker, 1976- editor. | Barbeau, Jeffrey W., editor.
Title: The image of God in an image driven age : explorations in theological
  anthropology / edited by Beth Felker Jones and Jeffrey W. Barbeau.
Description: Downers Grove : InterVarsity Press, 2016. | Includes index.
Identifiers: LCCN 2015050899 (print) | LCCN 2016000095 (ebook) | ISBN
  9780830851201 (pbk. : alk. paper) | ISBN 9780830899609 (eBook)
Subjects: LCSH: Theological anthropology—Christianity. | Image of God.
Classification: LCC BT701.3 .I44 2016 (print) | LCC BT701.3 (ebook) | DDC
  233/.5—dc23
LC record available at http://lccn.loc.gov/2015050899

P 25 24 23 22 21 20 19 18 17 16 15 14 13 12 11 10 9 8 7 6 5 4 3 2 1

Y 37 36 35 34 33 32 31 30 29 28 27 26 25 24 23 22 21 20 19 18 17 16

Dedicated to the Wheaton College Art Department

CONTENTS

ACKNOWLEDGMENTS

This book is the result of the twenty-fourth annual Wheaton Theology Conference, and organizing such an event—and editing the subsequent book—is no small feat. We're grateful to the many people who made it possible. We are especially thankful for the contribution of our friend and colleague Brett Foster, whose work will continue to remind us what it means to live as bearers of the divine image. Enormous thanks are due to Paula Anderson and Judi Nychay, whose tireless work on behalf of our department is much appreciated. Thanks are also due to Jeffrey Bingham, to our colleagues in the Biblical and Theological Studies Department, and to Hannah Considine and Chris Smith, whose work on the index made this book possible. Thanks to the team at InterVarsity Press, especially Bob Fryling and David Congdon. We're thankful for all the contributors to this volume, who together made this an extraordinary conference and valuable book.

The volume is dedicated to the Art Department at Wheaton College. These colleagues graciously collaborated with us on this project, and we have been blessed to learn from and with them. We're grateful for their faithful witness to the God whose image they bear.

INTRODUCTION

Beth Felker Jones and Jeffrey W. Barbeau

"Image," so the saying goes, "is everything." Look in any magazine, turn on the nearest television, or open an app on any smartphone: images abound. Colors, words, pictures, videos and advertisements reveal a world of intricate complexity, unveil sights from the farthest corners of the world and the outer reaches of space and give humanity shared access to what could once only be imagined. Public images are constructed through symbols of power or representations of beauty. Visual images in film or photography memorialize decisive moments in history—moments of celebration and discovery no less than those of war and famine—and shape our collective interpretation of major events. Individually, too, memories indelibly shape our sense of self in relationship with others. The mind's eye stores images that together construct the narrative of a life: a memory of a parent, an instant of tragedy, a moment of romantic love, a mental snapshot of the newborn child.

   Still, for all the ways that images help to shape our understanding of the self and the world in which we live, images often lead us astray and distort our relationships. Christians confess that humans have been created in the image of the living God, yet human beings chose to rebel against that God and so became unfaithful bearers of God's image. In the beginning, as John Wesley reflects, "Love filled the whole expansion of [the human] soul; it possessed him without a rival. Every moment of his heart was love: it knew no other fervor."[1] But the warmth that once vitalized the whole person was cast aside. Under the condition of sin, humans are still image-bearers, but the image of God is not as it should be. It is distorted, twisted, broken. We recognize that Adam's sin and fall has become our own: "The evil in me was foul," Augustine declares, "but I loved it."[2]

---

[1]John Wesley, "The Image of God," in *Works*, vol. 4, *Sermons IV*, ed. Albert C. Outler (Nashville: Abingdon, 1987), 294.
[2]Augustine, *Confessions* (London: Penguin, 1961), 47 (II.4).

Part of the good news of the gospel of Jesus Christ is that Jesus, who is the image of God, restores the divine image in us, partially now and fully in that day to come when "this perishable body puts on imperishability, and this mortal body puts on immortality" (1 Cor 15:54). Paul contrasts human beginnings with the human future, Adam with Jesus: "The first man was from the earth, a man of dust; the second man is from heaven" (1 Cor 15:47). Paul makes it clear that, just as we have shared in Adam's fallen image, we are meant to share in all that belongs to Christ: "Just as we have borne the image of the man of dust, we will also bear the image of the man of heaven" (1 Cor 15:49). The image on the cover of this book might lead us to meditate on this seemingly unfathomable promise. The cover shows a photograph of sculptor David Hooker's *Corpus*, in which he has covered a crucifix in literal dust, including the skin cells and the hair of those who "have borne the image of the man of dust." Jesus Christ shares all that is ours, including our mortality, so that we may share all that is his.

Beginning with the conviction that the doctrine of the image of God (often written using the Latin *imago Dei*) offers truth and health in a culture inundated with images, we invited Christian scholars from a variety of backgrounds to speak to these questions: How, in our time and place, might our understanding of what it means to be created in the divine image be challenged or distorted? In dealing with this situation, what corrective and constructive resources are available in the Christian faith? How can the Christian doctrine of the image of God inform and strengthen Christian witness in this image-driven age?

Too often the temptation is to respond to such questions in a negative tone. There is much about the present image-driven age that concerns Christians, and it would have been too easy to spend all the words of this volume articulating what wrongs have distorted this world. We need, of course, to tell the truth about the world's brokenness, and the essays in this volume do careful work in diagnosing our present disorder, but we are happy to report that the overall project avoids wallowing in the negative. In all cases, these essays also point to the hope and healing that are real in Jesus Christ, and they offer positive direction for witnessing to the goodness of God.

The Image of God in an Image Driven Age: Explorations in Theological Anthropology thereby offers a unified collection of essays—ecumenical in nature and catholic in spirit—exploring what it means to be truly human and created in the divine image in the world today. We have designed the volume for the use of a variety of audiences, including theologians who wish to learn from the conversation among colleagues recorded here as well as pastors and other church and parachurch workers who are interested in faithful witness. It also remains accessible for students who are learning about Christian doctrine in general and the doctrine of the human person in particular—the "theological anthropology" of the subtitle. No essay in this volume is a standard introduction to theological anthropology, but students who have a chance to read the whole will find something even more interesting: a variety of voices engaging with the heart of the Christian understanding of what it means to be human and conversing with one another and with the greater Christian tradition.

Introductions to theological anthropology usually claim that there are three primary ways in which theologians think about the image of God: image can be conceived as (1) something *substantial*—usually rationality—about the human being, (2) something about the *function*—usually as representatives of God the king—that humans are meant to fill within creation or (3) something about the way humans are mean to *relate* to God and one another, including the moral dimension of those relationships.[3] This is a helpful teaching tool, though it can be reductive. In this volume, though, students will find theologians actually entering into this conversation. Some of the authors prefer one of these three primary views; others prefer none or some combination thereof. For example, Catherine McDowell argues for a functional understanding of the image, though one transformed deeply by thinking about kinship. Craig Blomberg provides a New Testament theology of the image that strongly favors the moral and relational. Janet Soskice critiques, but in some ways adopts, a substantive account of the image, helping us to associate the centrality of language with what it means to be human and showing that speech is also inherently relational. No artificial unanimity has been imposed on the authors or their essays. Readers will see differences and areas of overlap between these arguments and will, ideally, return to the biblical texts that all this

---

[3]For such an introduction, see chapter 5, "Reflecting God's Image: Theological Anthropology," in Beth Felker Jones, *Practicing Christian Doctrine: An Introduction to Thinking and Living Theologically* (Grand Rapids: Baker Academic, 2014).

volume's authors are reading as they seek to better understand the doctrine of the *imago Dei*. Moreover, while there is much variety among these essays and difference of opinion about what constitutes the image of God in the human being, there is also a deep unity holding them together. The authors, though they come from different traditions within the body of Christ, are all committed to Scripture and to doing theology for the good of the people of God.

The Image of God in an Image Driven Age collects contributions from the twenty-fourth annual Wheaton Theology Conference, held at Wheaton College in Illinois and cosponsored by the college's Biblical and Theological Studies Department and InterVarsity Press. The conference flourished in the college's liberal arts context, and we were privileged to work in partnership with the Art Department. Speakers—now authors in this volume—included scholars from English and art history as well as from biblical and theological studies. Conference attendees viewed a series of six short theological films by Joonhee Park. Those films showed art faculty in the process of creating, of making images. "Marsh" focuses on painter Joel Sheesley in his careful attention to creation. "Messages," featuring Park's own work (though he does not appear on screen), looks at the despair that can overwhelm bearers of God's image in a fallen world. "Sweep" centers on David Hooker's performance art about the Underground Railroad, and "Witness" focuses on community art led by Leah Samuelson. "Passage" shows Jeremy Botts working on an art installation in and for his local church. Finally, "Stations" explores Greg Schreck's photographs representing the global church. We hope readers will access Park's films online and reflect on them in association with the essays here.[4] Additionally, two poems were written for and read at the conference and are printed in this volume. Jill Peláez Baumgaertner writes of a child in the image of God in "Zola, *Imago Dei*, on Her First Birthday," and the late Brett Foster's "Whiteout" explores the image subject to mortality, "compromised and glorious." In these films and poems, a theology of the image is worked out in wonderful ways as words and images unite.

The essays in *The Image of God in an Image Driven Age* are organized around four central themes of Christian faith and practice: canon, culture, vision and witness. In the first group of essays, the authors explore major biblical themes

---

[4]These videos are posted on the "Wheaton Art" YouTube channel, www.youtube.com/channel /UCD7X9wNCwuplMi1ISd-AHzQ.

related to the divine image and contribute to contemporary understanding of image-bearing today. The first chapter is an Old Testament theology of the image of God. Catherine McDowell ("'In the Image of God He Created Them': How Genesis 1:26-27 Defines the Divine-Human Relationship and Why It Matters") focuses on the first and most familiar *imago Dei* passage in Scripture, the Genesis proclamation that God created human beings in the divine image and likeness. She explains how understanding the context in which Genesis was written helps us to see something we might otherwise have missed: ancient kings set up images of themselves as reminders of their rule, and humans in God's image can be seen "as living 'statuettes' representing God and his rule." McDowell deepens this understanding, showing that Scripture also portrays humans as God's kin. In God's image, we are representatives of the divine, but we are also God's children. For McDowell, this means the doctrine of the image is about relationship and bears directly on ethics.

William A. Dyrness invokes the full arc of the biblical story in chapter two ("Poised Between Life and Death: The *Imago Dei* After Eden"). Dyrness offers a fresh reading of Genesis 1–3, showing the fecundity and goodness of original creation alongside the story of creation gone "tragically wrong" when Adam and Eve sinned. Gently chiding his own Protestant tradition, Dyrness reminds readers not to forget the goodness of creation in the image and the "trajectory of life," even as the temptation to idolatry, which leads to a "trajectory of death," persists. Human beings are imaginative creatures, in Dyrness's view— creatures who need to imagine the future of God's new creation. For this reason, he draws out interpersonal and environmental implications of that new creation for cultural renewal in the world today.

In chapter three, Craig L. Blomberg's essay ("'True Righteousness and Holiness': The Image of God in the New Testament") provides a careful analysis of theological anthropology in New Testament perspective. Blomberg meticulously examines various New Testament texts in order to better assess what it means to be created in the image of God. He considers all the Pauline texts related to the *imago* and argues that, for Paul, to bear God's image is to be like Jesus (who is the image). To be an image-bearer is to be Christlike. Blomberg is thus not persuaded by Old Testament scholars who argue that the image is functional; he finds a moral explanation of the image in the New Testament. As image-bearers, we are to reflect God's glory, which means to live sanctified, godly lives. In this way, human living in the world should fore-shadow life in the world to come.

The second part of the book, "Culture," includes contributions that explore the relationship between image-bearing, theology and the arts. Timothy R. Gaines and Shawna Songer Gaines take up the relationship between the image of God and human sexuality in chapter four ("Uncovering Christ: Sexuality in the Image of the Invisible God"). Sexual sin can distort our understanding of what it means to image God, but these pastor-scholars set this distortion in a biblical context of divine desire. They maintain that a biblical perspective affirms that sexuality is a good gift from God and part of God's good, creative intentions for human beings. Through examples from popular culture and Renaissance art they reimagine ways that sexuality contributes to the construction of the self.

In chapter five ("Culture Breaking: In Praise of Iconoclasm"), Matthew J. Milliner recovers the Protestant and ecumenical heritage of iconoclasm as a resource for resisting twisted images in an image-driven world. He diagnoses the contemporary obsession with images in modern culture as a flood of idols, renewing the depravity of ancient Babylon. While the art world wants to offer resistance to consumer capitalism, Milliner reads this as a place of failed resistance and calls Christians to a vision of resistance through reformed iconoclasm. He interprets the works of Wheaton College artists as examples of the best kind of such an iconic posture and contends that "genuine . . . resistance arises from the sincerity of their Christian faith."

Moving from visual artists to literature, in chapter six ("Carrying the Fire, Bearing the Image: Theological Reflections on Cormac McCarthy's *The Road*") Christina Bieber Lake examines the novel *The Road* as an example of how fiction can probe the depths of human personhood and suffering. While *The Road* is a bleak, postapocalyptic novel, Lake believes that McCarthy subtly shows the persistence of the image of God through the darkness of despair, tragedy and utter hopelessness. While other scholars have argued that God is nowhere to be found in American fiction, Lake identifies allusions to the biblical story of Job and its "metaphysical questions regarding personhood and suffering" in the text. She argues that the novel's beauty is a response to "the goodness of human persons as made in the image of God" and thereby challenges readers to engage in close readings of contemporary literature.

The third part of the collection, "Vision," takes up the Christian idea of Christ as the icon of God. In chapter seven ("What Does It Mean to See Someone? Icons and Identity"), Ian A. McFarland considers how Western Christians can better understand the image of God through an Eastern Orthodox theology of the icon. He worries that Western interest in icons too often relegates them to mere decoration and neglects their profound theological meaning. Through a closer look at the christological basis of Orthodox iconography, McFarland shows how icons can train us to see people rightly, arguing "that seeing a person involves looking them in the *face* and acknowledging that a face belongs to a particular *someone*." Icons remind us that, whenever we see bodies, we encounter persons made in the image of God. In this way, icons point to an eschatological future while at the same time challenging both a materialism that would reduce persons to bodies only and a dualism that would devalue bodies as mere containers of spirit.

Icon theology is also central to chapter eight ("Image, Spirit and *Theosis*: Imaging God in an Image-Distorting World"), where Daniela C. Augustine writes of the Spirit's work in sanctifying image-bearing human beings. She calls readers to intercessory prayer as a way of "making time and space for the other." Augustine draws on the traditional Eastern Orthodox distinction between *image* as something humans have and *likeness* as something into which we must grow in the process of becoming like God. Augustine reads icons as she explores God's "unconditional hospitality" for creation and contrasts Babel, as a "conversational exclusion of others," with Pentecost: a place where language is healed for communion between God and humans, and even among humans.

In chapter nine ("The God of Creative Address: Creation, Christology and Ethics"), Janet Soskice focuses on Jesus the image as the Word made flesh—Jesus as the image of a God who speaks the world into being and makes humans, too, into creative speakers. For Soskice the image is not only visual but even connected to the Word. She finds purely rational explanations of the image of God inadequate: they tend toward a kind of gnosticism and have proved inadequate for ethics. Soskice suggests that the human capacity for speech—imaging the speaking God—is connected to rationality but also solves these problems. Speech is embodied and is a "social possession"; even those humans who do not speak are wrapped in a community of speech. In this way, Soskice calls readers to a deep, grace-filled optimism about the possibility that humans may, like Jesus, shine forth with God's image.

The final part of the volume, "Witness," considers faith in a world where Christian proclamation and practice are ways of witnessing to the triune God. Aware of the goodness of creation and the promise of new creation, these essays challenge readers to take a sober look at the effects of sin on our ability to understand the image of God while witnessing to truth about the God who created us in the divine image. In chapter ten ("The Sin of Racism: Racialization of the Image of God"), Soong-Chan Rah exposes racism as the usurping of "God's rightful position in creation." Rah explores assumptions of white superiority and white American exceptionalism and argues that the norm for being human has been found, not in God, but in whiteness. Rah demonstrates ways that the doctrine of the image of God has been damaged by racism, especially through two sobering stories: depictions of the city and an account of black evangelicals and evangelist Tom Skinner.

Beth Felker Jones's essay ("Witnessing in Freedom: Resisting Commodification of the Image"), chapter eleven, encourages readers to think about the image of God as serving the purpose of witness. She maintains that to be in the image of God is to "show and tell" the truth about God to the world. The essay explores the contemporary cultural problem of human commodification, and Jones argues that the Christian doctrine of the *imago Dei* offers resistance to commodification. Jones claims that humans are universally made in God's image, and this requires a valuing of the diversity of human beings. The essay uses an example from sexual ethics to help readers think about ways that Christians can witness against the reduction of persons to market commodities.

The same truth of the *imago Dei* that informs that witness—the universality of the human being as created in God's image—is also enormously influential in global Christianity, especially among marginalized groups of people. In chapter twelve ("The Storm of Images: The Image of God in Global Faith"), Philip Jenkins shows how faith is always contextualized. Jenkins looks at examples of faith crossing cultural borders and shows ways that contextual factors are taken up into mainstream theology. Jenkins, a scholar of new, growing, global Christianity, describes the translation and inculturation of the image of God in terms of localizing the divine image, Catholic feminine images of the divine as related to Mary, images tied to the power of the Spirit and images of hope that affirm the dignity of every human being. Jenkins writes of people around the world who have been treated as less than human finding "a revolutionary new notion of human dignity" in the universality of the *imago*.

In all, *The Image of God in an Image Driven Age* offers diverse perspectives on the relationship between humans and the divine, the world and the future. Drawing on biblical, theological and cultural resources, these authors reveal the central place of theological anthropology in contemporary reflection on Christian faith and practice. The authors speak from different social, ecclesial and political backgrounds, but each uncovers new resources for new patterns of reflection and life in the world. We pray that God might use this book to continue to shape his people into faithful witnesses, true bearers of the image of Christ to a world in need.

Zola, *Imago Dei*, on Her First Birthday

Jill Peláez Baumgaertner

The dust swirls, did it unfurl
this girl, God's deep yearning
for her, once clay,
now *imago dei*?

Reach back to Adam,
in Eden's first mud and mire,
shaped whole but not entire,
given blood and bone
but made alone
with all his intricacies of marrow
and joint, a narrow
cage around his heart,
dreaming Eve and then upending
Eden with sin's smart?

The image, we all know, was smudged.
Was it play? Adam would say,
"Let's put it this way:
I am Eve's father
and her brother and her mate,
the result of God's hunger to create,
a mélange of rib and earth and breath,
at first no death, just promises kept.
God's own. His face was mine.
Mine, his. Mine, hers. Hers, his.
But we ate. And then we wept."

So into this stunned world, Zola
burst, at first indignant
at the dazzling light
after the dark tones
of her mother's heartbeat.
Tiny knob of nose, grey eyes,
a fierce grip, this bright sprite,
her face her father's.
They form each other's image.
He says, "Let's put it this way.
I am her father. For life.
This was not play. I,
a donor egg, and IVF,
then Heidi's belly stretched
beyond belief. But there she was,
the relief of birth, of breath.
Her face was mine. Mine, hers."

This spring, amidst Lent's
dirty snow, the cross's
promise still ahead,
the buds in trees still
tightly wrapped, the year's
potential yet untapped,
the branches filigreed
against the sky, baroque
their arms and fingers
pronged and split,
like roots inverted,
Zola's birthday. She is one.

In her purity of gaze,
delight of play,
her belly laughs
at small dogs' pranks,
she is God's hunger
and his plan, her mother's
longing, her father's yen.

Yet she will know
sin's twilight and its night,
and through it all
though sometimes dim
the gospel light.
We pray she reaches
for this unbroken gleam,
this holy bauble,
as she does her father's arms,
her mother's face,
and safe from harm
there find at least the trace
of Eden, wiping the film
from the dark glass,
to see Christ's face,
enigma, ambiguity,
until he is revealed,
the cross, his grace—
the mirror, resilvered
by his glory,
he alone
making God known.

And Zola, once abstracted
in a Petri dish,
becomes herself,
born flawed,
but still the dream of God,
himself, his image.

WHITEOUT

Brett Foster

(1973–2015)

The nurse practitioner who substitutes
for my regular doctor (thanks to a holiday)
amazed us with her free way of speaking.
We marveled at what she so freely revealed,
compared with my circumspect oncologist.

I remember most of all her description
of a CT scan when it's bad or "dirty," how spots
of white infiltrate the body's imagized
inner spaces. "Sometimes there is so much
white that it just lights up the whole scan,"
she said. And so this visualized blizzard
covers the body's fields and highways,
its needed and contained organic landscape.
A whiteout without an ounce of repose,
"snow-crash," like a television's blank face.

Where do we go, or what do we do,
when this is what we know or is thought
through? There's nowhere to go, I suppose,
and one must wear the leaden heaviness
of that whiteness, must be willing to be led
to that particular nowhere and bearing.

This is just one of one million images
that besiege our lives, along with God-
made *imago* that frames us, in which we thrive
in our being and growing and going, yet sometimes
allowing our belittling. What do we consist of

finally? And what do we permit to represent
our depths? Eventually everyone must see,

must be, a complicated, compromising image,
all the more esteemed in complication, still glorious
in its gift existence, compromised and glorious.

Part One

CANON

1

"IN THE IMAGE OF GOD HE CREATED THEM"

How Genesis 1:26-27 Defines the Divine-Human Relationship and Why It Matters[1]

Catherine McDowell

INTRODUCTION

Genesis 1:26-27 has long generated a tremendous amount of lay and scholarly interest, and rightly so. Not only does it hold pride of place, with the rest of Genesis 1, as the introduction to the Bible, but it also describes the creation of the first humans in relation to God himself using the unexpected terms *image* (*ṣelem*) and *likeness* (*dəmût*):

> God said, "Let us create humanity[2] in our image, according to our likeness. Let them rule over the fish of the sea and the birds of the sky and over the beasts, and over all the earth, and over everything that creeps on the earth." So God created humanity[3] in his image. In the image of God he created them.[4] Male and female he created them. (author's translation)

---

[1]A version of this chapter appears in my book *The Image of God in the Garden of Eden: The Creation of Humanity in Genesis 2:5–3:24 in Light of the mīs pî pīt pî and wpt-r Rituals of Mesopotamia and Ancient Egypt* (Winona Lake, IN: Eisenbrauns, 2015).

[2]The Hebrew noun is *ʾādām*. In this context, it refers to humanity as a whole, as indicated by the plural verb *wəyirdû* ("let them rule") and the reference to male and female in the following verse.

[3]Here, the noun is paired with the definite article (*hāʾādām*). This phrase refers specifically to *the* man Adam in Gen 2:7-8, 15-16, 18-23, 25, and Gen 3:8, 9, 12, 20, 22. However, it refers collectively to humanity (as opposed to the plant and animal orders) with singular verbs in Gen 6:1-2, 4. The same is true in Gen 6:5, where, presumably, both men and women had become increasingly wicked. Further, the possessive suffix in the phrase "his heart" (*libbō*) in Gen 6:5, as the ESV renders it, is grammatically masculine and singular because its antecedent, *hāʾādām*, is grammatically masculine and singular, not because "his" refers to the man Adam. The NIV attempts to make the meaning clear by translating the phrase as "the thoughts of the human heart," although this is a bit wordy in English.

[4]The object of the verb is the masculine singular pronoun *ʾōtô*, "him" or "it," because its antecedent, *hāʾādām*, is a third-person masculine singular noun. Here it refers, as does its antecedent, to human-

What the terms *image* and *likeness* mean has been debated for centuries. In this chapter I will suggest that to be created in God's image is to be God's kin, specifically, "son," with all the responsibilities and privileges sonship entails. I will then examine how Israel's status as "created in the image" was embodied in the law and what this can teach us about bearing the image of God in our world today.

INTERPRETATIONS OF GENESIS 1[5]

The dominant view throughout the history of interpretation has been that these terms refer to a spiritual or mental similarity to God with which humans were endowed at creation. One early proponent of this view is the first-century Jewish philosopher Philo of Alexandria. Philo argued that because God is a spiritual, nonmaterial being, to be created in his image and according to his likeness *must* refer to an immaterial, spiritual correspondence. This was the prevailing view during the first two centuries of the church. It continued in popularity with Augustine, who claimed that human likeness to God consists in human memory, intelligence (or understanding) and will, all of which are necessary for knowing, understanding and loving God.[6]

Martin Luther agreed. He concluded, "When Moses says that man was created also in the similitude of God, he indicates that man is not only like God in this respect that he has the ability to reason, or an intellect, and a will, but also that he has a likeness of God, that is, a will and intellect by which he understands God and by which he desires what God desires."[7]

---

ity as a whole. The ESV translates the object pronoun as "him." This may be faithful to the grammar (unless "it" is intended—see below), but can be misleading in terms of meaning. The NIV and NRSV opt for the plural object pronoun "them." This captures accurately the sense of the Hebrew but does not convey the underlying masculine singular Hebrew pronoun. We could translate the second part of Gen 1:27, "In the image of God he created *it*," where "it" refers to the singular *hāʾādām* (humanity) earlier in the verse. This preserves both the Hebrew grammar *and* its meaning, but it is a bit awkward in English. I choose to follow the NIV and NRSV for grammatical reasons: *hāʾādām* in 1:27a is a collective; therefore its object pronoun is best rendered in English as a plural.

[5]What follows is only a cursory introduction to some of the major interpretations of *image* and *likeness* in Gen 1:26-27. For a summary of the history of interpretation of this passage, see Gunnlaugur A. Jónsson, *The Image of God: Genesis 1:26-28 in a Century of Old Testament Research*, trans. Lorraine Svendsen (Lund: Almqvist and Wiksell, 1988); Claus Westermann, *Genesis 1-11: A Continental Commentary* (Minneapolis: Fortress Press, 1994), 147-58; and Edward Curtis, "Man as the Image of God in Genesis in Light of Ancient Near Eastern Parallels" (PhD diss., University of Pennsylvania, 1984), 1-60.

[6]Augustine, *The Trinity* 10.12, as quoted in Jónsson, *Image of God*, 13n21.

[7]Martin Luther, *Luther's Works, Vol. 1: Lectures on Genesis: Chapters 1-5*, ed. Jaroslav Pelikan,

This was also a common understanding among German scholars during the late nineteenth and early twentieth centuries. August Dillmann argued that because God is spirit, image and likeness simply could not refer to a corporeal resemblance. The likeness, he inferred, must consist in humanity's mental capacity and desire for the eternal, true and good.[8] Samuel Rolles Driver agreed, claiming that the image of and likeness to God was manifest in the human ability to reason and to comprehend moral and religious truth.[9] Although there are many nuanced views within the broader category of a nonmaterialistic interpretation of the *imago*, it has been and remains the most popular category for explaining image and likeness in Genesis 1:26-27.

There is much to commend this interpretation. Although God has appeared in anthropomorphic form, both in theophanies and visions of the Old Testament and in Christ himself (Col 1:5; 2 Cor 4:4), many argue that the incorporeality of God is implied by the fact that God exists as Spirit (Gen 1:2; Num 24:2; 1 Sam 10:10; 19:20; Ezek 11:24; Mt 3:16; Rom 8:9; 1 Cor 2:11), by prohibitions against image making (Ex 20:4; Deut 5:8), by direct references to divine formlessness (Deut 4:12, 15; Jn 5:37) and, perhaps most overtly, by John 4:24 ("God is spirit").[10] I argue, however, that God's spiritual nature does not preclude divine self-revelation in other forms. While commands in Exodus 20:4 and Deuteronomy 5:8 forbid the creation of idols, they do not claim that God has no form. Similarly, Deuteronomy 4:12, 15 (compare Jn 5:37) states that Israel saw no form of God at Horeb, not that God is formless. Finally, the statement in John 4:24 does not mean that God is manifest only as Spirit. As noted above, the incarnation belies this conclusion. And while it is true that human beings are endowed with godly qualities and capacities and with gifts of reason, these should be understood as *results* of being created in God's image and likeness rather than as *definitions* of the terms. In sum, I suspect the

---

Hilton C. Oswald and Helmut T. Lehmann (St. Louis: Concordia, 1999), 337, as quoted in Nathan Jastram, "Man as Male and Female: Created in the Image of God," *Concordia Theological Quarterly* 68 (2004): 12-13. However, Luther also understood the image of God to have a physical dimension. He believed that prelapsarian humanity was physically superior, having sharper eyesight and greater strength. The *imago*, according to Luther, referred to humanity's original righteousness, which was lost at the fall. Post-fall, humanity bears the image of sinful Adam.

[8]August Dillmann, *Genesis Critically and Exegetically Expounded* (Edinburgh: T&T Clark, 1897), 1:81-82.

[9]Samuel Rolles Driver, *The Book of Genesis* (London: Methuen, 1907), 32.

[10]I am not suggesting that Jn 4:24 defines God in his metaphysical being, only that this verse has been used, rightly or wrongly, to do so.

nonmaterial interpretations of image and likeness have more to do with Philo and Greek philosophy than with Genesis 1 and the biblical and ancient Near Eastern contexts, which are crucial for understanding these terms.

Despite the popularity of nonmaterial views of image and likeness, the idea that God has a form, and that the human body resembles it, is a prominent idea in rabbinic theology. The premier work on the subject remains Arthur Marmorstein's *Essays in Anthropomorphism* (1927), in which Marmorstein credits the followers of Rabbi Akiva and their literal reading of the biblical text with the development of an anthropomorphic understanding of God.[11] The argument, in short, is that God has a body because the Bible says so. At many points in the Old Testament, God is described in anthropomorphic terms: he redeems Israel with his outstretched arm (Ex 6:6), he smells the pleasing aroma of a sacrifice (Gen 8:21), his eyes run to and fro throughout the earth (2 Chron 16:9), the cry of the afflicted reaches his ears (Ps 22:24; Job 34:28), and so on. Further, the Old Testament reports theophanies in which God appears in human form. Ezekiel describes the Ancient of Days as having "a likeness with a human appearance" (Ezek 1:26 ESV). Daniel refers to God's clothing, the hair of his head and his being seated on a throne (Dan 7:9). In Daniel 7:13, the prophet describes the glorified Christ, ruler of God's kingdom, as "one like a son of man"—that is, with a human form.

Building on the idea that image and likeness refer to corporeality, Nöldeke relates the Hebrew term *image* (*ṣelem*) to its Arabic cognate (*ṣalama*), which means "to cut" or "to cut off" in reference to sculpture. He concludes that *image* in Genesis 1 thus refers to physical representation. This idea seems to be supported by Genesis 5:3, where Adam's fathering of Seth in his own likeness and after his image is analogous to God's creation of humanity in God's likeness (*dəmût*).[12] The German form critic Hermann Gunkel commented,

---

[11]Arthur Marmorstein, *The Old Rabbinic Doctrine of God*, vol. 2, in *Essays in Anthropomorphism* (New York: Ktav, 1968), 1-157, esp. 9, 32-35, 37, 56, 71. On the body of God see Meir Bar-Ilan, "The Hand of God: A Chapter in Rabbinic Anthropomorphism," in *Rashi 1040–1990: Hommage a Ephraim E. Urbach*, ed. G. Sed-Rajna (Paris: CERF, 1993); Alon G. Gottstein, "The Body as Image of God in Rabbinic Literature," *Harvard Theological Review* 87 (1994): 171-95. On precise measurements of God's divine body see Martin S. Cohen, *The Shi'ur qomah: Liturgy and Theurgy in Pre-Kabbalistic Jewish Mysticism* (Lanham, MD: University Press of America, 1983), and *The Shi'ur qomah: Texts and Recensions* (Tübingen: Mohr, 1985).

[12]T. Nöldeke, "ṣelem und ṣalmawet," *Zeitschrift für die Alttestamentliche Wissenschaft* 17 (1897): 183-87.

"God created Adam in his image; Adam begot Seth in his image. The second statement is very clear: *the son looks like the father; he resembles him in form and appearance. The first statement is to be interpreted accordingly: the first human resembles God in form and appearance."*[13]

This material interpretation of image and likeness may seem far-fetched to those of us accustomed to thinking of God only in spiritual terms. Is not anthropomorphic language applied to God simply a poetic way of rendering, within the limits of human language, an indescribable reality? Can we reasonably conclude from these texts that God has a physical form? The proponents of the material view are right, however, to insist that we interpret Genesis 1:26-27 in light of Genesis 5:1-3. Image and likeness in Genesis 5 must have something to do with these same terms in Genesis 1. The primary weakness of the material view is that it interprets the terms too narrowly. Indeed, image and likeness can refer to physical similarity, but they are not limited to it.

A third view is that of interpreting image and likeness in terms of relationship. The Swiss theologian Karl Barth perhaps best represents this idea.[14] This view notices that, when contrasted with the animals, humans are unique in their capacity to relate and respond to God, and, unlike the animals, they can enter into a covenant relationship with God. Two features of the creation account define this relationship. The first is the plural in Genesis 1:26, "Let us make," which Barth—following many others before him—interprets as a reference to the triune plurality of the one God. The second feature is the creation of humanity in two distinct genders (Gen 1:27). In being created male and female, humanity is both plural and differentiated and thus reflects relationship within the godhead.[15] In short, according to Barth, image in Genesis 1 does not refer to qualities or characteristics; neither is it about physical form. Rather, it consists in the "analogy of relation": the relationship between male and female is in some way analogous to the relationship among the persons of the Trinity.[16]

---

[13]Hermann Gunkel, *Genesis* (Macon, GA: Mercer University Press, 1997), 113 (my emphasis). However, he did not fully exclude the notion that the likeness includes a spiritual component (113).

[14]Karl Barth, *Church Dogmatics*, ed. G. W. Bromiley and T. F. Torrance (Edinburgh: T&T Clark, 1958), III/1, 182-206; hereafter cited as *CD* III/1. See also F. Horst, "Face to Face: The Biblical Doctrine of the Image of God," *Interpretation* 4 (1950): 259-70.

[15]See *CD* III/1, 197; see also Jónsson, *Image of God*, 72-73.

[16]C. Westermann also understood image and likeness to refer to the divine-human relationship. He comments, "The uniqueness of human beings consists in their being God's *counterparts*. The relationship

One strength of this view is that it recognizes the relational component that
the terms *image* and *likeness* imply. However, it falls short in that it fails to
ground its case *in the text* and within its biblical and ancient Near Eastern
contexts. The result is that implications (i.e., an intimate relationship that
humans enjoy with God but that animals do not) are mistaken for meaning.

A fourth and final view of the image is that of the "royal representative." In
1915, Johannes Hehn published an article explaining image and likeness in
Genesis 1 in light of Babylonian and Egyptian parallels, which defined the king
as the image of the god.[17] He concluded that, like their Babylonian and
Egyptian counterparts, these terms in Genesis are royal designations for humanity—that is, human beings are God's royal representatives on the earth.
Hehn's work and the work of those who have developed his ideas[18] have had
a powerful influence in *imago Dei* studies. This view now prevails among biblical scholars,[19] although regrettably it does not seem to have made its way into
the church in any significant measure.

The strength of the "royal representative" view is that it seeks to interpret
the terms in their ancient Near Eastern context. I suggest, however, that this
is another case of mistaking implication for meaning. Humanity's royal status
is, rather, derived from its identity as defined by image and likeness—that is,
humans are endowed with royal status *because* they are created in the image
and according to the likeness of God. Thus, while understanding these terms
in their ancient Near Eastern context was certainly an interpretive break-
through, the royal status and representative function result from—rather than
define—the image of God. The primary question of what it means that humanity is created in God's image remains unanswered.

---

to God is not something which is added to human existence; humans are created in such a way that *their
very existence* is intended to be their relationship to God" (*Genesis*, 156, my emphasis).

[17]J. Hehn, "Zum Terminus 'Bild Gottes,'" in *Festschrift Eduard Sachau zum siebzigsten Geburtstage*
(Berlin: G. Reimer, 1915), 36-52.

[18]G. von Rad, *Genesis: A Commentary* (Philadelphia: Westminster, 1972), 58; H. Wildberger, "Das
Abbild Gottes. Gen. I, 26-30," *Theologische Zeitschrift* 21 (1965): 255, 488; W. H. Schmidt, *Die
Schofungsgeschichte der Priesterschrift* (Neukirchen-Vluyn: Neukirchener-Verlag, 1964), and *The
Faith of the Old Testament: A History*, trans. John Sturdy (Philadelphia: Westminster, 1983), 194-
98.

[19]For example, D. J. A. Clines, "The Image of God in Man," *Tyndale Bulletin* 19 (1968): 53-103; and
Phyllis Bird, "'Male and Female He Created Them': Gen 1:27b in the Context of the Priestly Account of Creation," *Harvard Theological Review* 74 (1981): 129-59.

IMAGE AS CORRESPONDENCE, KIND AND KIN

Genesis 5:1-3. In Genesis 5, image and likeness express correspondence:[20]

This is the book of the generations of humanity. When God created humanity, he made it in the likeness of God.[21] Male and female he created them, and he blessed them and named them humanity when they were created. When Adam had lived 130 years, he fathered a son in his own likeness, after his image, and named him Seth. (Gen 5:1-3, author's translation)

Seth is in some way similar to his father, yet he is not Adam, just as Adam and Eve are like God in some way, yet they are not God. The author gives no explanation of what constitutes the likeness, but the plain reading of the text suggests that Seth resembles his father simply because his father begat him. By analogy, humans correspond to God because God creates them. Thus, this correspondence is intrinsic to the relationship between Creator and created.[22] When read in light of Genesis 1:26-27, to which Genesis 5:1-3 refers, the correspondence the author may have had in mind seems to be that of class. Seth is a human being, not a fish or a sheep, because his father is a human being. In short, to be created in Adam's likeness and according to his image means that Seth was created according to Adam's kind.

---

[20]This same pairing of terms appears in a bilingual Aramaic-Akkadian inscription on a statue of an Assyrian provincial official from the ninth century BC. The statue, found at Tell Fakhariyeh in Syria, is referred to in the Aramaic text as both "the likeness (*dmwtj*)" (line 1; "this likeness" [*dmwtj zjt*] in line 15) and "the image (*ṣlm*)" of Hadad-yis'i, the governor of Guzan. The Akkadian version renders both Aramaic terms with *ṣalmu*, suggesting, as many others have noted, that "image" and "likeness" may be synonyms, both here and in Gen 5:3. See A. R. Millard and P. Bordreuil, "A Statue from Syria with Assyrian and Aramaic Inscriptions," *Biblical Archaeologist* 45 (1982): 135-41; Randall W. Garr, "'Image' and 'Likeness' in the Inscription from Tell Fakhariyeh," *Israel Exploration Journal* 50 (2000): 227-34nn8-11.

[21]The traditional translation of this verse is, "This is the book of the generations of Adam. When God created him he made him in the likeness of God." This is certainly possible, and it may be the correct translation. However, is it equally possible, and perhaps more so given the context, that *'ādām* here refers to humanity as a whole? The object pronoun *'ōtô* would thus be rendered "it," referring to the human class. This seems to make better sense of Gen 5:1 in its context, especially in relation to the following verse (5:2) and Gen 1:26-27 (see footnote 4 above). Note that the ESV renders the first *'ādām* as "Adam," but the next *'ādām*, four words later, it translates as the collective "man," as it does again in v. 2. We must mention that all but one (Gen 10:1) of the other nearly identical genealogical notices in Genesis refer to the lineage of one person: Noah (Gen 6:9), Shem (11:10), Terah (11:27), Ishmael (25:12), Isaac (25:19), Esau (36:1, 9) and Jacob (37:2). However, even this does not preclude the translation of Gen 5:1 I have suggested, as the term *'ādām*, even when "humanity" rather than "Adam" is intended, is also a singular (albeit collective) noun. Thus if *'ādām* in Gen 5:1a refers to "humanity," it does not depart from the structure of the genealogical notice in Genesis.

[22]Westermann states that correspondence "is something given to humans by the very fact of existence" (*Genesis*, 356).

Genesis 9:5-6. In Genesis 9, the *imago Dei* appears as justification for the punishment of those who shed human blood:

> And for your lifeblood I will require a reckoning [demand an accounting]: from every beast I will require it. And from each human being I will require a reckoning for the life of another human being. Whoever sheds human blood, by humans shall their blood be shed, because in the image of God he [God] made humanity. (Gen 9:5-6 NIV, adapted)

The reason for requiring the life of the murderer is "because in the image of God he made humanity" (Gen 9:6), with "in the image of God" fronted for emphasis. What is it about the nature of humanity as created in God's image that requires the death of the murderer?

Genesis 9:6 states that when one pours out the blood of another, the Lord requires that the offender pay with his own lifeblood.[23] Second Chronicles 24 records one case in which this requirement is applied. As Zechariah the son of Jehoiada the priest dies, he cries out for the Lord to avenge his unjust death at the hand of the evil King Joash. God sends the Syrian army and even Joash's own servants to execute divine vengeance. Joash is killed "because of the shed blood of the son of Jehoiada the priest" (2 Chron 24:25, author's translation). Although God uses human agents, Zechariah understands that he is the divine avenger of Zechariah's blood, as revealed in his dying words: "May the LORD see and avenge!" (2 Chron 24:22). The psalmist ascribes this same role to God, proclaiming:

> Sing praises to the LORD, who sits enthroned in Zion!
>
> Tell among the peoples his deeds!
>
> For he who avenges shed blood [*dōrēš dāmîm*][24] is mindful of them; he does not forget the cry of the afflicted. (Ps 9:11-12 [Heb 9:12-13], author's translation)

To avenge a kinsman's blood was the role of the *gōʾēl*, often translated as "kinsman redeemer." The term is better rendered "to act as a kinsman,"[25] the

---

[23]Cf. Gen 42:22; Ezek 33:6, 10.

[24]The term for "blood" in Ps 9:13 is the plural *dāmîm*, referring to dispersed blood—that is, blood that has been shed, spilled or poured out. See Gen 4:10 and P. Joüon and T. Muraoka, *A Grammar of Biblical Hebrew* (Rome: Editrice Pontificio Istituto Biblico, 2006), §136b; Wilhelm Gesenius, E. Kautzsch and A. E. Cowley, *Gesenius' Hebrew Grammar* (Oxford: Clarendon, 1910), §124n; and B. K. Waltke and M. P. O'Connor, *An Introduction to Biblical Hebrew Syntax* (Winona Lake, IN: Eisenbrauns, 1990), 7.4.1b.

[25]Frank M. Cross, "Kinship and Covenant in Ancient Israel," in *From Epic to Canon: History and*

duties of which included not only defending and maintaining the welfare and rights of one's relatives but also avenging the blood of murdered family members (Num 35:19, 21, 24, 27; Deut 19:6, 12; Josh 20:3, 5, 9; 2 Sam 14:11). The specific title given to the avenger was "the *gō'ēl* of the blood" or "the kinsman of blood," usually rendered "the avenger of blood" in English Bibles. Nowhere in the Old Testament is God referred to explicitly with this title. However, Zechariah's cry for the Lord to "see and avenge" and the psalmist's identification of the Lord as the one who avenges shed blood indicate that God was understood as fulfilling this role.

What does this reveal about God's relationship to humanity? If God is indeed the divine blood avenger, then God is humanity's *nearest kin*. Human beings are members of God's clan and are therefore kin to one another. For this reason, shedding human blood is fratricide.[26] Furthermore, to murder one's kinsman is to slay a member of *God's* family. "One who touches you," says Zechariah, "touches the apple of [the Lord's] eye" (Zech 2:8). As the divine blood avenger, the Lord may rightly take the life of the offender, whether he does so directly through divine judgment or through an appointed human agent.

To summarize, in Genesis 5:1-3 *image* and *likeness* are terms that *classify*. Seth's being created in Adam's image and likeness identifies him as a human being. Seth is Adam's "kind." In Genesis 9:6, "kind" is also further specified as "kin." The Lord demands the life of a murderer because humans are made in God's image. Humans belong to God's family; and God, as the divine kinsman and therefore blood avenger, avenges their lives. How does this inform our understanding of image and likeness in Genesis 1?

Literature in Ancient Israel (Baltimore: Johns Hopkins University Press, 1998), 4.

[26]Gordon Wenham observes that Gen 9:5 "is the first time *'āḥ* 'brother' has been used since Gen 4, where the term is harped on to highlight the incongruity of Cain's action." He concludes, "*'āḥ* in Gen 9:5 is an allusion to Cain's murder of Abel" (Gordon J. Wenham, *Genesis 1–15* [Dallas: Word, 1998], 193). Kenneth Mathews also concludes that *'āḥ* in Gen 9:5 alludes to Cain's murder of Abel, and the reason he gives for the allusion is compelling: to demonstrate that "murder is fratricide by virtue of the inherent covenant all people have with God as created in his 'image.' We are to that fundamental degree all brothers and sisters in that we are all human" (Kenneth A. Mathews, *Genesis 1–11:26* [Nashville: Broadman & Holman, 1996], 404). Whether *'āḥ* in Gen 9:5 refers to brotherhood and/or kinship rather than a fixed idiom meaning "each human being" or "one another," I think we are on firmer ground to suggest that humanity is a family based on the phrase *baṣelem ĕlōhîm* in the following verse, Gen 9:6.

HUMANITY AS GOD'S "KIND"?

In Genesis 1:11-12, God creates vegetation, plants and fruit trees, all of which reproduce "each according to its/their kind." Three times in these two verses the phrase "according to its/their kind" is used to describe the correspondence between the plants and fruit trees that God created and the next generation of plants and fruit they produced. God also created the sea creatures and birds "according to their kinds" (Gen 1:21 ESV). He saw that it was good and commanded them to be fruitful and multiply in their respective domains.[27] God then made all the living creatures that inhabit the earth, each "according to its kind" (Gen 1:23-25), and saw that this, too, was good. In total, the phrase "according to its/their kind" is repeated ten times in these seven verses alone (Gen 1:11-12, 21-25).

Clearly, Genesis 1 emphasizes the creation and reproduction of each species according to its own distinctive type or class.[28] However, in the next two verses, the creation of the first human pair is not described as "according to its kind," as might be expected, but as "in the image of God." This juxtaposition of the repeated "according to its/their kind" with "in the image of God" suggests at least two things. First, Genesis 1 draws a sharp distinction between humanity (male and female) and the other created beings; second, just as the plants and animals were created according to their own type, humanity was made according to *God's kind*, metaphorically speaking. The author could have said this using the same words and grammatical construction (*lǝ + min*) as he did with the plants and animals, but he did not. Rather, he expressed human relationship to the divine using the terms *image* and *likeness*, terms that we know (Gen 5:1-3; 9:6) are *kinship* terms. Specifically, in Genesis 5:1-3 the terms denote the father-son relationship between Adam and Seth. Thus, it seems that to be created in the image of God is to be created as a "son" of God the Father.[29]

---

[27]The phrase "according to their kind" does not appear in Gen 1:22, but the implication is that the sea creatures and birds would respond to the command to be fruitful and multiply by reproducing according to their kind.

[28]See Ludwig Koehler and Walter Baumgartner, *Hebrew and Aramaic Lexicon of the Old Testament* (Leiden: Brill, 1995), 2:577; and G. Johannes Botterweck and Helmer Ringgren, *Theological Dictionary of the Old Testament* (Grand Rapids: Eerdmans, 1996), 8:289. To translate *lǝ + min* as "every kind," as the NRSV and NJPS do, misses the point that the plants and animals reproduce *within their own species*.

[29]This is not to say that humanity is in any way divine. Keep in mind that Genesis 1 is more liturgy

YAHWEH AS FATHER

The notion of God as father is well attested elsewhere in the Old Testament, where it denotes Yahweh's relationship to corporate Israel, referred to explicitly as Yahweh's child. In Deuteronomy 32:6, Yahweh is named as Israel's father who created, made and established them. Twice in Jeremiah Yahweh identifies himself as Israel's father (Jer 3:19; 31:9), and elsewhere Israel is described as Yahweh's firstborn son (Ex 4:22-23) whom he will carry, nurture and comfort (Is 66:12-13). Israel refers to Yahweh as father in Isaiah 63:16 and 64:7; in Malachi 2:10, God is identified both as Israel's father and as their creator,[30] indicating that Yahweh is deemed Israel's father because he created them.[31]

God is also identified as the father of the Israelite king. In 2 Samuel 7:14, God says in reference to Solomon, "I will be his father, and he will be my son" (NIV).[32] The psalmist goes further, using explicit birthing language to define the divine-royal relationship. Yahweh proclaims to the king, "You are my son; today I have begotten you" (Ps 2:7).

We must keep in mind, however, that humanity as a whole is nowhere explicitly described in the Old Testament as "God's son" or even "like God's son." However, the use of "image" and "likeness" to define the father-son relationship in Genesis 5:3, the comparison between the plants and animals as made "according to their kinds" and humanity made "in the image and according to the likeness of God" in Genesis 1:11-27, and the connection between the Israelite king as the son of God and humanity as God's appointed king over creation in Genesis 1 suggest that Genesis 1:26-27 may indeed define the divine-human

---

than genealogy (in contrast to Gen 5:1-3) and that, unlike Gen 5:1-3, it employs these terms *as a metaphor*. Further, this metaphor of sonship is not limited to males, as Gen 1:27 makes explicit. To describe the divine-human relationship in father-son terms is to employ a culturally significant metaphor; the weight of this metaphor would be lost if the text defined the woman separately as child or daughter. In other words, *in its ancient Near Eastern context the language of image and likeness implied sonship, and sonship entailed privilege and status that "child" or "daughter" did not*. By defining both male and female as created in the image and according to the likeness of God, and, hence, applying the metaphor of sonship to both male and female, Genesis 1 makes a most remarkable statement: *at creation, male and female shared equally in the status of "son" as it was defined in the biblical world.*

[30]See also Ps 27:10; 68:6; Prov 3:12.

[31]See also Hos 2:1; 11:1. This idea of divine parentage is also attested in Jer 2:26-28, where both the people and the leadership of Judah are condemned for considering other gods and goddesses as their parents.

[32]See also 1 Chron 28:6 and Ps 89:27-28.

relationship using the metaphor of father and son. The biblical evidence supports this theory, and it is reinforced by several extrabiblical references to the king as both the image and the son of the god.

IMAGE, LIKENESS AND SONSHIP IN THE ANCIENT NEAR EAST

The divine sonship of the king in the ancient Near East is an enormous topic. A few examples will suffice to demonstrate the link between image and likeness language and sonship: an ancient hymn about the Assyrian king Tukulti-Ninurta, a few lines from the Babylonian creation story known as *Enuma Elish*[33] and a Tenth Dynasty wisdom text from Egypt.

Beginning with Tukulti-Ninurta I (1243–1207 BC) the divine-royal relationship in Assyria was expressed in terms of statue manufacture and divine birth.[34] In the hymn from the Tukulti-Ninurta Epic, the king's body is likened to "the flesh of the gods," a phrase known elsewhere in the Assyrian Erra Myth as referring to the wood from which divine statues were made. He was "successfully engendered through/cast (*ši-pi-ik-šu*) into the channel of the womb of the gods" and, as a result, "He alone is the eternal image (*ṣalmu*) of Enlil," whom "Enlil raised . . . like a natural father, after his first-born son."[35] The combination of birthing and manufacturing imagery is striking. Not only is Tukulti-Ninurta's body likened to a divine statue, but the process of his creation is described both in terms of manufacture and procreation. Peter Machinist rightly concludes that here "image" identifies the physical body of the king with a divine statue.[36] However, in this context, "image" may have been intended as a double entendre, referring to the king both as a "living statue" of

---

[33]On the topic of divine sonship see Peter Machinist, "Kingship and Divinity in Imperial Assyria," in *Text, Artifact and Image: Revealing Ancient Israelite Religion*, ed. Gary Beckman and Theodore J. Lewis (Providence, RI: Brown Judaic Studies, 2006), 166-69; Jeffrey J. Niehaus, *Ancient Near Eastern Themes in Biblical Theology* (Grand Rapids: Kregel, 2008), 42-43; Ivam Engnell, *Studies in Divine Kingship in the Ancient Near East* (Uppsala: Almqvist & Wiksells Boktryckeri), 1945; and Scott Hahn, *Kinship by Covenant: A Canonical Approach to the Fulfillment of God's Saving Promises* (New Haven, CT: Yale University Press, 2009).

[34]Peter Machinist has demonstrated that these innovations were influenced by the royal theology of the Sumero-Babylonian south, where the idea of divine parentage and the king as the *ṣalmu* of the god is present in Sumerian hymns, royal inscriptions, rituals, personal names and legal texts ("The Epic of Tukulti Ninurta I: A Study in Middle Assyrian Literature" [PhD diss., Yale University, 1978], esp. 180-208).

[35]Text and translation from Machinist, "Kingship and Divinity," 160-61.

[36]Ibid., 163.

the god and also as Enlil's royal son.[37] Although the hymn avoids explicit deification of the king,[38] it certainly leaves the reader with the impression that
Tukulti-Ninurta I, unlike any other human being,[39] had a unique and special
relationship—which finds its closest analogy in sonship—with the god Enlil.[40]

The opening lines of the Babylonian creation story *Enuma Elish* reinforce
the idea that image and likeness terminology designated sonship. The account
begins with the creation of the primordial gods: Apsu and Tiamat beget
Lahmu, Lahamu, Anshar and Kishar. Anshar and Kishar then beget their
firstborn son, Anu, who is described as the likeness (*muššulu*)[41] of his father.[42]
The following line reads, "and Anu begot Nudimmud,[43] his image."[44] Both
examples define the father-son relationship in terms of image and likeness:
Anu is the *image* (*muššulu*) of his father Anshar, and Ea is the "likeness, effigy,
replica, image, resemblance, counterpart, or equivalent"[45] (*tamšilu*) of his
father, Anu. Although there are additional texts to which one could appeal, the
biblical and extrabiblical examples just noted are sufficient to demonstrate
that image and likeness language was indeed used in Mesopotamia to define
the relationship of a god to a royal or divine son.[46]

---

[37]Note, however, that the notion of the divine sonship of the king dates back to the late third mil-
lennium BC in the Babylonian south. See ibid., 163n38.

[38]His body is "reckoned with the flesh of the gods" but is not explicitly said to be made of divine
flesh. His name is written without the divine prefix (*dingir*), and Enlil is not *the* father but is described as "*like* (*ki-ma*) a natural father." Machinist makes these observations and concludes, "All
of these suggest, in sum, a certain hesitation on the part of Tukulti-Ninurta and his scribes as to
the full deification of kings that at least the late third and early second millennia of Babylonian
history offered. Evidently, the pull of a more conservative tradition . . . was still strong" (ibid.,
163-64).

[39]As Machinist notes, the language of divine sonship in Assyria was, with very rare exception, exclusively reserved for the king. See ibid., 168.

[40]The notion that the king was born of and/or nurtured by the gods originated in the Sumero-
Babylonian south and continued to appear in Assyrian royal texts long after Tukulti-Ninurta I's
death and in first-millennium BC royal texts from Babylonia. See ibid., 166-69.

[41]This term refers to likeness and, by extension, a mirror. It may mean "replica" and "representation";
see A. Leo Oppenheim and Erica Reiner, eds., *The Assyrian Dictionary of the Oriental Institute of
the University of Chicago* M² (Chicago: Oriental Institute, 1977), 281.

[42]Enuma Elish, Tablet I, line 15. See Philippe Talon, *The Standard Babylonian Creation Myth Enuma
Elish: Introduction, Cuneiform Text, Transliteration, and Sign List with a Translation and Glossary
in French* (Helsinki: The Neo-Assyrian Text Corpus Project, 2005), 33.

[43]Another name for Ea.

[44]Talon, *Standard Babylonian Creation Myth*, 33, line 16.

[45]*Chicago Assyrian Dictionary* T, 147-49.

[46]On the theme of the divine sonship of the king in Neo-Assyrian royal texts, see Machinist, "Kingship and Divinity," 166-69.

In a Tenth Dynasty wisdom text from Egypt, however, it is not the king but humanity that is defined both as the image and the offspring of the creator-god. The relevant portion of the text, known as "The Instructions for Merikare," reads:

> (Well) provided is humankind, the cattle of the god. It was for their sake that he made heaven and earth and repelled the "greed" of the waters. And it was so that their nostrils might live (breathe) that he made the winds. *They are his images which have come forth from his body,* and he shines in heaven for their sake. It is for them that he made plants, cattle, birds and fish (to) nourish them.[47]

While the term translated "images" (*snnw*) can refer to a statue, it also means "second,"[48] hence "likeness" and "image."[49] In this context, however, "images" denotes offspring.

The cumulative evidence from the early chapters of Genesis, the various biblical texts that identify God as the father of Israel and of the Israelite king, and the extrabiblical examples demonstrate that image and likeness terminology was indeed used in the ancient Near East to denote the relationship between father and son. Further, the Tukulti-Ninurta hymn shows that the terms could be used as a double entendre in which the relationship between god and king was framed both as royal image/statue and as son. I contend, as others have argued for different reasons, that this is how image and likeness are used in Genesis 1. Humanity is defined both as God's royal "son" and as living "statuettes" representing God and his rule in his macro-temple, the world. I have focused on the former because the connection between image and sonship has received far less attention in the commentaries and the secondary sources despite its fundamental importance for understanding what it means to be created in the image of God.

---

[47]The translation is from pages 131-32 in David Lorton, "God's Beneficient Creation: Coffin Texts Spell 1130, the Instructions for Merikare, and the Great Hymn to the Aton," *Studien zur Altägyptischen Kultur* 20 (1993): 125-55 (my emphasis). See also James Hoffmeier, "Some Thoughts on Genesis 1 & 2 and Egyptian Cosmology," *Journal of the Ancient Near Eastern Society* 15 (1983): 39-49, esp. 47. The text is published in L. Borchardt, *Allerhand Kleinigkeiten* (Leipzig: August Pries, 1933), 43-45, blatt 15; A. Volten, *Zwei altägyptische politische Schriften* (Copenhagen: Munksgaard, 1945); W. Helck, *Die Lehre fur König Merikare* (Wiesbaden, 1977); and J. F. Quack, *Studien zur Lehre für Merikare* (Wiesbaden, 1992).

[48]Hoffmeier, "Some Thoughts," 47. See also Adolf Erman and Hermann Grapow, *Wörterbuch der Aegyptischen Sprache* (Berlin: Akademie-Verlag, 1926–1961), 4:149. The Papyrus Carlsberg VI of Merikare dates to the New Kingdom (Eighteenth Dynasty).

[49]Raymond O. Faulkner, *A Concise Dictionary of Middle Egyptian* (Oxford: Griffith Institute, 1962), 232.

IMPLICATIONS: LIVING AS "SONS" OF GOD

One of the purposes of this volume is to consider ways that understanding the *imago Dei* can inform and strengthen our witness. Now that we have a clearer sense of what it means to be created in the image and according to the likeness of God, we will consider how Israel's sonship status manifested itself and what relevance this holds for the church today. Select laws from Leviticus 19 will serve as examples.

Israel's missionary calling included living as God's firstborn son before the nations. They were to be what Michael Goheen calls "a showcase people," whose very lives embodied their identity as images—that is, "sons"—of God:

> The nation of Israel was to be a display people, embodying in its communal life God's original creational intention and eschatological goal for humanity. He would come and dwell among them and give them his torah to direct their corporate life in his way. God's people were to be an attractive sign before all nations of what God had intended in the beginning, and of the goal toward which he was moving: the restoration of all creation and human life from the corruption of sin.[50]

In many English Bibles Leviticus 19 has a title like "Various Laws" (for example, NIV). At first glance, it does indeed seem to be a somewhat random collection of legal texts. However, the first two verses and the repetition of "I am the LORD" and "I am the LORD your God" (fifteen times in thirty-seven verses!) make it clear what binds these laws together: each of them highlights a particular manifestation of God's holiness that Israel was to imitate. In doing so, they were to be a living manifestation of God's original intention for humanity.

Israel was to live as God's royal sons and representatives before the watching eyes of the nations so that others would find a relationship with God irresistible (compare Zech 8:23). God's people were to live out their identity as image (that is, son and representative) not only through what we might consider the more obvious means—sacrifice, prayer, studying the Torah, abstaining from making and worshiping idols, observing religious feasts and festivals—but by the way they lived their lives, including how they dealt with money, how they treated their employees, how they conducted business and how they used their wealth to care for the poor. Their relationship with God

---

[50]Michael Goheen, *A Light to the Nations: The Missional Church and the Biblical Story* (Grand Rapids: Baker Academic, 2011), 25.

was to be conveyed through every aspect of Israel's life. Consider the following laws from Leviticus 19:

> You shall not keep for yourself the wages of a laborer until morning. (Lev 19:13)

> You shall not cheat in measuring length, weight, or quantity. You shall have honest balances, honest weights, an honest ephah, and an honest hin: I am the LORD your God, who brought you out of the land of Egypt. (Lev 19:35-36)

> When you reap the harvest of your land, you shall not reap to the very edges of your field, or gather the gleanings of your harvest. You shall not strip your vineyard bare, or gather the fallen grapes of your vineyard; you shall leave them for the poor and the alien: I am the LORD your God. (Lev 19:9-10)

Yahweh reveals himself in these laws. He cares for the worker who is to be treated with dignity by being paid in a timely fashion. He is also a God of truth and honesty. These qualities are to characterize his people in all spheres of life, including business. Israelites were not to defraud their customers through dishonest means of any kind.

The gleaning laws (Lev 19:9-10) display God's care for both the poor and the wealthy: "When you reap the harvest of your land, you shall not reap your field right up to its edge, neither shall you gather the gleanings after your harvest. And you shall not strip your vineyard bare, neither shall you gather the fallen grapes of your vineyard. You shall leave them for the poor and for the sojourner: I am the LORD your God" (ESV). Through their labor, the poor could provide for themselves and their families without having to beg. Further, these laws enabled the poor to participate in worship, as they would have something to offer God from their gleanings. Finally, these laws could prevent landowners from becoming greedy, self-sufficient, prideful and hardhearted. Leaving some of the produce behind was both a reminder of God's mercy and an expression of gratitude to God, the divine landowner, who had redeemed his people from slavery in Egypt, given them the land and provided for their sustenance. In short, Yahweh's original intent for creation, his redemptive plan and his eschatological vision for humanity was to be proclaimed not only through the written Torah but also through the Torah lived out.

Israel failed miserably at distinguishing herself from the nations. God's people spurned their sonship status, not only through the worship of foreign gods such as Baal and Asherah, but also by their idolatry of self. This was partially manifested in oppression of the poor and unjust business practices as reported by the prophet Amos, among others:

> For three sins of Israel, even for four, I will not relent. They sell the innocent for silver, and the needy for a pair of sandals. They trample on the heads of the poor as on the dust of the ground and deny justice to the oppressed. (Amos 2:6-7 NIV)

> Hear this word, you cows of Bashan on Mount Samaria, you women who oppress the poor and crush the needy and say to your husbands, "Bring us some drinks!" (Amos 4:1 NIV)

> You levy a straw tax on the poor and impose a tax on their grain. Therefore, though you have built stone mansions, you will not live in them; though you have planted lush vineyards, you will not drink their wine. For I know how many are your offenses and how great your sins. There are those who oppress the innocent and take bribes and deprive the poor of justice in the courts. (Amos 5:11-12 NIV)

> "When will the New Moon be over that we may sell grain, and the Sabbath be ended that we may market wheat?" Skimping on the measure, boosting the price and cheating with dishonest scales, buying the poor with silver and the needy for a pair of sandals, selling even the sweepings with the wheat. (Amos 8:5-6 NIV)

Long before Amos prophesied, in the days when the judges ruled, there was a man from the clan of Elimelek whose name was Boaz. Boaz is introduced in Ruth 2:1 as a *gibbôr ḥayil*, often translated "a worthy man" and understood to refer to a man of good repute. Although the story does prove Boaz to be a worthy man, this phrase more likely indicates (as the RSV, NASB and KJV translate it) that Boaz was rich! He was a wealthy landowner and businessman who adhered to God's covenant prescriptions as demonstrated in his treatment of Ruth and Naomi.[51] His compliance resulted in much-needed provision for those who gleaned in his fields. His obedience, during the days when there was no king in Israel and everyone did what was right in his own eyes, surely would have been a living testimony, an example of Torah lived out by one who was made "son" through redemption and covenant.

In Matthew 22:37-39, Jesus sums up the entire Old Testament law with two commands: "You shall love the Lord your God with all your heart, and with all your soul, and with all your mind" and "You shall love your neighbor as

---

[51]It is worth noting that in the case of Ruth, Boaz went well beyond what the Levitical law required.

yourself." Now, recall those "various laws" in Leviticus 19. Perhaps the title for that collection of laws should read instead, "How to love your neighbor" or "How to demonstrate the original creational intent and God's eschatological goal for humanity." Treating workers fairly and with dignity, abiding by honest business practices and showing mercy to the poor are not only acts of obedience but also manifestations of love—concrete examples of how the firstborn son was to love his divine father and reflect God to the nations, which would result in love and care for neighbor.

Like Boaz, we live in a time when everyone does what is right in his or her own eyes. Imagine companies, corporations, studios, public schools, law firms, real estate agencies, small businesses and artist communities inhabited by God's people who are living out a right understanding of their identity as images. Imagine a world in which people live as "sons of God," who faithfully represent him in the world. By so doing, they proclaim and demonstrate in every sphere of life God's original creational intent, his redemptive plan and his eschatological goal for humanity. This was Israel's mission, and it is ours, for the sake of the world.

2

POISED BETWEEN LIFE AND DEATH

The Imago Dei *After Eden*

William A. Dyrness

INTRODUCTION

To reflect on the image of God in light of the events of Genesis 3 is also to ask what it might mean to reflect God in twenty-first-century America. This is the two-part goal of this chapter. To be more specific, I want to ask how we could possibly image the triune God in a broken world. How can we image God in light of issues of resource depletion and climate change on one hand and the racial concerns associated with recent events in Ferguson, Missouri, on the other? As I ask these questions, I am struck by the way contemporary culture conspires to distract us from these urgent concerns of how to care for our planet and for each other.

Advertisers are anxious to find ways for us to feel good about ourselves, suggesting products and experiences that distract us from these depressing scenarios. Protestants, masters of suspicion, are quick to note the idolatrous longings in all this even as we grasp the smartphones in our pocket. If we are honest, for many of us the serpent's audacious promise, "you will be like God" (Gen 3:5), seems almost to have been fulfilled. I will return to a reason for suspicion below, but first I must ask what it could possibly mean, today, to be like God. I want to reflect on the first chapters of Genesis, which strike me with each rereading as enormously relevant to our understanding of the be-guiling images that surge around us. This is the original story of desire, mastery and relationship, and it is the story of our cultural discipleship. After looking at Genesis, I will ask how Christ, the new image of God, fills in and corrects the picture.

REREADING GENESIS 1–3

How better to tell of beginnings than through images and stories? This is what Genesis gives us: two versions of the story of how God brings about our world. All the ancient Near Eastern creation accounts are stories of the gods' struggles to form human society, but in the Genesis account God works uniquely and directly: by a word. The text anticipates the centurion's request of Jesus in Luke: "Just say the word and my servant will be healed" (Lk 7:7 CEB). Indeed, these chapters in Genesis are centrally about God, what God has done and what God continues to do by speaking and calling out to the creature.

God takes the initiative, planting a garden and then playing host to the man and woman created to live there. But even before that, God enjoys watching what is made—as though God is also amazed. Watch how the waters bring forth fish! See the way the earth brings forth oranges and roses, again anticipating Jesus, who clearly enjoyed watching the lilies grow (Mt 6:28). God loved what was happening in creation, and the more God worked on it, the more it could resemble its Creator, pleasing God even more.

Creation by the word emphasizes God's transcendence, but the language of Genesis 1 also stresses immanence: "let the earth put forth" (Gen 1:11), "let the waters bring forth" (Gen 1:20), and so on. David Fergusson has argued that Darwin is actually to be thanked for helping us see God as immanent in the process of creation; God is present and active throughout, taking personal delight in each detail. "The model here," Fergusson writes, "is of God's 'letting the world become itself' not in such a way as to abandon it but in the interest of a patient accompanying that seeks to work within and alongside creative processes."[1] And God is the first to take delight in all that is going on; it is as if he is saying, "My, this is good."

In Genesis 2, God bends down and forms Adam out of the soil and breathes into Adam "the breath of life" (Gen 2:7). Next, God plants a garden with every tree that "is pleasant to the sight and good for food" (Gen 2:9) and puts Adam there to care for it. But God, the gardener host, has instructions for Adam:

---

[1]David Fergusson, "Interpreting the Story of Creation," in *Genesis and Christian Theology*, ed. N. MacDonald, M. W. Elliott and G. Macaskill (Grand Rapids: Eerdmans, 2012), 170.

"You may freely eat of every tree of the garden; but of the tree of the knowledge of good and evil you shall not eat" (Gen 2:16-17). Then God notices that Adam is alone and observes that "it is not good that the man should be alone; I will make him a helper as his partner" (Gen 2:18). Surprisingly, God does not immediately create Eve but first makes the animals and brings them to Adam "to see what he would call them" (Gen 2:19). The man names the animals, and God continues to watch the world become itself. It turns out that none of the animals did the trick; the text points out that "there was not found a helper as his partner" (Gen 2:20). So God made a woman from a rib of Adam's and brought her to him, and they were both naked and unashamed.

This is clearly God's show. Adam and Eve have a starring role to play, but it is not only their story. Their roles are carefully set. First, they are defined by a set of relationships: with God who walks with them in the cool of the day, with the creation they are to name and care for, with each other. In relationship with each other, they discover one who is "bone of my bones and flesh of my flesh" (Gen 2:23); that is, they find themselves in knowing the other. Finally, Adam and Eve are defined by knowledge of themselves.

Let me linger a bit on this last relationship because it will be key to what I want to argue. When God came to create Adam in Genesis 1, the first-person plural appears: "Let us make humankind in our image" (Gen 1:26). Of all the suggested explanations of this phrase, the most convincing is to call this a plural of self-deliberation, stressing God's reflexivity.[2] As Karl Barth expresses this conception, here "we have to do with a concert of mind and act and action in the divine being itself."[3] Surely it is the whole person, embodied and breathed by God, that images God. But at the center of this wholeness stands the reflexive ability to both know and transcend oneself and to imagine a possible future.

So the human being is created in a dynamic set of relationships, each reflective of God's triunity. To leave things there might suggest this network of relations binds humans, but it is self-reflexivity that provides the ability to

---

[2] Jürgen Moltmann, Hans Walter Wolff and Umberto Cassuto have all suggested something similar. For an excellent summary of the discussion see Pascal Daniel Bazzell, "Toward a Creational Perspective on Poverty," in *Genesis and Christian Theology*, 233-34. As Barth notes, all this is best understood against the backdrop of God's triunity. See *Church Dogmatics* (Edinburgh: T&T Clark, 1958), III/1, 192; hereafter cited as *CD* III/1.
[3] *CD* III/1, 192.

respond appropriately to each relationship, to make something of the responsibilities each entails. Notice that the attractions for Adam and Eve were both aesthetic and moral; those lures invited them to make a world out of God's gifts. Moreover, the attractions were not the same in all directions; the pushes and pulls exerted pressures that were neither possible to resist nor easy to manage. Notice further that there were already limits and structure built into the working of things—not only between day and night, earth and sea, but also between the human and creation.

While there was plenty to see and enjoy, there was one place in the garden that was off-limits. Adam and Eve were not to eat of the tree of the knowledge of good and evil; God said, "In the day that you eat of it you shall die" (Gen 2:17). But God intended limits to represent permission and not simply constraint. As Flannery O'Connor described limits in relation to the creative process, "Possibility and limit mean about the same thing. It is the business of the writer to push his talent to the outermost limit, but this means to the outermost limit of the talent he has."[4] While tragedy did not strike until the next chapter, we observe already that frictions are intrinsic to the account in Genesis 2. John Goldingay writes:

> There was a tension built into the creation story. It issued from thought and it generated laughter, and it reflected a systematic week's work that was especially pleasing when completed. But it gave its key players a demanding task of managing a world that had a mind of its own.[5]

All it would take was a spark, a suggestion that "you will be like God" (Gen 3:5), and the damage would be done.

THE TWO TRAJECTORIES OF CREATION

How can something so good have such potential to go wrong? The key is to recognize that the account offers two trajectories that exist in tension with each other. This tension can be either creative or alienating, and it continues to inform human cultural projects. Let me suggest how this might be. The first

---

[4]Flannery O'Connor, *Mystery and Manners: Occasional Prose*, selected and ed. Sally Fitzgerald and Robert Fitzgerald (New York: Farrar, Straus, and Giroux, 1961), 170.
[5]John Goldingay, *Old Testament Theology vol. 1: Israel's Gospel* (Downers Grove, IL: IVP Academic, 2003), 131. Cf. Barth, "From the very first this place is not without serious problems" (*CD* III/1, 250).

trajectory is the trajectory of life: creation appears as fundamentally the good work of God. One comes away from reading these verses with a sense of delight and joy in all that was made and all that Adam and Eve were created to enjoy. This is the original goodness of creation. Many Protestants have been slow to recognize this; it often appears that Protestant theology begins at Genesis 3. By contrast, in Orthodox theology Adam is understood to have fallen not from a state of perfection but from a "state of undeveloped simplicity."[6] Timothy Ware describes this, quoting from and commenting on an Orthodox hymn sung at funerals:

> "I am the image of Thine inexpressible glory, even though I bear the wounds of sin." And because he still retains the image of God, man still retains free will, although sin restricts its scope. Even after the fall, God, "takes not away from man the power to will—to will to obey or not to obey."[7]

Orthodoxy has its hands on the trajectory of original goodness and its continuing influence.

Eden, after all, means "delight," and God's first command is to "freely eat of every tree of the garden" (Gen 2:16). The tone is one of permission, of fertility, of life and growth. Unlike the other local religions, the stars and sun are neighbors; the waters and animals are friends. Notice especially two dominant characteristics of this wondrous creation: separation and difference. God takes care to separate the night from the day and the dry land from the seas. God also creates abundance and difference; "birds multiply on the earth" (Gen 1:22), and the earth brings forth "living creatures of every kind" (Gen 1:24). Separation and difference are not problems to be solved, as they are in Greek thought; they are gifts to be savored in the same way the multiple gifts of the body of Christ are to be celebrated (1 Cor 12). It is impossible for us to know what it was like to live in such a world, but we might imagine it as a place with the freedom and opportunity, as Goldingay puts it, "to learn obedience and grow to moral maturity."[8]

A world that offers the conditions for growth into obedience and maturity also offers the opportunity to exercise genius and creativity. In such a world,

---

[6]Timothy Ware, *The Orthodox Church* (New York: Penguin, 1963), 228-29.
[7]Ibid., 228-29. The final quotation is from Dositheus's *Confession*, Decree iii.
[8]Goldingay, *Old Testament Theology*, 146.

humans wonder: what if we could find a way to ride those horses, or let that dog come and lie by our fire? What if we crossed this daisy with that one; what would that be like? This reflexive spark lies behind all creativity, all culture making. Paul Fiddes argues that this moral sense and creative imagination are responses to God. "The reaching of the imagination towards a new world," he says, "is the result of God's reaching toward us."[9] God wanted to see what Adam would call the creatures. In giving over this role, God allowed humans to make culture. But we can also see the danger here: such imagination can always head out on its own.

This is what happened in the second trajectory, which I will call the trajectory of death. Genesis 3 records the tragic event where permission was squandered and the reflexive imagination was unleashed for sinful purposes. Note that the serpent is identified as "more crafty than any other wild animal that the LORD God had made" (Gen 3:1). The use of wisdom language ("crafty"; "subtle" KJV) for one of God's creatures, and indeed the appearance of the serpent itself, implies that this temptation comes from within the goodness of creation. This wisdom appeals precisely to that imaginative capacity wherein the man and woman image God. Satan does not appear in this account; indeed, he does not show up until later in the Old Testament period and does not play a central role until John Milton retells this story in *Paradise Lost*. But we can be sure that something went tragically wrong and that it involved imagining some other goodness than what God provided in the ordered bounty of creation—the main tools in Satan's arsenal.

Notice that the serpent's appeal is made to humanity's reflexive imagination. The serpent wants Eve to wonder: What if you took the fruit from that tree? What if you really did become "like God, knowing good and evil" (Gen 3:5)? What would that be like? Later, we will hear an echo of this in the story of Christ, when the devil says to him in the wilderness, "All the kingdoms of the world . . . I will give you" (Mt 4:8-9). After all, the fruit was "good for food" and "a delight to the eyes" (Gen 3:6). This description of all the trees in Eden now perversely characterizes the one forbidden tree. T. S. Eliot has captured this moment:

---

[9]Paul Fiddes, *Freedom and Limit: A Dialogue Between Literature and Christian Doctrine* (New York: St. Martin's Press, 1993), 30.

Between the idea
and the reality
Between the motion
and the act
Falls the shadow: For Thine is the kingdom[10]

The suggestion turned out to be the father of the act. Eve took the fruit, ate it, gave it to Adam, and he ate. The text notes ominously that "the eyes of both were opened" (Gen 3:7). Immediately they become ashamed of their nakedness and they hide from God. Separation and difference are no longer friends; they become enemies. But God remains true, continuing to pursue them and asking, "Where are you?" (Gen 3:9), "Who told you that you were naked?" (Gen 3:11), "What is this that you have done?" (Gen 3:13). Notice that God is still letting the world reveal itself. The good news is that, despite this tragic turn, God does not give up on the man and the woman.[11]

The bad news is that now God—and all of us—must reckon with the fatal rupture that has occurred—what theologians call "original sin." However we understand this passage, clearly something happened in the course of the history of creation that has disrupted the good order of things.[12] The temptation to take the fruit of the tree of the knowledge of good and evil proved irresistible. The tension among the pressures of creation and the imagination of the man and woman was too great. Perhaps Adam and Eve would have grown into that knowledge in time.[13] But rather than trusting God to give what they needed, they reached out like Prometheus and stole what belonged to God.

Adam and Eve's disobedience involved a transgressing of limits and a despoiling of creation. The ordered life in which they had been created was now disordered, and they were set on the path of death. God had promised that in the day they ate of the tree they would die. Sure enough, death did enter, following disobedience like a shadow, as Paul notes in Romans 5:12. Instead of

---

[10]T. S. Eliot, "The Hollow Men," in *T. S. Eliot: The Collected Poems 1909–1963* (New York: Harcourt, 1963), 81-82.

[11]Goldingay notes, "God's knowledge of us comes about through having a relationship with us" (*Old Testament Theology*, 137).

[12]Cf. Marguerite Shuster, "Something intruded, in space and time, upon what God had made" (*The Fall and Sin* [Grand Rapids: Eerdmans, 2004], 5).

[13]This is Goldingay's suggestion, reflecting an Orthodox theme (Goldingay, *Old Testament Theology*, 146).

peace with the animals, there is enmity (Gen 3:15); instead of mutual care between the man and the woman, there is distorted desire and rule (Gen 3:16); care for the earth is challenged, and they eat their bread by the sweat of their brow (Gen 3:19).

Scripture insists that this disruption is universal. It affects everyone in all places and times. It has become, as Paul Fiddes notes, a universal fact and not an occasional problem.[14] Though it is a problem for each of us, it is also a fact for all of us together. Solidarity in sin inflicts our missteps on our children and even our neighbors. Worse, there is an inevitability to sin that, try as we might, we cannot contain. Indeed, we sense in ourselves and in the world around us a moral gravity, a historical momentum toward evil.[15] All of this is graphically illustrated in the subsequent chapters of Genesis: growing corruption and the loss of even the ability to imagine goodness. God is still the center of this story, and he watches this process with horror—grieving in his heart that "every inclination of the thoughts of [human] hearts was only evil continually" (Gen 6:5) and determining to intervene in the flood narrative. But after the flood, though "the inclination of the human heart is [still] evil from youth" (Gen 8:21), God will not destroy the earth. Instead, he will bless it and will bless the descendants of Noah, and of Abraham, and in Israel will hold out to the world a chance, as Moses tells his people, to "choose life" (Deut 30:19).

The biblical account captures precisely this situation of being poised at the intersection of the two trajectories I have sketched: between the original good and the original evil, between life and death. We cannot escape either, but neither can we find a way to reconcile them. Paul Fiddes concludes, "God has put us in a situation where it appears easier to resolve our anxieties in some other way than trust in God."[16]

NEW CREATION OF GRACE

Rather than sketch out the way Israel dealt with God's gifts of creation and liberation, I will move to focus on Jesus, the Son of David and Israel's messiah. As someone who has reflected for a long time on God's work in culture, I have

---

[14]Fiddes, *Freedom and Limit*, 60.

[15]On this, see the excellent pages in Cornelius Plantinga, *Not the Way It's Supposed to Be: A Breviary of Sin* (Grand Rapids: Eerdmans, 1995), 29-33. The historical momentum of sin is Plantinga's language.

[16]Fiddes, *Freedom and Limit*, 61.

struggled to know how to understand the work of Christ in light of our cultural calling. What social practices, if any, are implied in the work of Christ? The temptation is to see the spiritual call of Christ as superseding our more earthly responsibilities, as though becoming a new creature diminishes our call to heal the earth, but I am convinced that this impulse is deeply mistaken. I believe the work of Christ and the gift of the Spirit call us to a deeper engagement with the work of tending and keeping the earth, and thus a closer identification with its suffering. I will argue that Christ's work engages and fulfills these trajectories of creation and that this filling up has direct implications for our cultural responsibilities.

Remember that creation itself was God's good project intended to develop in ways God was eager to watch. This is what makes the disruption of Genesis 3 so critical. As Douglas Farrow notes:

> The love for God which is the life of man cannot emerge *ex nihilo* in full bloom; it requires to grow with experience. But that in turn is what makes the fall, however unsurprising, such a devastating affair. In the fall, man is "turned backwards." He does not grow up in the love of God as he is intended to. The course of his time, his so-called progress, is set in the wrong direction.[17]

The life of creation involves a forward movement. This is why, as Orthodox theology stresses, the true profile of what becomes of the image of God has to be worked out in the future. As created, the world was good; indeed, its purposes were perfect. But as Colin Gunton notes, this was not perfection in the sense of completion. The created order was heading somewhere, and that goal is to be seen only in Jesus Christ. As Gunton explains, "Jesus Christ recapitulates our human story in order that the project of the perfection of all things may be achieved."[18] His designation as the second Adam underscores the fact that the destiny of the first Adam is bound up with Christ, just as Christ's victory over sin and death is bound up with the renewal of all things, signaled by the resurrection and the pouring out of the Spirit.

Interestingly, though Old Testament references to the image of God outside of Genesis 1 are rare,[19] the term appears prominently in New Testament

---

[17]Quoted in Colin E. Gunton, *The Triune Creator: A Historical and Systematic Study* (Grand Rapids: Eerdmans, 1998), 201-2. Gunton's discussion is heavily dependent on the Eastern theologian Irenaeus.

[18]Gunton, *Triune Creator,* 202.

[19]Gen 9:6 and Jas 3:9 are the only two that do not refer to Christ.

discussions of Christ as the true image of God. The worldly gods have blinded the minds of unbelievers, Paul writes in 2 Corinthians 4:4, "to keep them from seeing the light of the gospel of the glory of Christ, who is the image of God." Colossians 1:15 describes Christ as the "image of the invisible God, the firstborn of all creation." Believers are transformed into this image by the work of the Spirit (Rom 8:29; 1 Cor 15:49; 2 Cor 3:18; Col 3:10). To learn what the image of God means for the Christian not only means going back to Genesis but also must mean going ahead to the story of Christ. There we see the true image of God, and this image deals with all the problems associated with stewardship of the goods of creation and human relationships. Jesus as the image heals all that is involved with the fundamental human calling to be stewards and neighbors.

This leads me to my central claim: the model we should have in mind is not the U-shaped model of Northrop Frye or John Milton—paradise, paradise lost and paradise regained. Rather, we should see ourselves as exiles. We should frame all our efforts, as Michael Edwards puts it, as "a search for the lost world of Eden."[20] We imagine a fulfilling life with this device, with that woman or in that exotic place, but what we really want is to discover a world of freedom and permission where distinctions and differences are gifts and God accompanies us in the cool of the day. This is not a return to Eden but something far better: a discovery, an entrance into God's imagination, what the New Testament calls "new creation." The proper model is not creation–fall–redemption, but creation–new creation.

In light of Genesis 3, we can see Christ's accomplishment in Romans 5. There, Paul says that "sin came into the world through one man, and death came through sin, and so death spread to all because all have sinned" (Rom 5:12). But in Jesus Christ, God matched this tragedy with a more comprehensive blessing—reminding us that, amid the curses of Genesis 3, there is a promise indicating that God's primary impulse is of mercy and not judgment. Paul says, "Just as by the one man's disobedience the many were made sinners, so by the one man's obedience the many will be made righteous" (Rom 5:19). One might think that the dominion of death brought about by sin had so corrupted both creation and human attempts at dominion that created goodness

---

[20]Michael Edwards, *Towards a Christian Poetics* (Grand Rapids: Eerdmans, 1984), quoted in Fiddes, *Freedom and Limit*, 49. As Fiddes notes here, the Old Testament "refuses pattern."

was lost. But God's re-creation not only insists on that goodness but also introduces into it a higher order of things that Paul describes, using words that recall Genesis 1, as grace exercising dominion "through justification leading to eternal life through Jesus Christ" (Rom 5:21).

To develop the implications of the above claim for cultural renewal, let me return to the two trajectories of creation: of bounty and limit, of life and death. In Christ these trajectories are taken up and lived out. But Christ embodies a radical inversion, a reversal that changes everything for our cultural engagement. The original Genesis account starts with life, the fulsome display of fertility and growth. All goodness is available except for restrictions placed on the tree in the middle: first came creation and life, then a promised death. Now in Christ, the order is reversed: first there is a death, then resurrection life.

The first trajectory in this new order of things is that of limit and of rupture. In the original account of creation, difference is a gift and limits are protections. Day is separated from night, sea from land. The animals are brought to Adam to be named and ordered; Adam and Eve are naked and not ashamed. One of the most important results of Adam and Eve's disobedience is that difference—including gender difference and the relationship between humans and the rest of creation—becomes problematic. The problem comes because power issues have distorted the created order. Notice the language prominent in Genesis 3:15-19: enmity, bruising, pain, rule. The way is open for the goods of creation and the most intimate relationships to become commodities, hostages to power struggles.

The irony is that we see these power plays as a means to life when in fact they lead to death. What the world regards as "knowing how to get ahead" is a working out of the disobedience of our first parents: "The getting of treasures by a lying tongue is a fleeting vapor and a snare of death" (Prov 21:6). Paul puts this more directly: in Adam we all die (1 Cor 15:22). We see this death-making at work even among Jesus' own disciples; in Mark, it is placed in the context of Jesus' prediction of his death.[21] In Mark 10, the disciples begin to wonder where they will end up in the new order that Jesus has

---

[21]An earlier prediction in Mk 8:31 is also closely connected to the challenge that all who want to save their lives must lose them; they must "say no to themselves" (Mk 8:34 CEB). That is, the death of Christ implies also our death.

announced. James and John want to continue their special relationship, and
the others become angry. Such political negotiations have become so much a
normal part of our life that we are not surprised at this exchange, but that is
the point. As Jesus indicates, ordering people around (Mk 10:42 CEB) is the
usual way of Gentiles; it represents the world we take for granted.

But that must change. Jesus goes on: "But it is not so among you; but
whoever wishes to become great among you must be your servant" (Mk
10:43). Why is this? Because of Jesus: "The Son of Man came not to be served
but to serve, and to give his life a ransom for many" (Mk 10:45). Notice that
Jesus gives the most prominent prediction of his death in the context of his
reordering of human power structures. Because of Christ's death, there will
be a new way to think about relationships that is based on mutuality and respect and that embodies God's unconditioned love for all.

The classic passage dealing with Christ's role in the reordering of power
structures is Philippians 2:5-10, likely based on an early Christian hymn. Paul
is concerned that the Philippians have a common mind, being "in full accord"
(Phil 2:2). This is possible only when the mind of Christ, the true image of
God, determines our way of relating to each other. Christ is the one who,
though he was God, "did not regard equality with God as something to be
exploited" (Phil 2:6). Here the temptation of the garden, repeated in the
devil's bogus offer to Christ in the wilderness, has been reversed. Rather than
claiming what was his by right, he was willing to give it up, to become "obe-
dient to the point of death—even death on a cross" (Phil 2:8). In Christ's
servant life among us, we find an image of what God wanted the first Adam to
be and what, by God's grace—that is, as a gift—we can become. The Philippians passage uses the verb "to exploit," the same word used in the Greek myth
of Prometheus,[22] which captures perfectly the contrast Paul expresses here.
Rather than seeking to claim what belongs to the gods, Christ—who is God—
gave up his claims and took on the role of a servant. Here is a new way of reflecting God: the way of mutual servanthood. Here, paradoxically, death to
self is the way to life. Just as Christ's death means that God lets go of the
charges against us, so as "we have been buried with [Christ] by baptism into
death" (Rom 6:4), we are enabled to let go, to forgive as we have been forgiven.

---

[22]See William Lynch, *Christ and Prometheus* (Notre Dame, IN: University of Notre Dame Press,
1970).

As I look at my life, my family, my community—even my Christian community—I continually ask if this is really possible. When Paul says, "Do nothing from selfish ambition or conceit, but in humility regard others as better than yourselves" (Phil 2:3), I am struck dumb. We glibly say this re-ordering of relationships can be realized only within the body of Christ, that we can only restructure our imaginations as formed by our baptism into Christ's death and by the exchange represented in the Eucharist. But let's be honest. Too often, it is within the body of Christ—and in representatives of that body—where difference has been dealt with through violent intervention rather than taken as a cry for understanding and reconciliation. I think that if this call to servanthood were all we had to go on, we would be, of all men and women, most miserable.

Fortunately, there is more to this story. By itself, Christ's call to live in a new way appeals only to the will; as long as we abide in death, it does not change anything. But three days after Christ's death comes resurrection, and with it the possibility of a new life for us. To fully appropriate this, however, we need to recall the theme of the bounty of God's goodness in creation. Christ came not only to forgive our sins or even to conquer the power of evil—though he did both of these—but also to bring us into the creative life of God. This is realized by his resurrection and by those growing into his likeness. Paul describes this process: "As Christ was raised from the dead by the glory of the Father, so we too might walk in newness of life" (Rom 6:4). He makes it clear that this newness is only worked out by the gift of the "Spirit of Life in Christ Jesus" (Rom 8:2) who frees us from the law of death. Life in the Spirit leads us to cry as God's children, "Abba! Father!" (Rom 8:15).

What are the social implications of this new creation? What does this mean for our vocation as God's children? Note that for Paul this new way of being is not a deliverance from the struggles of the world; rather, it summons to us to go more deeply into the yearning of creation. One cannot participate in God without sharing in the groaning of creation to be "set free from its bondage to decay" and death, and the longing of creation to "obtain the freedom of the glory of the children of God" (Rom 8:21). Going deeply into the created order, considering the lilies and the birds (Mt 6:25-34), we are at the same time encountering the Creator. When medieval mystic Julian of Norwich marveled that the small hazelnut survives and grows, God told her,

"It lasts, and ever shall last, because God loves it. And in this fashion all things have their being by the grace of God."[23]

So much in Christ's ministry recalls the trajectory of life, the original goodness of fertility and permission, and recalls the generosity of God who said, "You may freely eat of every tree of the garden" (Gen 2:16). The Gospel accounts emphasize the openhandedness of Jesus' healing power and his provision. Think of "the crowd" who "were trying to touch him, for power came out from him and healed all of them" (Lk 6:19), the miracle of feeding the multitudes with baskets left over, the miracle of the draught of fish so plentiful it couldn't be hauled into the boat. Christ reminds us that the disruption of Genesis 3 did not ruin this richness—the earth still produces its plenty, and the rain still falls on the just and unjust.

Though the earth produces its bounty, not everyone enjoys it equally. Bounty is appropriated by one or another power; it is distributed as a commodity and becomes a scarce resource. How can fertility and plenty be recovered? The scriptural accounts answer that recovery comes only in the intervention of the new economy of grace introduced by Jesus Christ, by the power of the resurrected Christ poured out on the world by the Spirit. Frances Young and David Ford have argued that this "new economy" is the organizing metaphor of 2 Corinthians.[24] Further, they describe an actual connection between global economies and "the economy of God." The basic argument of Paul's letter, according to Young and Ford, is that God is the central provider. Key passages emphasize this: 2 Corinthians 2:14 uses the imagery of God leading us in a "triumphal procession," like that of the emperor proceeding with the spoils of victory through the streets of Rome; in 2 Corinthians 5:18, after announcing "new creation" in Christ, Paul emphasizes that "all this is from God." He sums up the central argument of chapters 8 and 9 with this doxology: "Thanks be to God for his indescribable gift!" (2 Cor 9:15). And what is this gift? It is the overflowing grace of Jesus Christ poured out by the Spirit (2 Cor 1:22; 3:6).

Paul elaborates on this gift (*charis*) in chapters 8 and 9, where he makes the connection between the exchange of God's grace and human sharing of

---

[23]Julian of Norwich, *Revelations of Divine Love* (Garden City, NY: Image/Doubleday, 1977), 88.
[24]Frances Young and David Ford, *Meaning and Truth in 2 Corinthians* (Grand Rapids: Eerdmans, 1987).

finances.[25] Based on his argument wherein enmity, through Christ's reconciliation,[26] has been replaced with friendship (2 Cor 5), Paul uses the collection of funds by Macedonian believers for the impoverished saints in Jerusalem as a metaphor for Christ's new economy of abundance. The collection—which Paul calls *charis* ("grace" or "gift of grace")—subverts the traditional patron-client understanding of benevolence in which specific returns were expected. Collection as gift expresses a new understanding of economic abundance, embodied here in the exchange between Macedonian abundance and the needs of the poor in Jerusalem. This also involves a reversal in which a relatively poor area, Macedonia, is asked to support one that was ordinarily supplied with abundant imperial resources; this too illustrates that the new economy overturns normal expectations. Young and Ford comment that the "money seems to function like a sacrament both of the unity of Jews and Gentiles in the Church and the validity of Paul's apostolate in relation to the original apostles in Jerusalem."[27] The basis of this exchange is in what Jesus has done, in "the generous act of our Lord Jesus Christ, that though he was rich, yet for your sakes he became poor, so that by his poverty you might become rich" (2 Cor 8:9). This means that "God is able to provide you with every blessing in abundance, so that by always having enough of everything, you may share abundantly in every good work" (2 Cor 9:8).

We must be careful not to see this as supporting the notion that the gospel somehow promises material blessings. Nothing could be further from Paul's intention. Paul writes of a mutual exchange of gifts that flows from and reflects the boundless grace extended to us in Christ. Moreover, none of the participants Paul addressed were wealthy. Indeed, the Christians in Jerusalem were in dire straits due to a recent famine, and the Christians in Macedonia were anything but rich. The point, Paul stresses, is not that one should suffer at another's expense but that through a mutual sharing and the multiplication it allows that all might have enough. The grace of sharing replicates itself and lives off the grace extended in Christ; it is an extension of the resurrection life of Christ. The gifts of creation find their highest purpose in being offered in

---

[25]Young and Ford see 2 Cor 1:3-11 and Paul's exultation in 2 Cor 10–12 as also key to developing this metaphor (ibid., 174-75).

[26]Young and Ford point out that the original meaning of reconciliation referred to an exchange of money, a moneylender's profit or merchandise (ibid., 176).

[27]Ibid., 180.

the service of one another. The point is to allow the goods of creation to be taken, blessed and distributed in memory of the one broken for us. Creation is offered in the service of communion. This does not constitute an economic program, but it does suggest an impulse that would transform our thinking about just distribution of the earth's resources.

CULTURE AND IDOLATRY

I want to conclude by making some comments on the temptation to idolatry posed by our cultural situation and then give two concrete examples of interventions that reflect new creation. Both idolatry and creativity appeal to the same reflexive imagination, that ability to imagine a future that I have argued is a central component of the image of God. Advertisers are always appealing to our imaginative vision. They want us to agree with the stories they tell about the commodities they sell. They want us to concur that this is what matters; this is how it feels; this makes life better. The Christian imagination will tell a different story, but to image God is also to imagine a better future—a new way of being in the world. To image God is to ask, "What if my life, our life together, could be like this?"

Children of the Reformation are rightly suspicious of anything setting itself up to rival God in our lives, and it is true that the Reformers, in their context, had to stress that any visual mediation that could distract the heart from God is idolatry. Calvin defined idolatry as the tendency "to worship the gifts in place of the Giver."[28] We are not wrong to see that engagement—even constructive engagement—with our culture is prone to idolatry. Yet I believe that the temptation in our context is not to *replace* God with objects or relationships but to *fail to engage* them in pursuit of righteousness. A closer reading of the Reformers' reflections on idolatry suggests a deeper and more insidious sense in which humans are drawn to misuse the goods of creation, and the Reformers' often radical rejection of religious symbols needs to be seen in the light of their positive program. For Calvin, this more subtle sense of idolatry involves all that would distract us from our pursuit of visible righteousness in our lives—all that would distract us from performing what is good in the

---

[28]John Calvin, *Institutes of the Christian Religion*, ed. John T. McNeill, trans. Ford Lewis Battles (Louisville: Westminster John Knox, 2011), 4.17.36. See also William Dyrness, *Reformed Theology and Visual Culture* (Cambridge: Cambridge University Press, 2004), 32. For what follows see pages 144-45.

world. As Calvin puts it, "We have no right to follow the mind's caprice wherever it impels us, but, dependent upon his will, ought to stand firm in that alone which is pleasing to him.... Unless we would turn away from our Creator in impious ingratitude, we must cherish righteousness all our life."[29] This call is to order our imagination toward new creation relationships and work.

William Perkins insisted that human knowledge of God and of ourselves is neither symbolically mediated nor merely intellectually grasped; it is known "experimentally." It is something to be performed. Faith and confidence in Christ "are but fictions of the brain, so long as they are severed from amendment of heart and life."[30] Idolatry is, in part, an empty confession that bears no visible fruit.

New creation involves imagining a new way of life. The new mind operates at the level of that self-reflexivity that lies at the heart of our creation in God's likeness. In Christ the new creation is on full display: he is the true image of God who dies and rises again so that we are able to forget the things that are behind and move toward a new future. Becoming a new creation in Christ gives us the ability to imagine a new way of relating to each other and to the goods of creation. More than this, the Spirit empowers this new world, this Christian imaginary, so that it can be embodied. New creation can be made visible in our culture.

This Christian imaginary understands social relations not as power plays but as arenas of mutual service. Ethnic differences are not commodities to be bought and sold but are gifts to be savored and shared. Sexuality is a gift to be guarded and treasured. This seeks to embody the reconciling love of God revealed in Christ in actual social relations. What if we had the imagination to see the world in the light of the resurrection? What if we saw the resurrection as the original nonviolent intervention? Forgiveness is an extension of this pacific intervention. Nonviolence as a moral strategy may be the most important contribution of the twentieth century. It is connected to the vision of Martin Luther King Jr. and Gandhi, but behind them is the life and work of Christ, who "came not to be served but to serve, and to give his life a ransom for many" (Mt 20:28). Gandhi learned this from his careful reading of the New Testament he always carried with him, and King from his Baptist tradition.

---

[29]Calvin, *Institutes* 2.8.2.
[30]William Perkins, *Reformed Catholike* (Cambridge: John Legat, 1598), 115.

A powerful illustration of the possibility of the Christian imaginary is the story of Ruby Bridges as recounted by Robert Coles. Born in the early 1950s in Mississippi, she moved with her family to New Orleans when her father's job in the fields was taken over by a machine. He found work as a janitor, and Ruby's mother cleaned a bank every night after she tucked the children into bed. Every Sunday, the family went to church. "We wanted our children to be near God's spirit . . . from the start," Ruby's mother said.

All the schools in New Orleans at this time were segregated. In 1960, a judge ruled that four black girls would go to two white elementary schools, and Ruby Bridges was one of them. She was sent to first grade at William Frantz Elementary School. The family prayed together that they would have the courage to face the inevitable resistance to Ruby's presence. Every day, as federal marshals led Ruby to school, she passed angry crowds. White parents withdrew their children from the school. Wearing a clean dress and a bow in her hair, Ruby carried her lunch pail past the crowd and worked at her desk alone in Mrs. Henry's classroom.

One day, as Mrs. Henry watched Ruby approach from the window, she saw Ruby pause as though she was saying something to the crowd. Their shouting grew louder. Finally Ruby entered her classroom, and Mrs. Henry asked what she had said to them. "I wasn't talking to them," Ruby said. "I was praying for them." Ruby prayed for the people every day, but this day she forgot until she reached school. So she stopped and prayed: "Please God, try to forgive these people. Because even if they say those bad things, they don't know what they're doing. So you could forgive them, just like you did those folks a long time ago when they said terrible things about you."[31] Little by little, the white children returned to the school. Ruby later graduated from high school, married a building contractor, had four sons, and together they created an educational foundation to revitalize William Frantz Elementary School.

Ruby Bridges shows us that we are not just a collection of individuals. We are not on our own; we are in this together. Her life, each human life, is embedded in family and community in the same way that Christ was embedded in his Jewish community and in the good land that God had made. Just as Christ was among us as one who served, so by God's Spirit we can serve the

---

[31]The account of Ruby Bridges is available in a children's book by Robert Coles, illustrated by George Ford, *The Story of Ruby Bridges* (New York: Scholastic Inc., 1995).

community. Ruby's forgiveness was of a piece with the nonviolent intervention that Martin Luther King Jr. preached, reflecting the restored image of God.

In the Christian imaginary, the goods of creation become assets in the service of love. This love is defined by economy and embodied in an actual economy. The imagination has to reflect our hope for a new heaven and earth, and culture has to provide instruments for sharing goods. In hope, we can imagine what it would be like to treat the earth not as a possession to be used and hoarded but as a gift to be treasured and shared.

We have an illustration in those addressing climate change and resource depletion. Some time ago John Jeavons developed the notion of "biointensive" farming. He argues, in language that reflects Genesis 2:15, that our tilling of the soil should be a blessing and not a curse. Unlike most agriculture, which disrupts the biotic structure of the soil, biointensive farming seeks to preserve and enhance the biotic community.[32] Everything grown in this process is either eaten or composted and returned to the soil. Others have sought manufacturing processes that use biodegradable materials, glues and packaging. This process, sometimes referred to as "upcycling," returns materials to the organic process with improved rather than degraded quality. It preserves the nutrients so that nothing is lost; indeed, much is gained. Food produced in this way is healthier, both in that plants are grown organically and in that vitamins and trace minerals are preserved. The soil at the end of the process is more fertile than it was at the beginning. "Upcycling" is a reflection of a world where resurrection is a present reality, not only a future dream. It serves a world we all share, embedded in community and in creation, just as Christ came to be a servant of creation.

Forgiveness, upcycling, nonviolent intervention—these suggest we need not be satisfied with death and violence, either toward each other or the created order. We can imagine and work toward another order. As imagebearers, we can say, "What if the world were like that?" The mind of Christ can be our mind. Desire for such a world reflects the longing that is placed in all of us. What if the church saw one of its primary roles as nurturing such a desire?

---

[32]Jeavons has written a number of books; see, for example, *How to Grow More Vegetables* (Willits, CA: Ecology Action, 1978). I owe this reference to Rob Cahill, a biointensive gardener and pastor, formerly of Cosey Town, Pennsylvania.

3

"TRUE RIGHTEOUSNESS AND HOLINESS"

The Image of God in the New Testament

Craig L. Blomberg

INTRODUCTION

Denver Seminary, where I teach, has a Littleton, Colorado, mailing address. Few people had heard of Littleton until 1999. After that, even when I traveled overseas people would ask, "Isn't that where the shootings at Columbine High School occurred?" In 2012, another mass shooting occurred in nearby Aurora, in a movie theater showing the premiere of the film *The Dark Night Rises*. My younger daughter, home from college, had gone with a friend to a different theater for a showing of the same movie. After hearing the news, I found myself for the first time in years quietly opening her bedroom door to make sure she was there and alive. In 2013, a gunman shot and killed a girl at Arapahoe High School in Centennial, just blocks from our home. It was the school my older daughter graduated from. Even though she now lives in England, she saw the news ten minutes before we heard about it from a local friend. In places very close to us we experienced the depth of human evil and depravity.

These events can make even outspoken atheists grow quiet. As one such person said to me confidentially after the massacre at Sandy Hook Elementary School in 2012, "If the only thing keeping most of those parents going was the belief that they would see their children again in a life to come, who was I to take that away from them at such a tragic moment?"[1] Faced with the horror

---

[1] As my colleague Ray Prigodich once put it, our society doesn't believe in justification by faith; we

of death, few people are willing to believe that a person's consciousness has forever been extinguished.

While events like these highlight the very worst of humanity, the responses to them often show the very best of humanity. Police officers and firefighters risk and sometimes sacrifice their lives to stop criminals. Compassionate people donate resources to help those left homeless or displaced by tornadoes, hurricanes, earthquakes or tsunamis. In such times we often see the Christian church at its best. We lead in the nonprofit sector in providing relief for victims of tragedies on both small and large scales.[2] In many cases, faithful Christian efforts have dramatic positive effects.[3] But Christians fail too, and non-Christians also lead significant humanitarian efforts. The late Christopher Hitchens, an outspoken atheist, liked to challenge his opponents to name one good deed a Christian can do that other people cannot do.[4] Of course there are no such deeds, which led him to exult that he had disproved the value of religion. But the point is not to assess the behavior of any given individual but to consider the overall track records of people adhering to an ideology. On this point, Jonathan Hill has shown the enormous extent to which explicitly Christian foundations underlie the development of goods in law, science, medicine and other forms of health care, education and social justice.[5] Yes, Christians do wrong, but Christians have done much good in the world.[6]

What can account for the perplexing array of human behavior, very good and very bad, enacted throughout the world and across the centuries? I submit that only the Judeo-Christian notion of humans created in the image of God

believe in justification by death! With rare exceptions like Hitler or Osama bin Laden, when someone dies everybody says they are in a better place.

[2]See Scott C. Todd, *Fast Living: How the Church Will End Extreme Poverty* (Colorado Springs: Compassion International, 2011).

[3]August H. Konkel tells the story of journalist Brian Stewart's return to Christian faith after seeing Christian ministry in Poland, El Salvador, Ethiopia and elsewhere, in the worst examples of "hell on earth," where no one else was daring to try to make a difference for good. See Konkel, *First and Second Kings* (Grand Rapids: Zondervan, 2006), 463-66.

[4]"Hitchens vs. McGrath, Georgetown University," *Hitchens Debates Transcripts*, October 21, 2011, http://hitchensdebates.blogspot.com/2011/10/hitchens-vs-mcgrath-georgetown.html.

[5]Jonathan Hill, *What Has Christianity Ever Done for Us? How It Shaped the Modern World* (Downers Grove, IL: IVP Academic, 2005).

[6]See Paul Copan and Matthew Flannagan, *Did God Really Command Genocide? Coming to Terms with the Justice of God* (Grand Rapids: Baker Books, 2014), 288-98, and the literature there cited. Countering related objections and offering supplements to Hill, see David B. Hart, *Atheist Delusions: The Christian Revolution and Its Fashionable Enemies* (New Haven: Yale University Press, 2009).

can do so, and only when it is supplemented by the following affirmations: (1) sin has deeply and profoundly corrupted all human beings so that all people in their natural state have the potential for committing acts of unspeakable evil; (2) the image of God nevertheless remains strong enough in people outside of Christ that they likewise have the potential for self-sacrifice and actions of amazing goodness;[7] and (3) the process of salvation or redemption involves the partial re-creation of God's image in our lives as believers in this world and the full re-creation of that image in the world to come.[8] The image of God helps us understand what it means to be human, to face great tragedy and great beauty—but what is this mysterious image of God?

HISTORICAL APPROACHES

Overviews of the image of God often present three main approaches from the history of Christian theology: the substantial, the functional and the moral/ relational. The first view suggests that the image consists in a substantial likeness between humans and God. This is not a physical likeness; very few in the history of Christianity have argued that God is embodied.[9] Many have looked to structural characteristics of the human being—intelligence, rationality, the capacity for meaningful and abstract speech or self-reflection, the division of the psyche into cognition, volition and emotion, and so on—as evidence of the way in which we resemble God.[10] The substantial view is associated with Roman Catholicism, especially pre-Reformation Catholicism in the legacy of Augustine and Aquinas.[11] The view usually assumes that the

---

[7]John F. Kilner ("Humanity in God's Image: Is the Image Really Damaged?," *Journal of the Evangelical Theological Society* 53 [2010]: 601-17) represents a small minority of scholars who think the image was not damaged by sin. His laudable concern is to avoid giving grounds for concluding that physical and mentally challenged people are less in God's image than others, but these weaknesses are not sins so it seems that he has confused two separate categories. At the opposite end of the spectrum, especially in the Reformation tradition, a larger minority has argued that the image was completely lost at the fall (e.g., Grant R. Osborne, *Romans* [Downers Grove, IL: InterVarsity Press, 2004], 223), but this view does not seem to do adequate justice to Gen 9:6 and Jas 3:9.

[8]Similarly, Anthony A. Hoekema, *Created in God's Image* (Grand Rapids: Eerdmans, 1986), 32.

[9]Particularly Audius and his followers in the fourth century and the Church of Jesus Christ of Latter-day Saints today.

[10]For example, Gerald A. Klingbeil, "'He Spoke and It Was': Human Language, Divine Creation, and the Imago Dei," *Horizons in Biblical Theology* 36 (2014): 42-59; Aku Visala, "Imago Dei, Dualism, and Evolution: A Philosophical Defense of the Structural Image of God," *Zygon* 49 (2014): 101-20; Susan Windley-Daoust, *The Redeemed Image of God: Embodied Relations to the Unknown Divine* (Lanham, MD: University Press of America, 2002).

[11]Matthew Drever argues, nevertheless, for a relational element to Augustine's view as well; see

image of God is that which distinguishes the human species from the rest of the animal kingdom,[12] though scientific advances in understanding the most advanced forms of animal intelligence raise questions. In at least some respects, human capacities may be only quantitatively rather than qualitatively distinct from animals in cognition, language skills and various other mental processes.[13]

A second broad category understands the divine image as functional or representative; it can be found throughout the major theological traditions.[14] This perspective takes its cue from Genesis 1, noting that verse 28 calls on the first humans to be fruitful and increase in number. In this way, they can fill the earth and subdue it and rule over the other creatures God has made.[15] Humans, according to this view, were created to be God's vice-regents on earth, a view Psalm 8 seems to support. Especially in verse 5, the psalmist extols God for having made humans a little lower than God (MT; LXX has "angels"), crowning them with glory and honor to rule over all the works of his hands (Ps 8:6). This crowning may be a poetic way of referring back to the Genesis account of God creating humans in his image,[16] but this verse is not connected with the exercise of dominion in any way that allows us to specify a relationship between creation in the image and the function of dominion. Psalm 8, moreover, does not actually use either of the Hebrew words from Genesis 1 for "image" (*ṣelem*) or "likeness" (*dəmût*). Thus, although the psalm highlights a key purpose for which God created human beings, it does not explicitly identify this purpose as the definition of his image. If Psalm 8:5 is an oblique allusion to the *imago*, Psalm 8:6 appears to list a second feature of the creation of humans: we were made in his image; we were also created for

---

Drever, "Redeeming Creation: Creation Ex Nihilo and the Imago Dei in Augustine," *International Journal of Systematic Theology* 15 (2013): 135-53.

[12]See explicitly C. John Collins, *Did Adam and Eve Really Exist? Who They Were and Why You Should Care* (Wheaton, IL: Crossway, 2011), 95.

[13]Daniel K. Miller, "Responsible Relationship: Imago Dei and the Moral Distinction Between Humans and Other Animals," *International Journal of Systematic Theology* 13 (2011): 323-39; Celia Deane-Drummond, "God's Image and Likeness in Humans and Other Animals: Performative Soul-Making and Graced Nature," *Zygon* 47 (2012): 934-48.

[14]Stephen L. Herring, "A 'Transubstantiated' Humanity: The Relationship Between the Divine Image and the Presence of God in Genesis i 26f.," *Vetus Testamentum* 58 (2008): 480-94.

[15]William A. M. Beuken, "The Human Person in the Vision of Genesis 1–3: A Synthesis of Contemporary Insights," *Louvain Studies* 24 (1999): 3-20; Walter McConnell, "In His Image: A Christian's Place in Creation," *Asia Journal of Theology* 20 (2006): 114-27.

[16]Tremper Longman III, *Psalms* (Downers Grove, IL: InterVarsity Press, 2014), 81.

stewardship. There is synonymous parallelism throughout the psalm, but this is always between two parts of a single verse, not between consecutive verses. So too here: verses 5a and b parallel each other (made only a little lower than God/crowned with glory and honor) as do verses 6a and b (made rulers over God's works/put everything under their feet). This suggests that verse 6, in its entirety, is not merely repeating the contents of verse 5.

Neither does Genesis 1 specify a relationship between the *imago* and God's mandate to the first human couple. Genesis 1:26 presents God's determination to create humanity in his image. Genesis 1:27 narrates that he does so. Genesis 1:28 then summarizes that he blessed them and then gave them a series of commands: to be fruitful, to multiply, to fill the earth, to subdue it and to rule over all the other animals and plants. The commands to subdue and rule follow quickly after God's determination to create humans in his image, but they are only the last two commands in a series of five. Few scholars consider the notion of populating the planet with children to be what the image of God consists of, so why should exercising dominion be taken that way? None of these tasks is said to define the divine image. A task, moreover, is something that naturally flows from a characteristic of an entity rather than being equated with that characteristic itself.[17] Already in verse 26 a purpose clause reinforces this point: humanity is created in God's image *in order to* rule over the rest of the cosmos.[18] It makes no sense to say that God's image *is* this exercise of vice-regency; we would then have a statement equivalent to saying they rule on God's behalf in order to rule on God's behalf—a tautology. The *imago*, then, must be something different, something that enables the exercise of vice-regency.[19]

 The third major understanding of the image is alternately called the social, relational or moral view.[20] Here readings of Genesis 1 focus on the even more

---

[17]See esp. C. F. Keil and F. Delitzsch, *Commentary on the Old Testament*, repr. ed. (Grand Rapids: Eerdmans, 1985), 1:63. Cf. also Victor P. Hamilton, *The Book of Genesis: Chapters 1–17* (Grand Rapids: Eerdmans, 1990), 137.

[18]Bill T. Arnold, *Genesis* (Cambridge: Cambridge University Press, 2009), 45.

[19]Occasionally, the functional approach has defined the *imago Dei* as creativity, since Gen 1:26-27 comes at the climax of God's creative action. Representing him on earth could then be imagined to involve replicating, in a derivative sense, his creative gifts, but this inference relies on even less of a connection between the image and its definition than does the approach that takes the image to be the exercise of dominion. This move tends to appear more at the popular level. See, for example, several of the articles in *Sojourners* 25 (May–June 1996); the entire fascicle is entitled *In the Image of God: The Creativity of Faith*.

[20]Gerald R. Bray, "The Significance of God's Image in Man," *Tyndale Bulletin* 42 (1991): 195-225;

immediate context of the announcement that God will fashion humans after his image and likeness. Even before Genesis 1:27 ends, the narrator adds, "male and female he created them." Some theologians have suggested that one does not fully experience creation in God's image apart from social relationships among others of both genders.[21] Still others focus on the unique capacity humans have to relate to God.[22] This, in turn, leads some theologians to focus on our identity as moral beings. As Mark Twain famously put it, "Man is the only animal who blushes. Or needs to."[23] The moral understanding of the image is associated particularly with the Protestant Reformers, especially Calvin and Luther,[24] while the social emphasis has been articulated more recently and influentially by Karl Barth.[25]

This three-part taxonomy is simplistic, as attempts to categorize a large number of positions on a topic debated over time usually are. Some systematicians would not group the relational and moral views together at all,[26] or they see the capacity for human relationships as something akin to cognition, volition and emotion with the capacity for relationship with the divine as more resembling the moral view.[27] Other, less frequently held views do not fall neatly into these categories. Alistair McFadyen encourages us to think about image more as a verb than a noun, so that "theological anthropology might be a matter of performance rather than definition: actively imaging God."[28] Paul Sands speaks of a vocational understanding of the *imago* in an attempt to give

---

Stanley Grenz, "The Social God and the Relational Self: Toward a Theology of the *Imago Dei* in the Postmodern Context," *Horizons in Biblical Theology* 24 (2002): 33-57; Oswald Bayer, "Being in the Image of God," *Lutheran Quarterly* 27 (2013): 79.

[21] For example, Paul Niskanen, "The Poetics of Adam: The Creation of אדם in the Image of אלהים," *Journal of Biblical Literature* 128 (2009): 417-36; cf. Hoekema, *Created in God's Image*, 99.

[22] For example, Andreas Schüle, "Made in the 'Image of God': The Concepts of Divine Images in Gen 1–3," *Zeitschrift für die alttestamentliche Wissenschaft* 117 (2005): 19.

[23] Mark Twain, *Following the Equator* (New York: Harper & Brothers, 1899), 264.

[24] On Luther, see Nathan Jastram, "Man as Male and Female: Created in the Image of God," *Concordia Theological Quarterly* 68 (2004): 5-96; on Calvin, see Randall Zachman, "Jesus Christ as the Image of God in Calvin's Theology," *Calvin Theological Journal* 25 (1990): 45-62.

[25] Joan E. O'Donovan, "Man in the Image of God: The Disagreement Between Barth and Brunner Reconsidered," *Scottish Journal of Theology* 39 (1986): 433-59.

[26] See Sinclair B. Ferguson, "Image of God," in *New Dictionary of Theology*, ed. Sinclair B. Ferguson, David F. Wright and J. I. Packer (Downers Grove, IL: InterVarsity Press, 1988), 329.

[27] See Stanley J. Grenz, *Theology for the Community of God* (Nashville: Broadman & Holman, 1994), 230-31.

[28] Alistair McFadyen, "Imagining God: A Theological Answer to the Anthropological Question?," *Zygon* 47 (2012): 918.

primacy to exercising dominion as caring stewardship while also subsuming under that exercise both the substantial and relational views.[29] Still others affirm all the major positions simultaneously. Bruce Demarest and Gordon Lewis, for example, conclude that God's image includes metaphysical, intellectual, moral, emotional, volitional and relational dimensions.[30] In an attempt to sort through the options, the rest of this essay will be devoted to a closer examination of key biblical texts.

OLD TESTAMENT TEXTS

Old Testament scholars gravitate toward the functional or representative position,[31] accepting the consensus that the Hebrew terms for "image" and "likeness" are synonyms and noting that they reflect the ancient practices of kings erecting statues of themselves for others to worship and of the crafting of visible idols to represent gods and goddesses.[32] In the case of royalty, statues usually had a physical resemblance to the person represented. In the case of gods and goddesses, idols had either a human or an animal-like appearance that may or may not have corresponded to what people thought the divine beings actually looked like, if indeed they conceived them in embodied form. Most Old Testament scholars take the role of the image to be the human exercise of God's royal rule as his visible representatives on earth.[33] But neither Genesis nor any other Old Testament book ever defines God's image in so many words. I believe the relationship between Genesis 1:26-27

---

[29]Paul Sands, "The *Imago Dei* as Vocation," *Evangelical Quarterly* 82 (2010): 28-41.

[30]Gordon R. Lewis and Bruce A. Demarest, *Integrative Theology* (Grand Rapids: Zondervan, 1990), 2:142-60. They suggest that the *imago* can be identified in examining everything involved in what it means to be human rather than seeing it as *one dimension* of humanness (160). Likewise, more explicitly, J. Wentzel van Huyssteen, "Human Origins and Religious Awareness in Search of Human Uniqueness," *Studia Theologica* 59 (2005): 122.

[31]For example, David J. A. Clines, "The Image of God in Man," *Tyndale Bulletin* 19 (1968): 53-103; Guunnlaugur A. Jónsson, *The Image of God: Genesis 1:26-28 in a Century of Old Testament Research* (Stockholm: Almqvist & Wiksell, 1988); Hendrik Bosman, "Humankind as Being Created in the 'Image of God' in the Old Testament: Possible Implications for the Theological Debate on Human Dignity," *Scriptura* 105 (2010): 561-71.

[32]Moisés Silva, *New International Dictionary of New Testament Theology and Exegesis* (Grand Rapids: Zondervan, 2014), 2:102-5. Cf. Gordon Wenham, *Genesis 1-15* (Waco, TX: Word, 1987), 30-32, 38.

[33]Cf. Richard S. Hess, "God and Origins: Interpreting the Early Chapters of Genesis," in *Darwin, Creation and the Fall: Theological Challenges*, ed. R. J. Berry and T. A. Noble (Nottingham: Apollos, 2009), 95-96. John H. Walton combines the functional and the ontological perspectives in *Genesis* (Grand Rapids: Zondervan, 2001), 131.

and verse 28 is most likely one of cause and effect.[34] As noted above, it is *because* humans are endowed with God's image that they are prepared to act as his vice-regents, stewarding creation. For this reason, the image cannot be equated with our role as stewards; it must be what makes us uniquely qualified to exercise that role.

Moreover, the second occurrence of the image or likeness of God in humanity in the Hebrew Bible points us in a slightly different direction. In Genesis 5:3, Seth is said to be created in Adam's likeness just as humans were made in God's likeness (Gen 5:1). Here family lineage and fatherly attributes comprise Adam's image, which he passes on to his son.[35] This points away from a functional or representational approach and toward the relational, with a touch of the substantial thrown in. On the other hand, nothing says that humans must be made in God's image *exactly* as children are in their parents' image. Again, in Genesis 5:2, the reference to making humans male and female intrudes as something we might not have expected. We still cannot be confident that we have an unambiguous definition of God's image in this passage.

The only other Old Testament text that bears directly on the nature of God's image is Genesis 9:6. Bolstering his declaration that whoever sheds human blood should be similarly put to death, God declares that "in his own image God made humankind." This clause by itself only means that humans were *originally* created in God's image.[36] But, given the context, it is hard to escape the conclusion that the point of this observation is to insist that even in fallen, sinful form, humans remain to some degree in the image of God. The insistence on capital punishment for murder would not have been needed in the absence of sin. The rationale for such punishment in a fallen world makes sense only if all human beings, however wicked, still reflect God's image in some fashion, so that murdering them proves unusually wicked and, at least under the old covenant, worthy of retaliation.[37]

---

[34]In other words, because humans were made in God's image, they could be given dominion over the rest of creation. But exercising dominion did not itself comprise the *imago*. See esp. G. C. Berkouwer, *Man: The Image of God* (Grand Rapids: Eerdmans, 1962), 71. Cf. also John T. Mueller, *Christian Dogmatics* (St. Louis: Concordia, 1934), 208.

[35]Cf. Kenneth A. Mathews, *Genesis 1–11:26* (Nashville: Broadman & Holman, 1996), 170.

[36]So that one could argue that the image is entirely lost in the fall. For example, see James D. G. Dunn, *Romans 1–8* (Dallas: Word, 1988), 495.

[37]In other words, from Gen 9:6 we can deduce the dignity that belongs to all human beings. See Dale Moody, *The Word of Truth: A Summary of Christian Doctrine Based on Revelation* (Grand Rapids: Eerdmans, 1981), 227.

Perhaps surprisingly, the concept of humanity formed in God's likeness does not play a significant role in the rest of the Old Testament.[38] The majority of uses of the words for "image" and "likeness" refer to humans inappropriately crafting or worshiping idols of wood or stone (e.g., Deut 4:16; 2 Kings 11:18; 2 Chron 33:7). These passages do not, therefore, help us in identifying God's image in humanity. A small number of commentators explicitly acknowledge that the image of God is never defined in the Old Testament.[39] Perhaps this is deliberate. The Old Testament contains numerous open-ended or incomplete presentations of themes as its writers look ahead to a future time when God would fulfill his promises. Perhaps the image of God is one of these. Maybe we are meant to gain a clear understanding of God's image only by turning to the New Testament.

NEW TESTAMENT TEXTS: GOSPELS AND ACTS

The only uses of the Greek words for "image" (*eikōn*) or "likeness" (*homoiōma*) in the Gospels come in the context of Jesus' reply to the Pharisees and Herodians who tried to trap him by asking about paying taxes to Rome. In Mark 12:16 and parallels, Jesus asks whose image appears on the coin used to pay the tax. The answer, of course, is Caesar's, which leads him to articulate his famous principle about giving to Caesar what is Caesar's and to God what is God's. As with the image of kings in Old Testament times, the image here refers to the engraved representation that was impressed on each coin. But this exchange teaches us nothing more about the image of God in humanity. Acts 17:29 and 19:35 make references to gods or goddesses whose image is represented in human sculptures, but these texts also do not help us in our quest to understand God's image.

NEW TESTAMENT TEXTS: GENERAL EPISTLES AND REVELATION

At the other end of the New Testament, the book of Revelation ten times refers to the image of the beast or antichrist that many will worship in the end

---

[38] I. Howard Marshall, "Being Human: Made in the Image of God," *Stone-Campbell Journal* 4 (2001): 50. Anticipating our conclusions, however, we note that when the image is understood in moral or relational categories, then it becomes central (even though the term itself is not) throughout the Old Testament. See W. Sibley Towner, "Clones of God: Genesis 1:26-28 and the Image of God in the Hebrew Bible," *Interpretation* 59 (2005): 354.

[39] For example, Richard S. Briggs, "Humans in the Image of God and Other Things Genesis Does Not Make Clear," *Journal of Theological Interpretation* 4 (2010): 111-26.

times (Rev 13:14, 15 [3x]; 14:9, 11; 15:2; 16:2; 19:20; 20:4). Here is another example of an image as a representation of a false god. Revelation 9:7 uses "likeness" ("appearance" in the NRSV) more loosely to describe what the demonic locusts looked like in John's vision. Hebrews 10:1 denies that the law creates a true image or form of the good things to come. None of these references adds to our understanding of the image of God in humans.

That leaves only the use of the words *eikōn* ("image") or *homoiōma* ("likeness") by Paul and James. Dealing briefly with James 3:9, we can see that it is important because, like Genesis 9:6, it reminds us that even unbelievers are made in and still remain in God's likeness.[40] For this reason, James explains, it is the height of inconsistency to praise God and curse any human being. The bulk of what we can learn about God's image and likeness from New Testament texts comes from Paul.

NEW TESTAMENT TEXTS: LETTERS OF PAUL

Likeness, form and representation. In Paul we see a helpful pattern of uses that supplies us with the constituent elements for forming a definition. To be sure, Paul also can use "likeness" to refer to an idol of a false god (Rom 1:23) or as a type of something yet to come (Rom 5:14). He can apply "likeness" to our crucifixion with Christ (in the "likeness of his death," Rom 6:5 KJV). But more helpfully for our purposes, he also uniquely identifies Jesus as having been sent "in the likeness of sinful flesh" (Rom 8:3). Paul knows that Jesus was not sinful (2 Cor 5:21), but he also recognizes that Jesus became fully human, thus closely approximating the experience of sinful human beings.[41] In experiencing human temptation and never yielding, Jesus' struggle against sin might be described as more acute than it is for any sinful human being. We succumb to sin frequently, at which point the struggle to resist temptation ends for a time.[42]

---

[40]Scot McKnight, *The Letter of James* (Grand Rapids: Eerdmans, 2011), 293-94; Dale C. Allison Jr., *A Critical and Exegetical Commentary on the Epistle of James* (New York: Bloomsbury T&T Clark, 2013), 553-54.

[41]Augustine phrased it nicely centuries ago: "What does sinful flesh have? Death and sin. What does the likeness of sinful flesh have? Death without sin. If it had sin it would be sinful flesh; if it did not have death it would not be the likeness of sinful flesh. As such he came—he came as Savior. He died but he vanquished death." Translation is from Gerald Bray, ed., *Romans,* rev. ed., Ancient Christian Commentary on Scripture (Downers Grove, IL: InterVarsity Press, 1998), 197.

[42]Leon Morris, "Hebrews," in *Expositor's Bible Commentary*, ed. Frank E. Gaebelein (Grand Rapids: Zondervan, 1981), 12:46.

That Jesus became fully human and yet did not sin recalls Genesis 1–2. However one interprets the story of Adam and Eve, it teaches the theological lesson that humans were created good (Gen 1:31) and therefore were not inherently sinful from the beginning. Despite Alexander Pope's famous epigram, "To err is human; to forgive, divine,"[43] it is possible to be fully human without being sinful; but because of the fall, only Jesus has lived a sinless human life.

A likeness can be a very close approximation without exact identity. This fits the concept of humans created in God's likeness and forestalls claims that this doctrine must lead to humans actually being deified. In other places, however, "likeness" *can* mean the exact representation or identical form of something, as in Philippians 2:7, where Jesus' taking upon himself the likeness of humanity means becoming *fully* human. *Homoiōma* ("likeness") in that passage appears in synonymous parallelism with *morphē* ("form" or "nature"), as the first part of the verse speaks of Christ taking the very *nature* of a servant. *Morphē* has already appeared in Philippians 2:6, affirming Christ's full deity as well.[44] Different terminology but identical concepts emerge in Hebrews 1:3, in which the Son "is the exact imprint (*charaktēr*) of God's very being."[45]

Christ as the image of God. From the remaining texts in Paul, a key contribution to a New Testament theology of the image of God appears in those passages that speak explicitly of Christ as God's image. In 1 Corinthians 15, Paul contrasts the natural (*psychikos*) body with the spiritual (*pneumatikos*) body (1 Cor 15:44). English translations have often misled readers to imagine Paul is contrasting something tangible with something intangible. It is hard to believe Paul envisioned the resurrected state of human existence as disembodied if he is using the word *body* (*sōma*) to describe it. Jewish hope consistently looked for a future bodily resurrection (see especially Dan 12:2),[46] and the immediate context of this verse makes plain that Paul is contrasting corruptible and incorruptible, mortal and immortal (1 Cor 15:42-43). Recent commentators have frequently suggested that the contrast in English would better be expressed by the adjectives "natural" and "supernatural."[47] Paul goes

---

[43]Alexander Pope, "An Essay on Criticism," Part II, line 525 (1711).

[44]Paul D. Feinberg, "The Kenosis and Christology: An Exegetical-Theological Analysis of Philippians 2:6-11," *Trinity Journal* 1 (1980): 29.

[45]Peter T. O'Brien, *The Letter to the Hebrews* (Grand Rapids: Eerdmans, 2010), 55.

[46]See esp. N. T. Wright, *The Resurrection of the Son of God* (Minneapolis: Fortress, 2003), 108-206.

[47]William L. Craig, "The Bodily Resurrection of Jesus," in *Gospel Perspectives*, vol. 1, ed. R. T. France

on to contrast Adam, the natural man, with Christ, the supernatural man, each prototypical of those who bear their image (1 Cor 15:45-48). The passage concludes, "Just as we have borne the image of the man of dust, we will also bear the image of the man of heaven" (1 Cor 15:49). We could summarize all of these parallel contrasts in another way: "Just as we have all been sinful, one day we will all be sinless." By bearing the image of Christ who is fully God, we bear the image of God, which will be perfected in us in the eternal state.[48]

Of all the options for understanding that image, this summary supports the moral or relational interpretation. We were created with the capacity for moral behavior and accountability. We abused that privilege and fell into sin. We are being redeemed as that capacity is progressively restored, though we will die before we have gotten terribly far in the process. In the resurrection life to come, the *imago* will be perfectly restored in what Paul refers to as our glorification (Rom 8:30).[49] Then we will be free from sin. The contrasts in 1 Corinthians 15 support Paul Wells's summary:

> The human image of God exists within a relationship: either in Adam or in Christ, and within them, there is relationship with God, one's neighbour, and other creatures. In the New Testament, the image refers essentially to the new community of Christ. Therein exist men and women recreated by the Spirit in the image of the Image, in an eschatological dynamic of progress and of hope.[50]

Tying the restoration of God's image to glorification proves significant, because we will see the concept of God's glory in the near or immediate context of every remaining reference to the image of God in Paul, beginning in 1 Corinthians 15:25-48.[51] Verses 40-41 contrast various kinds of "glory" (*doxa*)—both on earth and in heaven. Verse 43 contrasts the natural person with the supernatural person using the language of dishonor versus glory.

---

and David Wenham (Sheffield: JSOT, 1980), 58-59; Craig L. Blomberg, *1 Corinthians* (Grand Rapids: Zondervan, 1994), 316; Gordon D. Fee, *The First Epistle to the Corinthians*, 2nd ed. (Grand Rapids: Zondervan, 2014), 869.

[48]Steven Hultgren, "The Origin of Paul's Doctrine of the Two Adams in 1 Corinthians 15.45-49," *Journal for the Study of the New Testament* 25 (2003): 367.

[49]C. E. B. Cranfield, *A Critical and Exegetical Commentary on the Epistle to the Romans* (Edinburgh: T&T Clark, 1975), 1:432; Colin G. Kruse, *Paul's Letter to the Romans* (Grand Rapids: Eerdmans, 2012), 356.

[50]Paul Wells, "In Search of the Image of God: Theology of a Lost Paradigm," *Themelios* 30 (2004): 38.

[51]Douglas R. de Lacey stresses the way image and glory are parallel throughout much of Paul: "Image and Incarnation in Pauline Christology," *Tyndale Bulletin* 30 (1979): 3-28.

Quoting verses 42-43 together, "So it is with the resurrection of the dead. What is sown is perishable, what is raised is imperishable. It is sown in dishonor (*en atimia*), it is raised in glory (*en doxa*). It is sown in weakness, it is raised in power." Where we might have expected a contrast between dishonor and honor, we get one between dishonor and glory, suggesting that glory in this context is closely related to honor.[52] Acting honorably includes acting in accordance with God's will—that is, morally. Thus when we bear the image of the "man of dust" (1 Cor 15:49)—and 1 Corinthians 15:56 makes it clear that it is the image of the fallen, earthly man that we bear—we act dishonorably or immorally; when we bear the image of the heavenly man, we act honorably or morally.[53]

Paul also discusses Christ as the image of God in Colossians 1:15. There we read that "he is the image of the invisible God, the firstborn of all creation." There is widespread consensus that "firstborn" here means preeminent in rank, not the first being the Father created.[54] Paul is ascribing to Jesus divinity equal to that of the Father (cf. Col 2:9—"For in [Christ] the whole fullness of deity dwells bodily"). Christ displays in himself, eternally, the complete image of God, and he retained that image fully even as he took on human nature.[55] This alone should disqualify any substantial or physical definition of the *imago* that depends on humanity being embodied to possess it; Christ was the image before his incarnation. This should also exclude functional or representational

---

[52]Roy E. Ciampa and Brian S. Rosner, *The First Letter to the Corinthians* (Grand Rapids: Eerdmans, 2010), 824: "The concepts of glory and image are probably linked throughout these texts such that we are to understand that the image of the earthly man lacks the glory with which it was previously created and is now an image of impermanence, weakness, ignobility, and of earthly humanness while the image of the heavenly man reflects God's glory in its incorruptible, powerful, honorable, and spiritual nature (cf. vv. 42-44)."

[53]Ben Witherington III, *Conflict and Community in Corinth: A Socio-Rhetorical Commentary on 1 and 2 Corinthians* (Grand Rapids: Eerdmans, 1995), 309: "Now believers manifest in part the moral likeness of Christ and have the taste of the Spirit as an *arrabōn*; after the resurrection they will manifest both the outer and inner likeness of Christ."

[54]See esp. David E. Garland, *Colossians/Philemon* (Grand Rapids: Eerdmans, 1998), 87. Cf. also James D. G. Dunn, *The Epistles to the Colossians and to Philemon* (Grand Rapids: Eerdmans, 1996), 97-98.

[55]Everything else Paul predicates of Christ in the first half of this "hymn" (Col 1:15-17) refers to attributes or functions Christ had by the time of creation, so it would be unusual if this were the lone exception. David W. Pao notes that Wisdom as well as Genesis lies in the background, so that "for Paul, Jesus as the true Wisdom is and always has been the image of God, and through him God's nature and will are made known." *Colossians and Philemon* (Grand Rapids: Zondervan, 2012), 94-95.

definitions that require the existence of the created universe; Christ was the image before anything existed apart from the triune God. We are left with the moral or relational cluster of definitions.[56]

Colossians 1:16-20 goes on to enumerate points about the person and work of Christ but does not define God's image. The context, however, gives us some clues. Paul, in his prayers for the Colossians (Col 1:9-14), asks God to grant them increased knowledge and understanding to live a God-pleasing life, even as God strengthens them for the task "that comes from his glorious power" (Col 1:11). The subsequent context (Col 1:21-27) also refers to glory, when Paul concludes, "To them God chose to make known how great among the Gentiles are the riches of the glory of this mystery, which is Christ in you, the hope of glory" (Col 1:27). As Christians are progressively redeemed, they increasingly share the glory of Christ, the one who personifies the complete image of God, and they look forward to full glorification in the future life. Colossians 3:4 returns to this future hope, proclaiming, "When Christ who is your life is revealed, then you also will be revealed with him in glory."[57]

It would be easy to imagine this glory as some kind of visible radiance, supernatural aura or mystical revelation. After all, Colossians 3:1-3 commands believers, because they have been raised with Christ, to set their hearts on things above "where Christ is, seated at the right hand of God" (v. 1). The same mandate appears a second time in only slightly different words: "Set your minds on things that are above, not on things that are on earth" (v. 2). The rationale for this is that "you have died, and your life is hidden with Christ in God." Far from this turning out to be some esoteric or transcendent experience, Colossians 3:5-17 demonstrates that Paul is talking about holy, moral and upright living.[58] We are to put off "whatever in you is earthly: fornication, impurity, passion, evil desire, and greed" (v. 5), to rid ourselves of "anger, wrath, malice, slander, and abusive language" (v. 8), to clothe ourselves "with

---

[56]Likewise David H. Johnson, "The Image of God in Colossians," *Didaskalia* 3.2 (1992): 11. Donald Fairbairn makes the helpful distinction that we as humans "are not the very image of God itself" but we "bear the image of God. The exact image is Christ, the Son." *Life in the Trinity: An Introduction to Theology with the Help of the Church Fathers* (Downers Grove, IL: IVP Academic, 2009), 61.

[57]R. McL. Wilson notes that this fourth use of *doxa* in the letter finally discloses its full significance as we await precisely the glory that Christ in his resurrected humanity possesses. *A Critical and Exegetical Commentary on Colossians and Philemon* (New York: T&T Clark, 2005), 240.

[58]Garland, *Colossians/Philemon*, 214. Cf. further John R. Levison, "2 Apoc. Bar. 48:42-52:7 and the Apocalyptic Dimension of Colossians 3:1-6," *Journal of Biblical Literature* 108 (1989): 93-108.

compassion, kindness, humility, meekness, and patience" (v. 12) and to "let the peace of Christ rule" in our hearts (v. 15). The result of sharing Christ's glory turns out to be living moral and upright lives.

Believers in God's image. Five remaining verses in Paul speak about believers in God's image. The first two are closely related.

Colossians 3:10 and Ephesians 4:24. We should not be surprised, then, when we turn to the remaining Pauline texts on the image of God in humanity and discover one of them tucked into Colossians 3:1-17. Verses 9-10 command believers not to lie to each other, "seeing that you have stripped off the old self with its practices and have clothed yourselves with the new self, which is being renewed in knowledge according to the image of its creator." Here "Christ is all and in all" (v. 11). The logic of 3:1-8 is thus repeated in verses 9-15. A particular reality of our new creation (raised with Christ, the new self) supplies the reason Paul can call us to act in accordance with our new natures or selves (set your hearts on things above; do not lie to each other—vv. 1, 9). At first that new behavior seems to include a mysterious dimension (your life is hidden with Christ in God; Christ is all, and in all—vv. 3, 11) and is defined as sharing a key aspect of Christ's transcendence (appearing with him in glory, being renewed in the image of the Creator—vv. 4, 10). But any triumphalism is countered when that transcendence is defined in terms of the humdrum of moral living in an ungodly world (vv. 5-8, 12-15).[59]

Ephesians 4:24 confirms even more clearly that Paul believes the human embodiment of the *imago Dei* is disclosed in adhering to God's standards of morality. Ephesians and Colossians are remarkably similar in structure and content, so that one can often talk about parallel passages in those epistles as one does with the Synoptic Gospels.[60] Ephesians 4:22-24 closely parallels Colossians 3:9-10. Both occur approximately one third of the way through the second, ethical half of the letter, after the first half has provided the theological—and specifically Christological—basis for Paul's ethical injunctions. Both speak of putting off the old self and its wicked practices and putting on

[59]Douglas J. Moo observes in the context of 3:3 that we have not been transported to heaven nor do we look any different from those still of the world around us. But "Paul's point in this context is that we certainly need to behave differently." *The Letters to the Colossians and to Philemon* (Grand Rapids: Eerdmans, 2008), 250.

[60]E.g., Harold W. Hoehner, *Ephesians: An Exegetical Commentary* (Grand Rapids: Baker Academic, 2002), 611.

the new self with a new attitude or understanding. Instead of likening this to re-creation in God's image, as in Colossians, Ephesians uses the clause "created according to the likeness of God in true righteousness and holiness." The Greek for "like God" is *kata theon*, literally "according to God." But it is widely recognized that this expression is synonymous with "in the image of God."[61]

Unlike Colossians, however, Ephesians then adds the prepositional phrase that clinches the moral interpretation of the *imago*. We are not created to be like God in what theologians have come to call his incommunicable attributes: omnipotence, omniscience, omnipresence, aseity and so on. We are created to be like him "in true righteousness and holiness." We are called to increasingly exemplify ethical standards of godly living, empowered by the Spirit to do so, though we are fully capable of rebelling, quenching the Spirit and losing ground. Just as in Colossians, Paul in Ephesians also turns immediately to the moral implications of his statement: "So then, putting away falsehood, let all of us speak the truth to our neighbors" (Eph 4:25). Related injunctions follow throughout this ethical portion of the epistle.[62]

1 Corinthians 11:7. Only three references to God's image remain to be surveyed. One appears in that puzzling passage in 1 Corinthians 11:2-16 about head coverings for men and women during worship. Verse 7 may be the most understudied verse in an otherwise exhaustively examined passage. Paul has just finished explaining why he wants the men to pray or prophesy with their heads uncovered and the women to pray or prophesy with their heads covered. While most scholars assume external head coverings are in view, a good case can be made for Paul wanting men to have short hair and women to have long hair, as in verses 14-16.[63] Whatever the specifics, two themes unify proposals for why this was an issue in Corinth: proper and improper head coverings signified either sexual or religious faithfulness versus faithlessness.[64]

---

[61]F. F. Bruce, *The Epistles to the Colossians, to Philemon, and to the Ephesians* (Grand Rapids: Eerdmans, 1984), 358-59; Ernest Best, *A Critical and Exegetical Commentary on Ephesians* (Edinburgh: T&T Clark, 1998), 437.

[62]Frank Thielman, *Ephesians* (Grand Rapids: Baker Academic, 2010), 306-7; Clinton E. Arnold, *Ephesians* (Grand Rapids: Zondervan, 2010), 290.

[63]A. Philip Brown, "Chrysostom and Epiphanius: Long Hair Prohibited as Covering in 1 Corinthians 11:4, 7," *Bulletin for Biblical Research* 23 (2013): 365-76; David E. Blattenberger, *Rethinking 1 Corinthians 11:2-16 Through Archaeological and Moral-Rhetorical Analysis* (Lewiston, NY: Mellen, 1997).

[64]Craig L. Blomberg, *1 Corinthians* (Grand Rapids: Zondervan, 1994), 215. Cf. also Mark Finney, "Honour, Head-Coverings and Headship: 1 Corinthians 11.2-16 in Its Social Context," *Journal for the Study of the New Testament* 33 (2010): 31-58.

Verse 7 reads, "For a man ought not to have his head veiled, since he is the image and reflection of God; but woman is the reflection of man." A common interpretation of this statement has assumed that Paul is in some way indicating female inferiority. Some have even imagined that Paul was claiming that only the man was made in the image of God.[65] But this is not the perspective held by the most influential patristic or Reformation writers, and it is rightly almost entirely abandoned today. Paul knew Genesis 1:26-27 and believed, like most Jews and early Christians, that male and female alike were created in God's image. Most likely this is the very reason Paul does not repeat the word *image* and say "woman is the *image* and glory of man."[66] But in what way is man the glory of God while woman is (only?) the glory of man?

Philip Payne believes the issue behind this passage is hair length: Paul proscribes long hair for men because it sometimes signified homosexuality in the Greek world.[67] Short hair on women could suggest a lesbian relationship.[68] Asserting that woman is the glory of man would then be the alternative to man being the glory of man.

Perhaps more likely, given the clear allusion to the creation stories in 1 Corinthians 11:8-9, is that woman appears as man's glory in contrast to the animals that man named but that could not serve as his helpers.[69] In other words, it would be a reminder that man and woman match each other in ways that animals and humans do not. Paul's statement would not demean women but should be read as a reference to the creation of women as the completion of the creation of humanity, as an equal partner with the man. In 1 Corinthians

---

[65]Astonishingly, Pheme Perkins still believes Paul did not think women were created in God's image, as if this Pharisaic Jew had no knowledge of Genesis 1:26-28! See *First Corinthians* (Grand Rapids: Baker Academic, 2012), 138.

[66]Kenneth E. Bailey, *Paul Through Mediterranean Eyes: Cultural Studies in 1 Corinthians* (Downers Grove, IL: IVP Academic, 2011), 307. Creatively, Bailey thinks that looking at a man without a head covering in Corinth would have led to praising God who created human beings, while looking at a woman without a head covering would have led to praising the woman for what makes her gender attractive, thus deflecting attention from God. But this requires taking "man" in the first instance as "humanity" and in the second as "male" or "her husband," which seems unlikely in a context with so much parallelism.

[67]Philip B. Payne, *Man and Woman, One in Christ: An Exegetical and Theological Study of Paul's Letters* (Grand Rapids: Zondervan, 2009), 176.

[68]Gordon D. Fee, *The First Epistle to the Corinthians*, 2nd ed. (Grand Rapids: Eerdmans, 2014), 563-64nn84-85.

[69]Ibid., 570-72. Cf. Anthony C. Thiselton, *The First Epistle to the Corinthians* (Grand Rapids: Eerdmans, 2000), 833-37.

11:14-15, we learn that long hair dishonors a man but brings glory to a woman. So the same behavior—grooming in culturally appropriate ways that represent sexual or religious fidelity—brings glory or honor to oneself as well as to one's "head." Obviously, Paul believes that one can bring glory to more than one person or being at a time.[70]

What is more pertinent for our purposes is the explicit linkage of "image" and "glory" in the first part of 1 Corinthians 11:7. It is apparent that reflecting God's glory is an important component of possessing the divine image, perhaps deriving from Psalm 8:5.[71] It is too easy for us to imagine that glory here has something to do with beauty, because we often think of long hair on women as something beautiful. Short hair on men, though, is less likely to conjure up the concept of attractiveness, both then and now. Instead, we should think of glory as that which brings honor because the person's external appearance signals his or her sexual or religious faithfulness, and this lands us squarely back in the moral or ethical realm. Bringing glory to God when one is made in his image means behaving in a holy and righteous way, which is indicated in part by grooming or dress that signifies faithfulness according to the standards of a given culture.

2 Corinthians 3:18; 4:4. We have only Paul's use of "image" in 2 Corinthians 3:18 and 4:4 left to consider. Both appear in the same subsection of the epistle, in which Paul is contrasting the lesser glory of the law with the greater glory of the new covenant (2 Cor 3:7–4:6). Here, many English translations (e.g., CEB, HCSB) have used the expression "fading glory" to refer to the aura on Moses' face (2 Cor 3:7, 13) despite the lack of any hint in the Hebrew Bible that this light ever gradually disappeared.[72] The NIV deals with both verses better by translating, "The Israelites could not look steadily at the face of Moses because of its glory, transitory though it was" (2 Cor 3:7) and "We are not like

---

[70]See David E. Garland, *1 Corinthians* (Grand Rapids: Baker Academic, 2003), 523, who goes on to note that image and glory were consistently closely associated in Jewish exegesis. For the view that only husbands and wives are in view here, see P. T. Massey, "Gender Versus Marital Concerns: Does 1 Corinthians 11:2-16 Address the Issues of Male/Female or Husband/Wife?," *Tyndale Bulletin* 64 (2013): 239-56.

[71]Preben Vang, *1 Corinthians* (Grand Rapids: Baker Books, 2014), 148.

[72]Cf. "glory . . . fading as it was" (NASB); "brightness . . . fading away" (NLT); "brightness . . . fading as this was" (RSV). Correctly capturing the sense, on the other hand, are ESV—"glory . . . being brought to an end"; NET—"a glory which was made ineffective"; and NRSV—"a glory now set aside."

Moses, who would put a veil over his face to prevent the Israelites from seeing the end of what was passing away" (2 Cor 3:13). In the latter verse, Paul's point is that it was the old covenant that was passing away, not the glory surrounding Moses' face.[73]

When we come to 2 Corinthians 3:18, then, we read, "And all of us, with unveiled faces, seeing the glory of the Lord as though reflected in a mirror, are being transformed into the same image from one degree of glory to another; for this comes from the Lord, the Spirit." Paul has already insisted that the old covenant was glorious (2 Cor 3:9), making the new covenant that much more glorious, so much so that the earlier glory pales in comparison (2 Cor 3:10-11). The "one degree of glory to another" in verse 18 is literally "from glory to glory," possibly reflecting this growth in glory from the old to the new covenant.[74]

But what is this glory that grows as we are increasingly transformed into God's image as believers? Second Corinthians 4:1-6 helps us. We renounce secret and shameful ways, we do not use deception and we do not distort God's word (v. 2). Positively, we set forth the truth plainly, commending ourselves to everyone's consciences in God's sight (v. 3). Once again, we are confronted with moral or ethical categories.[75] Another way to put it could have been, "Because of our being remolded in God's image we live as upright, holy and God-pleasing lives as possible, even when everybody else, especially the competition, is unethical and immoral."

Second Corinthians 4:4 returns to the theme of Christ who is the image of God. In fact, "glory" and "image" seem virtually interchangeable in this verse:

---

[73]Linda L. Belleville, *Reflections of Glory: Paul's Polemical Use of the Moses-Doxa Tradition in 2 Corinthians 3* (Sheffield: JSOT, 1991), 295.

[74]Most commentators reflect the less-precise NIV and assume that Paul simply has increasing sanctification in view. But Paul B. Duff paraphrases verse 18 as follows: "So all believers can clearly see (i.e., 'with unveiled faces') God's power (i.e., 'the glory of the Lord') in the resurrection of the executed Christ. We believers can see this in ourselves (i.e., 'as in a mirror') because we are being transformed into the same image, the image of the resurrected Christ. Like Christ, we are being transformed from (the ministry of) death to (the ministry of) life (i.e., 'from glory to glory') because Moses' glorious ministry brought condemnation and the sentence of death upon us but my ministry (i.e., the ministry of the Spirit and righteousness) brings reconciliation with God which is tantamount to life. All of this has come about because the Lord (i.e., God who raised Christ) is also the Spirit who is present in my ministry." "Transformed 'from Glory to Glory': Paul's Appeal to the Experience of His Readers in 2 Corinthians 3:18," *Journal of Biblical Literature* 127 (2008): 774. For this same contrast between the glories of the two covenants, see Paul Barnett, *The Second Epistle to the Corinthians* (Grand Rapids: Eerdmans, 1997), 208; and Frank J. Matera, *II Corinthians: A Commentary* (Louisville: Westminster John Knox, 2003), 96.

[75]Colin G. Kruse, *The Second Epistle of Paul to the Corinthians* (Grand Rapids: Eerdmans, 1987), 104.

"The god of this world has blinded the minds of unbelievers, to keep them from seeing the light of the gospel of the glory of Christ, who is the image of God."[76] But that glory is not just Christ's. Verse 6 quickly adds that God has "shone in our hearts to give the light of the knowledge of the glory of God in the face of Jesus Christ." As we conclude our survey of the relevant New Testament data, it appears that the moral view of the *imago Dei* has emerged as a clear winner for understanding this important concept.

Having seen how regularly Paul associates glory with God's image, we may recall a key Old Testament text: Exodus 33:18–34:7. While no mention is made of God's image or likeness, God's glory plays a central role. As Moses is preparing to ascend Mount Sinai and receive God's law, he requests to see God's glory (v. 18). God replies that no fallen human being could see his glory and survive the exposure (v. 20), but he does promise to cause all his goodness to pass in front of Moses (v. 19). When Moses stands on the mountain, the Lord passes in front of him and declares that he is "merciful and gracious, slow to anger, and abounding in steadfast love and faithfulness, keeping steadfast love for the thousandth generation, forgiving iniquity and transgression and sin" (vv. 6-7). To the extent that God is revealing his glory to Moses as promised, and to the extent that God's glory discloses his image, we find once again that image is expressed in fundamentally ethical categories.[77] Given the close relationship between image and glory, this text sheds considerable light on the *imago Dei*.

Conclusion

Love (or mercy) and justice, the communicable attributes of God, thus summarize the heart of the *imago*. The human desire for both love and justice is deeply embedded in every culture. Moral or ethical living that stems from a capacity to relate to the divine sets humans apart from all other species. Ludwig Feuerbach, the nineteenth-century atheist philosopher, opined that if God did not exist, humanity would have had to create him,[78] but he did not

---

[76]Philip E. Hughes, *The True Image: The Origin and Destiny of Man in Christ* (Grand Rapids: Eerdmans, 1989), 26.

[77]I owe this emphasis on Exodus 33–34 as a key contributor to a biblical theology of the *imago* to my former colleague and chair of the psychology department at Palm Beach Atlantic College in 1983–1985, Ward Wilson. See R. Ward Wilson and Craig L. Blomberg, "The Image of God in Humanity: A Biblical-Psychological Perspective," *Themelios* 18.3 (1993): 8-15.

[78]Ludwig Feuerbach, *The Essence of Christianity*, repr. ed. (Amherst: Prometheus, 1989), 118 and throughout.

explain what would have given humanity the capacity to create the concept of the divine. Precisely because it is unique to humanity, it could not have come through the evolutionary processes that have given us numerous other facets of our nature.

There is no evidence that any other creature conceives of God or has the capacity to do so. Whether there is an innate sense of right or wrong in monkeys or dolphins, whether learned behaviors can lead to such a sense, there is no evidence that any species but our own can philosophize and reflect on their capacity for ethical and unethical living, where that capacity came from and what it might imply about a creator.[79] Nor would it make any sense to impose human accountability mechanisms on other species. For example, even with the most advanced community of gorillas, how could we imagine that one that had turned violent would be tried before a jury of its peers?

If it makes little sense to envision other animals providing justice for one another, what about love? To be sure, animals, especially parents, show devotion and affection in numerous ways, but to attribute to another animal Christian love—voluntary self-giving for the sake of the other, regardless of response, especially in light of one's awareness of the divine—seems inconceivable.[80] Love *and* justice—moral living, with divine rewards and punishments for the respective presence and absence of these attributes—uniquely define the human being. They uniquely represent the image of the divine in humanity. It makes sense, then, if Christians want to maximize their impact in advancing God's kingdom on earth, that we would seek to model before a watching world the most loving and just lifestyles possible.[81] In an era when most inhabitants of our planet have been let down by human authorities, we urgently need more models of genuine Christian love.

A generation ago Albert Hobbs wrote, "If there is anything which characterizes man more surely than his capacity for moral choice it is his unending

[79]Jason P. Roberts, "Emerging in the Image of God to Know Good and Evil," *Zygon* 46 (2011): 471-81.

[80]See esp. Lewis B. Smedes, *Love Within Limits: Realizing Selfless Love in a Selfish World*, rev. ed. (Grand Rapids: Eerdmans, 1989).

[81]Douglas P. Baker, "The Image of God: According to Their Kinds," *Reformation and Revival Journal* 12 (2003): 102-4, 106. Cf. Piet van Staden, "Image (of God) as Ethical Injunction: A Social-Scientific Perspective," *Theological Studies* 51 (1995): 279: "The faith of adherents to the community of believers finds expression in distinctive behavior—that is, in conduct that clearly identifies them as reflecting the image of God."

search for ways to evade his responsibility to choose—the responsibility which is the essence of his birthright."[82] Hobbs could as easily have said that *the image of God in which all humanity is created is the capacity for moral living.* This is where our research has led us.

Hobbs's observation seems truer today in our culture of victimization, in which we blame everybody and everything for our failures except ourselves. When we do acknowledge wrongdoing, we say we made a mistake, misspoke or made poor choices. We are reluctant to use the biblical word *sin* because it reminds us of the accountability we have.[83] At the same time, humans of many different ideological stripes still perform remarkable feats of heroism, self-sacrifice and love.

Christopher Hitchens was right when he noted that there is nothing good exclusive to Christians and nothing wicked that Christians cannot do. A half century ago, the great Dutch theologian G. C. Berkouwer commented that "anyone who attempts to combat humanism" by denying these claims "must necessarily underestimate the actuality of God's gifts to fallen man." He added, "We can be safeguarded against two extremes—a superficial optimism which deadens our alertness, or a simple pessimism which convinces no one—only when we see the divine limitation of the dark dynamic of corruption functioning not only through an external bridling of the effects of evil, but also through the endowments God has given to mankind."[84]

The next time a shooter or a terrorist strikes, we should not be surprised at the depths of evil or the heights of good that humanity, regenerate or unregenerate, is capable of. But we should expect Christians to take the lead in modeling the most moral, loving and sacrificial response. A fully biblical doctrine of the image of God, climaxing in the New Testament theology of the *imago,* produces both a lack of surprise at evil and an expectation of good.[85]

---

[82]Albert H. Hobbs, *Man Is Moral Choice* (Westport, CT: Arlington House, 1979), 247.

[83]Contrast Donald G. Bloesch, *Essentials of Evangelical Theology* (New York: Harper & Row, 1978), 1:95: "True human nature as we find it in Jesus Christ is without sin, and therefore sin is rightly seen as a deviation from human nature. It signifies the unnatural of man, the abnormal which has now become natural. The *imago Dei,* the reflection of the being of God in man, is defaced, but it is not destroyed. Man is still responsible before God, though his freedom has been considerably impaired."

[84]Berkouwer, *Man: The Image of God,* 186.

[85]Cf. esp. Norma V. Harrison, *God's Many-Splendored Image: Theological Anthropology for Christian Formation* (Grand Rapids: Baker Academic, 2010).

Part Two

CULTURE

4

Uncovering Christ

Sexuality in the Image of the Invisible God

Timothy R. Gaines and Shawna Songer Gaines

Human persons are—fundamentally and primordially—lovers.

James K. A. Smith, Desiring the Kingdom

Introduction

The images driving our age communicate messages about the nature of human sexuality. Popular Christian responses to the proliferation of sexualized imagery tend toward the denial and repression of sexuality; it is as if Christians, at least in the public sphere, are uncomfortable that sexual imagery exists at all. But in an age driven by visual images, particularly sexualized images, the Christian tradition has far more to offer than a bald disdain for sexuality. Christians cannot respond to sexualized images simply by saying what we ought *not* to do, see, wear or desire. If Christians wish to find a way beyond this kind of response, then we must engage in sustained, patient and informed reflection on how sexuality is to be understood faithfully.

A response beyond negation is possible when rooted in a Christian affirmation and celebration of sexuality as itself being assumed by God. Sexuality has been taken up and redeemed in the incarnation of Christ. This essay explores aspects of the Christian tradition's long history of attempting to make sense of sexuality, desire and the image of God in light of Christ's incarnation. We believe the rich resources found in the doctrines of creation and the incarnation open a world of possibility for understanding sexuality in light of the image of God, which is enfleshed in the person of Jesus. The Christian tradition is not opposed to the imaging of sexuality, and this is evident particularly in Renaissance-era depictions of Jesus. These Christian images stand in stark contrast to modern attempts to construct an image of human sexuality.

Understood systematically, read literarily and confessed creedally, Christian theological reflection begins with creation in God's image, moves to incarnation and culminates in the redemptive and creative power of God's Holy Spirit. Our first step is thus to take account of creation: we will explore the primacy of desire in the doctrine of creation in God's image. Our second step is to illustrate the incarnation as the fulfillment of God's desire for creation. In the third step, we will take account of the path we have walked and then analyze the offering presented to us by late modernity, including the option of constructing sexuality in our own self-made images. Should we bypass this diversion, a fourth step awaits us on the other side: the sanctification of the image.

CREATION IN THE (DESIRING) IMAGE

We were created in love at God's desire and by God's design. We were created in the image of the triune God who is eternal, self-giving love among Father, Son and Holy Spirit, three persons who are intimately poured out in one life, one God. God's creative act of love hints that desire is an elemental divine characteristic. While the writer of Genesis 1 provides no definitive motivation for God's creative act, the hovering of the Spirit over "the surface of the deep" suggests an anticipation fueled by love—God's own plentitude of desire. In the same way that God's Word rides on the breath of the wind (rûaḥ), so too does God's creative fiat process on God's creative desire.

"Desire," theologian Sarah Coakley explains, "is an ontological category belonging primarily to God, and only secondarily to humans as a token of the createdness 'in the image.'"[1] The pangs of longing for the things of life point us toward our created nature. We desire as created beings; we desire in the image of the Creator. This is a necessary step along our journey because "desire is more fundamental than 'sex.'"[2] Or, as Augustine noted, the human

---

[1] Sarah Coakley, *God, Sexuality and the Self: An Essay 'On the Trinity'* (Cambridge: Cambridge University Press, 2013), 10.
[2] Ibid., 10.

experience is one of desiring because we have been created to desire something other than ourselves: "You made us for yourself," he confesses to God, "and our hearts find no peace until they rest in you."[3] Sexuality is predicated upon that most basic desire. Before we are male or female, we desire. Before we are single, married, virgin or sexed, we desire. Before we are turned toward any sexual orientation or identification, we are desiring, erotic beings. And this is in God's image.

The Christian Scriptures tell the narrative of God's pursuit of a beloved creation and the broken bride's feeble attempts to be embraced and embraceable. Our story begins with God creating in a free expression of God's own desire. Though the triune life of God did not need any addition, God's love flowed outward in an act of freedom and desire. God's desire echoes through the remainder of the story as those created in God's image express their own desire. We remember Jacob's fourteen-year toil on behalf of the woman he desired; this desire was juxtaposed with God's favoring of Leah, the undesired one, through whom the line of David was born and from which also came the Messiah. The Psalms reverberate with themes of desire: "I seek you, my soul thirsts for you; my flesh faints for you," the psalmist sings to God (Ps 63:1). "As a deer longs for flowing streams, so my soul longs for you, O God. My soul thirsts for God, for the living God" (Ps 42:1-2).

Against the objections of those who were convinced by gnostic tendencies toward the denial of desire, the church included the Song of Solomon in the canon, partially because of the way its themes of desire testify to the completeness of God's creation. In Hosea we have an analogy that points to the primacy of desire in our relationship with God. Then there is Jesus himself, moved to tears over Jerusalem and enraged by temple politics. Even in giving himself over to death, he arranged a familial union between Mary and the disciple whom he loved (Jn 19:26-27). The beloved disciple's message would establish desire and redemption in the same divine movement: "God's love was revealed among us in this way: God sent his only Son into the world so that we might live through him" (1 Jn 4:9).

We humans are created as creatures who desire, vested with the image of a desiring, loving God. For this reason, James K. A. Smith makes an

---

[3]Augustine, *Confessions*, trans. R. F. Pine-Coffin (New York: Penguin, 1961), 21.

anthropological and epistemological claim that is at home in the Christian tradition: "Human persons are not primarily or for the most part thinkers, or even believers. Instead, human persons are—fundamentally and primordially—lovers."[4] Western Christians, inheritors of a vision of humanity established on reason, logic and a tendency to think of bodily desires as base or vulgar, could be helped by reaching back into the Christian tradition and recovering a view of desire as part of what it means to be created in God's image. To love and to desire in our bodies is very much what it means to be made in the image of God. We image the Creator in our desires, for the very impetus for our creation was God's divine desiring.

INCARNATION OF THE IMAGE

God's desire for this creation became manifest through the Holy Spirit's work in the womb of Mary—the conception of the Savior, God with us in flesh. The Christian faith is bold in its insistence that God became flesh, and for good reason. The incarnation is the fulfillment of all we have longed for, as the Word dwelled in creation and we could behold his body. In the incarnation, Jesus perfectly embodied the image of the divine, particularly in that his desire was entirely God-directed.

The church has insisted and continues to insist on the full humanity of Christ as including his desires. "I am thirsty," Jesus' labored request from the cross in John 19:28, not only calls to mind the image of souls panting for God as a deer pants for water (Ps 42) but also enflames our imaginations to consider the fullness of God's humanity in Christ, *complete with desire*. John's account of the resurrected Jesus asking the disciples to bring him the fish they caught as a morning meal signals to us that even in the resurrection bodily desire for things like food is still present in some way (Jn 21:10).

Jesus' redemptive desire is demonstrated in Luke's account of the Last Supper, which includes Jesus' words, "I have eagerly desired to eat this Passover with you before I suffer" (Lk 22:15). Both Matthew and Luke include Jesus' longing lament over Jerusalem: "Jerusalem, Jerusalem, the city that kills the prophets and stones those who are sent to it! How often have I desired to gather your children together as a hen gathers her brood under her wings, and

---

[4]James K. A. Smith, *Desiring the Kingdom: Worship, Worldview, and Cultural Formation* (Grand Rapids: Baker Academic, 2009), 41.

you were not willing!" (Mt 23:37; cf. Lk 13:34). The image the Gospel writers wished to convey of Jesus' incarnation both before and after his resurrection did not preclude the possibility of Jesus having, experiencing or entertaining desire. In the fullest expression and embodiment of humanity, desire was not eradicated; it was enfleshed.

The incarnation of Christ not only assumes desire but also orients it toward redemptive and holy ends. Where we see Jesus express desires, those desires point toward the goods of redemption. Jesus' longing to gather the residents of Jerusalem to himself, for example, is also a longing for the restoration and redemption of humanity. In this case, a desire to gather his people to himself is also a desire to lead them away from the destructive patterns of their current lives.

The incarnation of Christ is itself the embodiment of God's desire for the redemption of creation. John's theology of incarnation cannot be separated from the divine motivations revealed in the sending of the Son: "For God so loved the world that he gave his only Son, so that everyone who believes in him may not perish but may have eternal life" (Jn 3:16). The pattern we are given begins not with the sending of the Son but with the divine love and self-giving passion of God, ecstatically moving out toward creation in love.

In affirming both that desire is the basis of sexuality and that desire was not dismantled in the incarnation, we can now say that sexuality itself meets its fulfillment in the incarnation of Christ. Locating the theological consideration of human sexuality within the doctrine of the incarnation opens the discussion of human sexuality beyond the other doctrinal locations where it is so often treated systematically, pastorally and practically. If theological discussions of human sexuality gravitate toward either creation or sin without considering Christological resources, we will be at an impasse: the doctrine of creation alone would suggest that sexuality is part of our created makeup and ought to be affirmed and celebrated, while the doctrine of sin alone would remind us that all our activities and desires are marked by the effects of sin and that sexual desires are especially prone to malformation, misuse or abuse, especially in an image-driven age. Further, if we think only of sin, the sexualization of the image of God becomes a problem.

The sexual aspect of the *imago Dei* cannot be problematic, however, if Christians recover the full humanity of Jesus of Nazareth, the image of the invisible God. If sexuality, which is based on desire, remained in the incarnation of Jesus, it was taken up in him; in him it was fulfilled and redeemed. Sexuality finds its fullest expression in the incarnation of Christ. In the incarnation, the "restless heart" of Augustine's confession is stilled as desire itself comes to rest in Christ's complete devotion to the Father in the infilling power of the Holy Spirit. It is in the power of the Spirit that the Son is fully devoted to the Father and his desires take on a single-mindedness, turning away from the malformation of lust that characterizes sinful human sexuality.

Eugene Rogers offers a fascinating definition of lust as the sin of overreaching or "attempting to take by force what God would give in time."[5] Lust is desire that forgets its direction, failing to trust in God's answer to human desire. It is being ashamed of our creatureliness and attempting to fulfill our own desires in spite of our createdness; it is acting on our desires while forgetting that those desires have a good and proper aim. Rogers argues that Adam "counted divinity a thing to be grasped," acting upon his desire but reaching beyond the bounds of his placement as a creature in the garden.[6] Adam's sin was an act of grasping and taking rather than waiting and receiving.

By contrast, the second Adam "does not try to be God."[7] Because Jesus' life is completely and perfectly "in the Spirit," his eager desire to eat with the disciples culminates in his offering a gift to them. He does not grasp, nor does he withhold. "I have eagerly desired to eat this" immediately becomes "this is my body, which is given for you" (Lk 22:15, 19). In the Spirit, Jesus' desire is the reversal of Adam's desire. Rather than attempting to breach the boundaries of his humanness, Jesus' desire translates into an act that demonstrates that he "did not consider equality with God as something to be exploited" (Phil 2:6). In the incarnation, desire is fulfilled as it is given and not grasped. As the foundation of sexuality, desire "in the Spirit" is that which motivates human persons toward receiving the gifts of God that are most fully exemplified in the life of the Son, the image of the invisible God.

The first Adam fell into a state of shame. As Rogers explains, shame follows from lust. Adam's shame stems from the fact that he overreached—he strove

---

[5]Eugene F. Rogers Jr., *After the Spirit: A Constructive Pneumatology from Resources Outside the Modern West* (Grand Rapids: Eerdmans, 2005), 171.
[6]Ibid.
[7]Ibid.

to be more than a creature. His exposure in the garden is an exposure of his nakedness, now shameful as he grasps at knowledge beyond what was granted to him.

Theologians and artists, especially during the Renaissance, have given the redemption of this shame significant attention, especially in and around the images of the incarnation. Works of art spanning from Montagna's *Holy Family*, which portrays Jesus in his infancy, to Michelangelo's *Risen Christ*, envisioning Jesus in adulthood, expose him in ways that sent Adam seeking leaves. These images show Jesus' genitals, not to shock the viewer but for theological purposes. These artists carefully withdrew the cover of clothing in order to say something about the nature of sexuality in the incarnation of Christ.

The artists' point was that sexuality was assumed in the incarnation, taken up by Christ and redeemed in its fullness. "If Michelangelo denuded his *Risen Christ*," Leo Steinberg maintains, "he must have sensed a rightness in his decision more compelling than inhibitions of modesty; he must have seen that a loincloth would convict these genitalia of being 'pudenda,' thereby denying the very work of redemption which promised to free human nature from its Adamic contagion of shame."[8] The innocence of the Christ child in a collection of fourteenth-century Madonnas is punctuated by the child's nakedness, sometimes exposed by the child himself, other times revealed by Mary. This signals a goodness stronger than the need for modesty, a purity negating the need for denial. The "unabashed freedom" of these Renaissance artists and the freedom of the subjects of the images "conveyed a possibility which Christian teaching reserved only for Christ and for those who would resurrect in Christ's likeness: the possibility of human nature without human guilt."[9]

Steinberg also examines a number of sixteenth-century works of art that were later repainted, covering up Christ's nakedness. Baroque additions to Michelangelo's *Risen Christ*, which had demonstrated Christ's victory over lust in his assumption of sexuality, cover his nakedness and obscure the original artist's theological meaning. Subsequent cleanings of the paintings have restored many of these works, but the implication is that humans have not yet

---

[8] Leo Steinberg, *The Sexuality of Christ in Renaissance Art and in Modern Oblivion* (Chicago: University of Chicago Press, 1996), 21.
[9] Ibid., 21-22.

been able to embrace the image of the invisible God in such a way that his sexuality fulfills sexuality for the rest of humanity created in God's image.[10]

The incarnation of Christ provides the essential foundation for the redemption of human sexuality. In the image of the invisible God, desire is taken up, redeemed and made whole. The incarnation teaches us that desire need not reach beyond what it has been created to be. Christ's coming in human likeness continues to demonstrate that the desires given to humanity are gifts directed toward good ends. As a subset of desire, so too is sexuality.

CONSTRUCTION OF THE IMAGE

Even so, humans continue to overreach, grasping at our own images and ignoring the fact that God has given God's own image to us. While humans have been created in the image of a desiring God, our greatest desire has turned toward constructing an image for ourselves. There is a difference between creation and construction. Only God can create something out of nothing; we can merely rearrange what we have been given—and so often we do, constructing an image that is a mockery of the one gifted to us.

The drive toward self-construction is nothing new. The invention of lust was Adam's attempt at grasping good and evil, bringing them under his control and defining "good" according to his own desires. This approach has flourished in the late modern era; consciously or not, human persons consider themselves to be the result of their own self-construction, largely guided by self-defined desires. Especially in an image-driven age, we are prone to construct an image for ourselves rather than seek to be renewed in the divine image.

In the Western world, self-construction takes place largely through consumption of goods, materials and brands. For example, the shoe manufacturer and marketing powerhouse Nike has launched a customizable line of shoes based on 31 different parts and 82 different materials, providing thousands of unique options. But consumers are being allowed to do more than customize a shoe: they can now create a unique image and life experience. These shoes, so Nike marketers would have buyers believe, are one more step toward projecting a desired self-image to the world. Each color, contour and eyelet gives buyers more material to construct for themselves an image.

---

[10]Ibid., 184-95.

Marketers, Smith has pointed out, are not oblivious to the desiring nature of humanity. "Desire is a structural feature of being human," and marketers have not ignored this reality.[11] We are lovers down deep, goes the logic of marketing, and so the goal of advertising is not to convince the consumer that the product being advertised is the best. The goal is to pique the consumer's desire for the image the product can create.

The images of our age are directly connected with this "structural feature." These images are often sexual, intended to evoke a consumer's desire. Marketers know that if they can raise desire and associate a product with that desire, they can probably get the consumer to buy the product. "If you link sex and advertising, you have a powerful one-two punch," advertising analyst Tom Reichert explains. "Companies deliberately link their products with sexual information: because of our biology we can't help but be drawn to it."[12] What does sex have to do with rice, beer, deodorant or hamburgers? The answer is very little, until we see a commercial or billboard bringing the two into an unholy union of erotic desire. Suddenly we want both—but *why*? The marketing imagery of sex signals to us that the products sold alongside a partially nude model will help us achieve some kind of sexual fulfillment. "If you buy this deodorant," the logic goes, "you can create yourself into the kind of man for whom beautiful models rip off their clothes. So buy this deodorant."

These marketing strategies point to our deeper brokenness; our desire has been directed away from our Creator and toward constructing for ourselves an image. The difference between consumerism and the Christian tradition, however, is that the Christian tradition assumes that human desires find their good end in God while marketers suggest to consumers that satiating our desires is a good end in itself. In the absence of a divine end for our desire, we quickly move toward a mode of self-construction in which the images that shape our understanding of the good life play a role. We pick and choose images that we believe will help us achieve the good end we desire based on the images that court our desires. From there, it is only a few short steps toward a vision of humanity that is dependent upon a self-constructed image rather than being made in the image of God. Our desires themselves become the fabric of the image in which we are made.

---

[11]Smith, *Desiring the Kingdom*, 51.
[12]Tom Reichert, *The Erotic History of Advertising* (Amherst: Prometheus, 2011), 22.

Consider the difference between a contemporary clothing advertisement and Michelangelo's *Risen Christ*. The clothing ad shows models wearing very little; it focuses in on body parts without showing faces, without showing whole people. While *Risen Christ* is far more explicit in terms of the amount of human anatomy on display, the juxtaposition of these images reveals the vastly different ends to which they are directed. In *Risen Christ*, Jesus' nudity suggests a peaceful comfort in his own incarnation, a comfort that neither denies his embodied state nor makes it a source of anxiety. Any shame, guilt or lust has been overcome such that his sexuality is not in conflict with a life of holiness.

The clothing ad, on the other hand, features anxiously poised bodies on the verge of a sexual act. The image hints at clothing, but only in passing; sexual desire is clearly the subject and the highest good. Sexual desire serves no purpose other than its own celebration; in this way, it sells the clothing that will ostensibly achieve this end for the consumer. The underlying message is that if you would construct your image by purchasing these clothes, you will have the ability to express and experience this kind of heightened sexual desire. The anxiety in the image suggests that these desires will not be *fulfilled* but only *experienced* (and probably as much as possible). *"Be the creator of your own image,"* it calls, "and experience what can be possible when you reach for sexual gratification." Oddly enough, the nudity we see in *Risen Christ* would be more jarring in the clothing ad precisely because of the ad's logical end: self-construction unto lust.

Not long ago, we sat down with a teenager under our pastoral care who was at times enthusiastic about Jesus but whose commitment to the practices of faith was occasional and sparse. We finally asked her, "Why are you a Christian?" She told us, "It's just part of what makes me, me. I like to sing and dance, I like chocolate and I like Jesus." Jesus and chocolate could easily appear side by side on her social media feed, mere expressions of desiring an image that must be constructed according to personal preference. In her estimation, Jesus is not the image of the invisible God but a fragment of her own project of self-construction.

Sexual images are no different in the late-modern context. Believing ourselves to be projects of constant construction, improvement and flux, we are prone to constructing a sexual image for ourselves. Our desires lead us in this ongoing project; that which we desire is adopted into our sexual identity as a piece of that identity. Who I am is defined by what I desire: sex, men, women, Jesus, chocolate.

Self-construction offers many things to many people. It is good news to those who are seeking liberation from outdated mores and moralism. But self-construction is not in the kenotic pattern of the incarnated Christ. Self-construction is not self-emptying. So long as we are tempted to follow Adam's pattern of overreaching, of placing ourselves in the position of image-makers, we relegate the good desires of our creaturely existence to lust. So long as we busy ourselves with constructing an image in the likeness of our desires, we miss the goodness of lodging our desires in divinity and allowing our practices to follow.

As our desires have been directed toward creating for ourselves an image, and the images we use in our self-creation are increasingly sexual, the image of human sexuality has become more complicated and subjected to malformation. We think that if a runner can create a shoe that matches her unique form and style, shouldn't we be able to create language to identify a person's unique sexual expression and way of being in one's body? There are more and more categories to give expression to sexual behavior and desire: a casual hookup, a three-way exchange, exclusive sexual permission, commitment to live together, commitment in marriage, cheating in marriage. In addition, there are ways to define and distinguish sexual orientation, sexual identity and sexual expression. There have never been so many options to create for ourselves a unique image of sexuality. To an extent, all these variations point us toward the fact that we were created in the image of an incarnational, embodied God who we were created to desire with our bodies. But that desire only finds peace and true satisfaction in the Creator. Apart from the divine source, that desire will restlessly create, adjust and recreate an image for itself.

On a regular basis, pastors, church leaders and those giving guidance and counsel around the issues of sexuality in an image-driven age encounter a number of complications in the ways persons envision their sexual identity. They must be aware that what many of those in their care are learning to desire—more than God, more than intimacy, even more than sex—is a self-made image. Theirs is the sin of Adam: acting upon desire by attempting to take sexual expression under their own control and to create a sexual identity as an act of overreaching rather than of gracious reception. Still, the desire that drives their pursuit is God-given. Sexual images themselves are not the problem for Christians. It is sexual images in the absence of holy purposes that are problematic, especially when those images suggest to us that we can be made in their likeness as fleeting and momentary opportunities for gratification. What we are witnessing, then, is a society's attempt to construct an identity around those images, an ongoing and never-ending attempt to find identity based upon a nihilistic project of constant self-construction.

The theological issues underlying this enterprise reflect the way persons understand the source of those images. It is a theological decision to try to build an identity on the gratification of our desires rather than looking beyond ourselves in hopes of receiving an image upon which our identity will be patterned. Whether it is advertising, pornography or any other sexual image directed toward self-construction or gratification, the late-modern, image-driven age offers us but a single tree in the midst of a fruitful garden. It is Christian doctrine that offers real hope for our embodied desires.

SANCTIFICATION OF THE IMAGE

We come now to the final leg of our journey, a constructive proposal in which Christian doctrine points to a way forward for our understanding of human sexuality in an image-driven age. Expressions of sexuality meet their good end as they are sanctified and drawn into God's purposes for the fulfillment of creation. The image of God in which humans are created is not compromised or desecrated when it is sexed, but it must continually participate in the same creative impulse that drove the desiring Creator to speak creation into being.

Christ's desires met their unspoiled and good end as he was perfectly open to being in the Spirit. The same Spirit now hovers over the face of chaotic human desires, ready to sanctify them, empowering them toward their good end. The Spirit not only directs human desires but also draws them into the flow of the trinitarian life of God. This is not to say that humans become divine in the way that God is divine; rather, the divine life was broken open to creation in the incarnation. The wound in Christ's body from which the fluids of life poured now stands open as the entry point into the goodness of God. The triune life of God, characterized by eternal love in desire, was opened by the very desire that marks God's life, drawing human persons into the eternal love of the Father, Son and Holy Spirit and redeeming their desires, enticing them into the redemptive flow of God's love and desire.

Embodied desires are a gift from the Creator. Receiving those desires as a gift recognizes and acknowledges that we are not self-constructed beings; our desires are not the materials given to us for the task of self-construction. Our desires are a gift of love, and so are the orientations of those desires. In the power of the Spirit those desires are directed toward God; sexual desire is a sanctified subset of desiring the goodness of the divine. And those desires are sanctified in bodies—good, created bodies—just as Christ took on flesh and became for us sanctification (1 Cor 1:30).

Our proposal depends on directing persons into the redemptive rhythms of the way of Jesus Christ, who entrusted his desires to the Father in the power of the Spirit. Our recommendation is to embrace desire while constantly being reminded that the image in which we were created is given to us as a gift. We must also remember that desire quickly turns to lust when we attempt to create our own sexuality in the image of anything other than God or when we treat the satisfaction of desire as a good end in itself. A holy sexuality, then, is not defined by a suspension of desire but a sanctified directing of that desire in the power of the Spirit.

All too often the first lesson young people learn from the church about sexuality is that they must wait for it. The evangelical abstinence campaigns of the 1990s were perhaps the most recognizable and formative teaching on Christian sexuality for young people in recent history.[13] At its best, this movement sought to guide a young generation away from late-modern patterns of sexual expression as a means to self-construction. However, one of the pernicious unintended consequences of this teaching is that it promotes the idea that desire ought to be suspended or forsaken; true love must wait because its highest form of expression is sexual. Therefore, a holy expression of our desires is to suspend them until they can be properly channeled toward a spouse.

There is nothing overtly Christian about this approach. In the logic of some evangelical abstinence programs, one's spouse could idolatrously be exchanged

---

[13]One study demonstrating the formative power of such campaigns through cultural and rhetorical analysis of evangelical abstinence campaigns is Christine J. Gardner, *Making Chastity Sexy: The Rhetoric of Evangelical Abstinence Campaigns* (Berkeley: University of California Press, 2011).

for God and marriage itself could become yet another image constructed to express a particular brand of human sexuality. The biblical story tells us that we are created as desiring beings by a God who desired to create bodies and desired to enter into flesh. Therefore, we cannot wait to be sexual, nor can we put our desires on hold. To do so grates against our very createdness and obscures the image of God, creating frustration, repression, shame and sexual disorders. Furthermore, if our embodied desires are a gift from our Creator, why should we leave them shrouded by the leaves of Adam's shame?

At the same time, sanctified sexual desires are not the unbounded expression of sex acts in the absence of a good goal. Again, Christ demonstrates to us what holy desire looks like. As the one for whom equality with God was not something to be exploited, Jesus did not use his human body for his own gain or gratification; he offered up the whole of his bodily existence in an act of self-emptying, trusting the Father to exalt and glorify his sacrifice. Commending that pattern is a worthwhile pastoral approach to aid those wading through an image-driven age, questing for an image in which they can be made. Christian women and men, made in the image of God, need not attempt to take by force what God is freely giving to us. The fulfillment of every desire God created within us is found in Jesus Christ, the fullness of God who became flesh. We wait only for the full consummation of his lordship over creation. In our waiting, we groan as we eagerly anticipate the redemption of our bodies (Rom 8:22-23). Sanctified sexual desires compel our bodies to wait on the Lord.

Comedian Jim Gaffigan strikes a chord with churchgoers when he confesses to lusting after women in the congregation as he passes the peace of Christ.[14] Perhaps the truth behind this observation is its insistence that our sexual desires do not wait outside until we have finished with our asexual worship. Passing the peace has been retained by the Christian tradition partly because we need to touch and be touched by one another in holy ways. We long for intimacy in the body of Christ as we wait for resurrection.

If we believe that we are made in the image of God—that our desires are a gift from God and that they can be sanctified through Christ who became sanctification for us—then surely there is no need to check our sexuality at

---

[14]"Jim Gaffigan - Jesus - *Beyond the Pale*," YouTube video posted by jimgaffigan, March 13, 2009, www.youtube.com/watch?v=2k_9mXpNdgU.

the door of the church. Pews are a perfect place for breast-feeding mothers, weeping widowers and the young and sexually restless. Indeed, pastors and worship leaders have the great task of engaging both the bodies and desires of worshipers. For far too long, evangelical worship has tended to engage the mind over the body as if those two could somehow be detached. As Smith rightly points out:

> The church has been duped by modernity and has bought into a kind of Cartesian model of the human person, wrongly assuming that the heady realm of ideas and beliefs is the core of our being. These are part of being human, but I think they come second to embodied desire. And because of this, the church has been trying to counter the consumer formation of the heart by focusing on the head and missing the target: it's as if the church is pouring water on our head to put out a fire in our heart.[15]

Truly, women and men created in the image of God are burning to engage in their faith with their bodies, longings and desires. Instead of telling single people to wait before their desires can be satisfied and doing our best to extinguish the flames, we ought to be fanning those flames in worship and service in ways that direct our desires and our bodies toward the God who created us. In doing so we cease our relentless attempts to create an image for ourselves. When our bodies are given over to the endless flow of love between Father, Son and Holy Spirit, they are set free from an image-driven age that would exploit the flesh God created.

Sanctification does not make our bodies sexless. On the contrary, it frees our sexual desires to be oriented toward the one who is redeeming our bodies in the consummation of all creation. Therefore, our proposal is not a program that we can construct for ourselves. We are arguing for a deep trust in the work of the triune God to sanctify the desires of our flesh. Sanctification calls us to live in Christ, the image of the invisible God who desires to create us anew. In the power of the Spirit, we surrender our bodies in the likeness of Christ to be part of this sanctified creation, bringing glory to the Father.

CONCLUSION

How might we express creation in God's image to a culture that increasingly defines sexuality in image-driven ways? Maybe we could say something like

---

[15]Smith, *Desiring the Kingdom*, 76-77.

this: The gift of God is waiting for you, the sanctification of your flesh. You need not take by force what God is freely giving. We are first and foremost creatures of desire and lovers of God. God desired to come to us in love in the person of Jesus, the fullness of God in unashamed flesh. God gives us not only sexual desires but the fulfillment of those desires in the flesh of Christ, crucified, emptied and resurrected. While in our own power we are capable of nothing more than shoddy self-construction, the gift of sanctification is truly a new act of creation that only God can conceive and only God can desire into being. Be set free, you lovers, to find peace for your burning hearts in desire for your Creator.

5

CULTURE BREAKING

In Praise of Iconoclasm

Matthew J. Milliner

*All Christian images are born broken. When they are not, they are broken in
another meaning of the word: they are so bad that they are ready for the bonfire!*

BRUNO LATOUR, "HOW TO BE ICONOPHILIC IN SCIENCE, ART, RELIGION"

*We build paintings before You like walls
so that thousands of them now surround You—
for our pious hands veil You whenever
our hearts simply open to behold You.*

RAINER MARIA RILKE, *PRAYERS OF A YOUNG POET*

BABYLON

"Cinema, advertising and magazines push at us a quotidian flood of 'ready-
made' images, which are to the order of vision what prejudice is to the
intelligence."[1] The great modern artist Henri Matisse said those words when
Manhattan's Times Square was a relatively quaint collection of hand-painted

---

[1]Henri Matisse, "Il faut regarder toute la vie avec des yeux d'enfants," in *Henri Matisse: Écrits et
propos sur l'art,* ed. Dominique Fourcade (Paris: Hermann, 1992), 321 (author's translation).
Matisse's remarks, first published in 1953, seem to contain a dig at Marcel Duchamp's "ready made"
(*toute faites*) art.

billboards. Today, the menacing power of its dazzling images only confirms the artist's insight, moving some theorists to call our own era an "optocracy" in which we are ruled by what influences our eyes.[2] It takes courage to detach ourselves from such influence, claims Matisse. He believes genuine art can accomplish such detachment, and in the course of this chapter I will discuss what I believe to be failed and successful examples of such liberation.

Success in resisting our image-driven age, I will argue, comes less from the macro-art world than from micro-art worlds like that of the Art Department at Wheaton College, where I teach and where the conference that this publication is based on was held.[3] As an art historian, I hasten to point out that well-wielded words can facilitate resistance as much as can genuine art. "Nothing is worse for the image's influence," writes Jacques Ellul, "than to be taken apart and analyzed by language. The word produces disenchantment with the image; the word strips it of its hypnotic and magical power."[4] Finding Ellul's critique of the present visual regime to be far more stinging and effective than ones that depart from strictly secular premises,[5] I begin by using words to analyze one particular droplet from the rising flood of contemporary images.

On a winter morning in 2015, the carefully controlled algorithms of Facebook delivered to my eyes a news story through Britain's *Daily Mail* about the Islamic State destroying ancient artifacts in the Mosul Museum.[6] The link

---

[2]Marie-José Mondzain, *Image, Icon, Economy: The Byzantine Origins of the Contemporary Imaginary* (Redwood City, CA: Stanford University Press, 2005), 162.

[3]Against any challenge that I am merely discussing the artists closest to me, let me note that this is no different from practices of the macro-art world. Consider the fact that New York's two most influential critics, Jerry Salz and Roberta Smith, are married to each other (Sarah Thornton, *Seven Days in the Art World* [New York: Norton, 2008], 171). Or consider this headline, conveying the breadth of the American gallery scene: "Almost one third of solo shows in US museums go to artists represented by five galleries" (Julia Halperin, *The Art Newspaper*, April 2, 2015). Or ponder Ai Wei Wei's assertion that "the art market is like the stock market except that it is smaller, so it can be controlled by an even smaller group of people" (Sarah Thornton, *33 Artists in 3 Acts* [New York: Norton, 2014], 13). Nearly all major commentators on the art world eventually get around to commenting on its *smallness*.

[4]Jacques Ellul, *The Humiliation of the Word* (Grand Rapids: Eerdmans, 1985), 142.

[5]Mondzain, for example, opposes theology, considering Byzantine icon theory to be the origin of the present image regime: "There are no great differences," she asserts, "between submitting to a church council or to CNN" (*Image, Icon, Economy*, 223). Ellul claims the opposite: "The triumph of things visual involves a radical negation of Christianity" (*Humiliation of the Word*, 198). For Ellul, our attachment to images is connected less to Byzantine iconophiles than it is to Genesis 3. Images, after all, are "pleasant to look at, good to eat, and capable of waking intelligence" (ibid., 149).

[6]Julian Robinson, "ISIS Thugs Take a Hammer to Civilisation," *Daily Mail*, February 26, 2015, www .dailymail.co.uk/news/article-2970270/Islamic-State-fighters-destroy-antiquities-Iraq-video.html.

took me to the *Daily Mail* webpage where I was tantalized by video footage of the destruction. But before I could view the video—which was carefully branded by both ISIS and the *Daily Mail* in the upper right and left corners respectively—I was obliged to watch a Cover Girl makeup advertisement featuring singer Katy Perry dressed like a flower.

A distinguished, disembodied British accent queries, "Katy Perry, quite contrary, how do your lashes grow?" "Soft and full like a flower's," Perry responds. "That's the power of [this] mascara." And quite a power it is, for the advertisement then takes a Kafkaesque turn as petals begin to grow from Perry's eyelids. The voice then posits that this metamorphosis must be due to Perry having "met someone new." This person is "you," the viewer. Following this intimate turn, the phrase "Lash me and lash me not" infuses fifty shades of grey into this overwhelmingly pink commercial, to which the voice responds, "That's hot." At this point, Perry raises her floriated skirt in a cancan-like kick, which I take to be the moment at which the virtual union of Perry and viewer is complete. Finally, in a fascinating evocation of that archetypal image of Rococo frivolity, Jean-Honoré Fragonard's 1767 *The Swing*, Perry launches across the screen before she falls back exhausted into a bed of flowers. Immediately thereafter, the ISIS statue-smashing begins.

No one, so far as I know, planned this curious juxtaposition. There was no executive at the *Daily Mail* determining that all who wished to watch ISIS destroying images should see Katy Perry first.[7] Our current flood of images is less a conspiracy than the uncontrollable tyranny of the possible.[8] Let me nevertheless describe this unpalatable conflation as bluntly as possible: If I want to see images of people destroying images, I have to see images that some might consider worthy of being destroyed. More provocatively, in order to see ISIS destroy images associated with the original Babylon, I am obliged to witness images of our present Babylon as well.

---

[7] The advertisement, which ran in February 2015 in the wake of Perry's Super Bowl performance, was later replaced by other advertisements preceding the same ISIS video, including Ziploc bags (March 2015) and Olive Garden (April 2015).

[8] "We produce images only because we have certain equipment. . . . The universe of images is a result of technique alone, and not of some human intention, some philosophy or economic structure, a need for profit, the class struggle, or the Oedipus complex." Ellul, *Humiliation of the Word*, 148. Compare George Steiner's similar remarks in *In Bluebeard's Castle* (New Haven: Yale University Press, 1974): "We shall, I expect, open the last door in [Bluebeard's] castle even if it leads, perhaps *because* it leads, onto realities which are beyond the reach of human comprehension and control" (140).

The suggestion that twenty-first-century America is a Babylon of sorts is supported by another Perry coincidence, this time a liturgical one. Her 2015 Super Bowl halftime performance fell on Septuagesima, the Sunday in the Christian year that commemorates the Babylonian captivity (seventy days before Easter, paralleling the seventy years of captivity). Indeed, Babylon seems the most immediate biblical parallel to the spectacle that American Super Bowls present. Suggesting as much is not to single out American culture for unique censure; it is only to point out that segments of every society will map onto the city types in the book of Revelation: oppressive Babylon or liberating New Jerusalem.

Part of the spectacle included Perry riding on top of an enormous, faceted golden tiger, both her outfit and the tiger's eyes aflame. The biblically trained imagination makes connections when seeing a woman riding atop a beast, and it is not the New Jerusalem passages that spring to mind. This is not to seriously suggest that Perry is the Babylonian "woman sitting on a scarlet beast" of Revelation 17:3. Instead, it is an attempt to imagine what it would be like to watch the Super Bowl with early Christians like Clement of Alexandria, who did not pull punches when it came to critiquing the visual culture of his day.[9]

To readers who understandably wonder what is inherently oppressive about selling makeup or watching sporting events, I offer the example of the Church of the Holy Communion in New York City. The building, which still stands in Manhattan, was a forerunner of high-church evangelicalism fused with social justice. Eucharist was celebrated weekly, women were prominent in their ministries and the first convention of black Episcopal clergymen met there in 1883.[10] By 1983, however, the Church of the Holy Communion had become the Limelight nightclub, center of the recreational drug trade in New York. It was "pagan Rome on acid," as one participant put it. "Degeneracy without consequences."[11] But whereas intense partying is necessarily short-lived, the consumer lifestyle endures. The building's current inhabitant, Lime-light Shops, is disturbing in a different way, offering a literal illustration of

---

[9]The inclusion of Missy Elliot and Lenny Kravitz in the same performance strikes me, to borrow terms used by Willie Jennings in his presentation at the conference that led to this volume, as more "counterpunctual" rather than "counterhegemonic" resistance.

[10]David W. Dunlap, *From Abyssinian to Zion: A Guide to Manhattan's Houses of Worship* (New York: Columbia University Press, 2004), 36-37.

[11]"Limelight - Move Trailer (2011) HD," YouTube video posted by Movieclips Trailers, August 11, 2011, www.youtube.com/watch?v=D1Ntoy-RKdY.

James K. A. Smith's observation that the cultural liturgy of the mall competes with the church.[12] In this case, the mall colonizes the church. Fashion ads plastered on Richard Upjohn's stonework beckon outsiders to be transformed within; conversion has been replaced with confession-booth dressing rooms; surviving stained-glass windows of the good Samaritan clothing the poor now look down on the rich clothing themselves. The Eucharist has been replaced with what the Limelight website describes as a "slice of heaven" from the in-store pizza shop (see figure 1).

Figure 1. Limelight shops in the former Church of the Holy Communion, New York City.
Photos by Matthew Milliner.

[12]James K. A. Smith, *Desiring the Kingdom: Worship, Worldview, and Cultural Formation* (Grand Rapids: Baker Academic, 2009), 23.

All this is to say that whether or not Christians consider consumer visual culture something to be resisted, the fact that it resists Christianity is, in this case at least, rather clear. Evangelicals have spent the last half century embarrassed of their iconoclastic heritage and attempting to make themselves culturally serious. This was and remains important work. But the challenge that is so clear in the case of Limelight Shops might spur us to reactivate our iconoclastic heritage as well. Our charge may be not only to go about culture making[13] but to do some culture breaking as well, for breaking is what the people of God do when they find themselves in Babylon.

This is not to endorse the destructive actions of ISIS. As the captives of Israel were marched through the Ishtar Gate, they would have been killed had they foolishly attempted to deface the animals and dragons. The Babylonian captivity was a time when Israelites did not have the power to break images, and so they broke them rhetorically instead. Jeremiah, for example, does not need to destroy images, because he, like Paul (1 Cor 8:4), doesn't *believe* in them: "Do not be afraid of them, for they cannot do evil, nor is it in them to do good" (Jer 10:5). Jeremiah and Paul offer a framework that transcends the ISIS/Cover Girl dichotomy of literal destruction or thoughtless embrace. Their biblical witness generated the ecumenical heritage of iconoclasm that is uniquely equipped to help us navigate a hitherto unprecedented ocean of images.

Modern art, moreover, can be an ally in making sense of our bewildering new condition. Contrary to what might be assumed, to suggest that we live in a Babylon whose visual features must be seriously resisted is not to be a philistine. The Philistines were creators of idols (2 Sam 5:21)! As Matisse understood, thoughtful artistic practice should oppose, rather than endorse, the deleterious aspects of our image-driven age.

FAILED RESISTANCE

To substantiate the claim that art resists mass culture, imagine a young person, distraught by America's visual superficiality, retreating into the Art Institute of Chicago for refuge. There she finds that the museum has recast its world-class modernist collection under the theme "Shatter Rupture Break."[14]

---

[13]Andy Crouch, *Culture Making* (Downers Grove, IL: InterVarsity Press, 2008). I consider this paper to be complementing, not opposing, this important book.

[14]The exhibition, the first in a Modern Series that aims to recast the museum's holdings in this area, ran February–May 2015.

Modern art, she learns from the gallery label, "disrupted traditional conventions of depth and illusionism, presenting vision as something fractured."[15]
Upon entering the exhibition, she is confronted with a projection of Fernand
Léger's *Ballet Mécanique*, the 1924 film that used the new medium of the
moving picture to rearrange and juxtapose human features in order to reveal
them anew. Léger thereby attacked the slick surface effects of mass culture, but
this was not a purely cynical enterprise. He believed that the masses "have the
right to demand that the time's revolution be carried out, and that they in their
turn be permitted to enter the domain of the beautiful."[16] In the opening se-
quences of the film, our young viewer even sees the neo-Rococo Katy Perry
advertisement subverted. The same swinging woman appears, but not in a way
that entrances in order to sell makeup. Instead she is upside-down and dis-
jointed. Impressed by Léger's critical take, our viewer then finds the film on
the Internet to study it more closely. But in order to do so, she must—as with
Katy Perry introducing ISIS—first watch sexy dancers in gold sequins and
people being showered with money (an advertisement for *Dancing with the
Stars*).[17] The question arises whether Léger's early efforts to neutralize mass
culture are sufficient for *our* times. Can the present visual regime be resisted
by Léger's artistic descendants?

Certainly one of the primary impulses of contemporary art is to do precisely that—to subvert. Take, for example, Christopher Williams's *The Production Line of Happiness*, a solo show that began in Chicago and traveled to
Manhattan's Museum of Modern Art. On the surface, it might seem that Williams is imitating the features of consumerist culture. He depicts, for example,
a beautiful smiling woman with a yellow towel bundled on her head, fit for a
soap advertisement.[18] Closer investigation, however, shows that he is actually
pulling back the curtain to reveal advertising techniques. In the same image,
he shows the color strips employed to attain the right photographic effect. The

---

[15]"Shatter Rupture Break" exhibition description, www.artic.edu/exhibition/shatter-rupture
-break.

[16]Fernand Léger, "The New Realism Goes On," in *Art in Theory: 1900–2000*, ed. Charles Harrison
and Paul Wood (Malden, MA: Blackwell, 2003), 505.

[17]"Fernand Leger - Ballet mecanique (1924)," YouTube video posted by iconauta2, January 20,
2013, www.youtube.com/watch?v=2QV9-l-rXOE. The advertisement has since been replaced by
a different one.

[18]The image's full title is "Kodak Three Point Reflection Guide, © 1968 Eastman Kodak Company,
1968. (Meiko Laughing), Vancouver, BC, April 6, 2005."

art lets us catch the advertiser in the act, causing us (one hopes) to question the constructed nature of the images around us.

Williams has garnered much praise for his technique, but we can be forgiven for wondering if this is enough. *Artforum*, the art world's magazine of record, proudly featured versions of Williams's work on its cover, but *Artforum* is itself so choked with advertisements that it has been nicknamed *Adforum*. Can well-educated, generally wealthy gallery-goers, after paying significant entrance fees to see Williams's show and maybe picking up a catalog and other gift shop items, really mount a full-scale resistance to the power of consumer culture?

But it would be too easy to dismiss contemporary art's efforts at resistance by pointing to museum admission fees and the existence of gift shops. Some artistic efforts at countering the dominant visual regime are as massive as the image culture they aim to oppose. In January 2015 NASA claimed to have made the largest image ever created, a Hubble telescope photo of the Andromeda galaxy that consisted of 1.5 billion pixels.[19] Many dutifully clicked the links and were given a desktop tour of the deepest reaches of the known universe. No doubt such images are impressive, but it is also noteworthy how we take them at face value, assuming that our computer screens are really giving us some kind of unquestionable truth.[20]

The Italian artist Paola Pivi, however, is in the process of making an image that is a good bit "larger" than NASA's. In so doing, she refuses to assent to these new maps of the cosmos as pure visual fact. Pivi took a photograph of Alicudi, a small island off the coast of Sicily, and attempted to create a 1:1 ratio installation of that image in a gallery. This would be the perfect image—the equivalent of the thing itself—and the attempt is a deliberate comic failure. The first of 3,742 massive PVC rolls necessary to create this perfect image

---

[19]"Sharpest ever view of the Andromeda Galaxy," www.spacetelescope.org/images/heic1502a/. Similar claims are made by mappings of the supercluster of galaxies known as Laniakea, within which the Milky Way is placed. Brad Plumer, "This is the most detailed map yet of our place in the universe," *Vox*, February 11, 2015, www.vox.com/2014/9/4/6105631/map-galaxy-supercluster-laniakea -milky-way.

[20]Moreover, images such as the Laniakea supercluster map seem to confirm Heidegger's observation that "the world picture does not change from an earlier medieval one into a modern one, but rather the fact that the world becomes picture at all is what distinguishes the essence of the modern age [*der Neuzeit*]." Martin Heidegger, *Questions Concerning Technology*, trans. William Levitt (New York: Harper Torchbooks, 2013), 130.

barely fit inside the massive main hall of the large venue for contemporary art, the Hamburger Bahnhof in Berlin (see figure 2).

Figure 2. Paola Pivi, Alicudi Project at the Hamburger Bahnhof, Berlin. Photo by Matthew Milliner.

Other artists like Hito Steyerl are deeply concerned with the advent of satellite maps, which began as military surveillance technology. She questions our "visual culture saturated by military and entertainment images from above."[21] Steyerl names this a "vertical sovereignty," which is a "radicalization— though not an overcoming—of the paradigm of linear perspective."[22] She challenges this development with disjunctive films that educate the public about the history of such technology, bringing levity to the topic—but also a level of dread.[23] Steyerl cites Achille Mbembe, whose discussion of the "occupation of the skies"[24] calls to mind the New Testament reference to the "ruler of the power of the air" (Eph 2:2). Especially consanguine with Christian image theory is Steyerl's appeal to the "poor image" that "insists upon its own imperfection, is popular but not consumerist, committed without becoming

---

[21]Hito Steyerl, *The Wretched Screen* (Berlin: Sternberg Press, 2012), 22.
[22]Ibid., 23-24.
[23]Hito Steyerl's film is titled *HOW NOT TO BE SEEN: A F**king Didactic Educational .MOV File*. It was featured at the Museum of Modern Art, where I viewed it in October 2014.
[24]Achille Mbembe, "Necropolitics," trans. Libby Meintjes, *Public Culture* 15, no. 1 (Winter 2003): 29. Cited by Steyerl, *Wretched Screen*, 23.

bureaucratic."[25] All this is to say that one strategy of contemporary art is not just to create images, but—like the angel wrestling with Jacob—to strategically wound them as well.[26]

But resistance is just one of several vectors in the practice of contemporary art. The more our imaginary young person explores the macro-art world, the more she might also conclude that while the mainstream of contemporary art might claim to be iconoclastic, it has found this an impossible task. Mainstream art may have even completely surrendered to the dominant consumer culture. Take, for example, Marina Abramović and Jeff Koons. Abramović is a daring performance artist whose stunts questioned not only the wider culture but the place of art within it. "Art must be beautiful. Artist [sic] must be beautiful," she chanted ironically in a 1975 performance, mock combing her hair. Léger would, I think, be proud, and Cover Girl perhaps a bit threatened. Today, however, Abramović is less ironic in her claim that artists must be beautiful. In an interview for PBS's Art 21, she looks back on a time of strict refusal to wear makeup or appear beautiful. She then announces her retirement from this posture because she just wants to laugh and "be female again." "I didn't need to prove anything to anybody anymore.... I think I'm okay artist [sic], I can now really enjoy myself, embrace fashion."[27] She admits her appearance on the cover of fashion magazines is "totally vanity."[28] She revels in the contradiction of her enduring a grueling performance-art session and then appearing at an event in her Ricardo Tishi dress made from 101 snakes. Perhaps, as she halfheartedly suggests, the fact that she is crashing fashion magazine covers in her sixties indicates that there are still flickers of resistance in her strategy.[29] A more straightforward reading, however, is that she has given in. This reading is far clearer in the case of Jeff Koons.

If our young person were to have viewed a Koons retrospective, at first she would have found an artist intent on critiquing the establishment. The early

[25]Steyerl, Wretched Screen, 39.

[26]Even a painter as prominent as Gerhard Richter could be said to use this strategy. Robert Storr explains how he inflicts violence on his images, and "the more vulnerable the subject, the more alarming this violence can be." Robert Storr, Gerhard Richter: Forty Years of Painting (New York: Museum of Modern Art, 2002), 73. I am grateful to Kate Penkethman for this reference.

[27]"SHORT: Marina Abramović: Embracing Fashion," from the series "Exclusive," Art 21, www.art21.org/videos/short-marina-abramovic-embracing-fashion.

[28]Ibid.

[29]Ibid.

Koons put vacuum cleaners in glass cases as if they were reliquaries; surely he must be mocking a world that seeks salvation in consumer products. Next she would have seen images that offer young men hope through basketball stardom placed next to a cast-iron life jacket and raft, provocatively suggesting that hoop dreams offer false hope. But moving further into the retrospective, she would learn that the artist gave up on his subversive quest long ago, offering an apotheosis of consumer capitalism instead. Koons, a former stockbroker, has taken his trade to more trustworthy markets, evidenced by his replacing the artist's traditional bohemian garb with a business suit.[30] He adroitly alters his image for respective art magazines: he can be an elementary school teacher imparting his "Banality as Saviour" message to children, be a bathrobed playboy for *ARTnews* or give a confessional close-up for *Flash Art*.[31] Any semblance of critique—any hint of Léger—has been eviscerated, even while he claims to be "a continuation of the avant-garde."[32] Moreover, he cannot critique because his most consistent rhetorical theme is universal acceptance. Koons never judges anything but "keeps everything in play."[33]

But one thing he does *not* keep in play is the Christian narrative. In an interview with singer and producer Pharrell Williams, Koons describes seeing Masaccio's painting of the expulsion of Adam and Eve from the Garden of Eden in the Brancacci Chapel in Florence. Koons says the painting caused him to want to "make a body of work that would help remove that kind of guilt and shame."[34] Koons's strategy to overcome the Christian narrative was to create billboard-size pornographic images of his wife (now ex-wife), a former porn

---

[30]Thornton, *33 Artists*, 5.

[31]Ibid.

[32]Ibid., 81.

[33]Some have pushed Koons on his rhetoric of acceptance. "Is it about the acceptance of everything?" asks Sarah Thornton. "Marxist and historians and Nazi skinheads, Occupy Wall Street protesters and Republican anti-evolutionists?" In response, Koons offers a childhood anecdote about self-acceptance and another about accepting others. Before she can press him, Thornton relates, "the PR pops her head around the door. My half hour is up." Thornton, *33 Artists*, 108.

[34]"Jeff Koons & Pharrell: Affirmation Abstraction Acceptance | ARTST TLK™ Ep. 11 Full," YouTube video posted by Reserve Channel, November 22, 2013, www.youtube.com/watch?v=YcjqajvmkxM. The producers of the interview, however, were sufficiently encumbered with Christian "guilt and shame" that they blurred out the naked woman whose job it was to refresh Koons's and Williams's beverages (Massacio remarks begin at 15:00, blurred waitress at 16:49). For my take on the Brancacci Chapel paintings, during the writing of which I poured all my own beverages, see Matthew J. Milliner, "The Brancacci Chapel and Academia's 'Religious Turn,'" in *Art as Spiritual Perception: Essays in Honor of E. John Walford,* ed. James Romaine (Wheaton, IL: Crossway, 2012), 90-107.

star and Italian parliamentarian. He claims there has to be "a [discreet] place for adults to look at those type of images," forgetting that the initial location was a billboard on Madison Avenue.[35] In justifying these images, Koons showed a doctrine concealed underneath his rhetoric of keeping everything in play: "The only true narrative," he claims, "is the biological narrative."[36]

Figure 3. Babylon's Ishtar Gate at the Pergamon Museum, Berlin. Photo by Matthew Milliner.

Or perhaps the rationale for these images is even less exalted than that. Koons may simply be acting on the words of Tobias Meyer, chief auctioneer at Sotheby's: "Obscenity sells."[37] If this is the case, Koons might be the perfect illustrator of our new Babylon.[38] His fifty-million-dollar balloon dogs even resemble the dragons on Babylon's Ishtar gate, and his kitsch sculptures lined in procession offer the real production line of happiness—this time without any semblance of critique (see figures 3 and 4).

This condition causes some of the most astute theorists of contemporary art to throw in the towel. Even art-world insiders such as Jerry Salz have lamented

[35]"Jeff Koons & Pharrell," 16:00; Thornton, 33 *Artists*, 5.

[36]Thornton, 33 *Artists*, 106.

[37]Don Thompson, *The $12 Million Stuffed Shark: The Curious Economics of Contemporary Art* (New York: Palgrave Macmillan, 2010), 251.

[38]Matthew Milliner, "The Five Stages of Grieving the Art of Jeff Koons," *First Things*, October 28, 2014, www.firstthings.com/web-exclusives/2014/10/the-five-stages-of-grieving-the-art-of-jeff-koons.

that the art museum has become "a revved-up showcase of the new, the now, the next, an always-activated market of events and experiences. . . . How did the museum go from being a contemplative quiet car to the very center of a commercial frenzy?"[39] It might be thought that the postcolonial art of Samuel Fosso or the subversive feminism of Cindy Sherman might nevertheless deliver a

Figure 4. Jeff Koons's sculptures at the 2014 Whitney Museum retrospective. Photo by Matthew Milliner.

bracing critique of the status quo, but one authoritative guide to contemporary art claims that they, too, have failed to offer lasting detachment. Surveying the globalized "art world" composed of biennial exhibitions, international art magazines and a very familiar cast of artists, Nick Mirzoeff concludes:

> The art world perceives itself as a space of contestation of global capital, while being almost completely an expression of that capital and its free flow into immaterial labor. . . . For it was the project of the avant-gardes to find a way of moving from the inside of bourgeois society to an outside vantage point from which a critique against the value of this society could be mounted . . . [but] there is . . . no longer such an "outside" view to be had. The aesthetic project of modernism—to act as a moral counterpoint to mass culture—has collapsed, for better or for worse, such

---

[39]Jerry Salz "The *New* New Museum," *Vulture,* April 19, 2015, www.vulture.com/2015/04/jerry-saltz -on-new-whitney-museum.html. However, Salz does see hope in the new Whitney Museum.

that art works are now promoted through this globalized niche market as luxury commodities (in this sense, as a kind of specialized mass culture).[40]

But wasn't this commodified condition precisely what conceptual art aimed to avoid? Hito Steyerl, however, claims that while such movements began "as a resistant move against the fetish value of visibility . . . the dematerialized art object turns out to be perfectly adapted to the semioticization of capital, and thus to the conceptual turn of capitalism."[41] Consider the fact that one of actor James Franco's pieces of "Non-Visible art" sold for $10,000![42] In light of this condition, Mirzoeff calls for "a better way to rekindle the emancipatory potential of the work of art,"[43] and I take the distant biblical echo of his prose to be an invitation to show a "more excellent way" (1 Cor 12:31). It is a way that George Bataille had already seen the need for in the 1930s when he—as an atheist—pointed to early Christianity as an example of true revolution that could avoid the perpetual compromising of the supposed avant-garde.[44]

FIRM RESISTANCE

Let us return to our imaginary young person one last time. Looking for enduring resistance to the regime of images, she visits the Art Institute of Chicago again. She notices that real classical images are very unlike the glistening remakes of Jeff Koons.[45] Time has had its way with the goddess of love in the Hellenistic collection, Aphrodite of Knidos, but others hastened its erosion along. Wandering into the exhibition of Byzantine icons, she notices a different head of Aphrodite that has been deliberately vandalized. It is quite the crowd pleaser; hence Greece often sends it around, blaming the defacement on "early, fanatical Christians."[46] Aphrodite's nose has been knocked away, her forehead marked with a cross. This cross, however, is more nuanced

---

[40]Nick Mirzoeff, "'That's All Folks': Contemporary Art and Popular Culture," in *A Companion to Contemporary Art Since 1945*, ed. Amelia Jones (Malden, MA: Blackwell, 2006), 507-9.

[41]Steyerl, *Wretched Screens*, 41-42.

[42]Cary Hodges, "James Franco Sells $10,000 Piece of Non-Visible Art," *Paste*, July 19, 2011, www .pastemagazine.com/articles/2011/07/james-franco-sells-ten-thousand-dollar-piece-of-no.html.

[43]Nick Mirzoeff, "That's All Folks," 509.

[44]Sven Lütticken, "Secrecy and Publicity: Reactivating the Avant-Garde," *New Left Review* 17, September/October 2002.

[45]Many of his sculptures are copies with a twist of the ancient Hellenistic statues to which early Christians were so opposed.

[46]Anastasia Lazaridou, ed., *Transition to Christianity: Art of Late Antiquity, 3rd to 7th Century AD* (New York: Onassis Public Benefit Foundation, 2011), 148.

than ISIS's rampant demolition. Indeed, the cross on Aphrodite's forehead is the first move of the Christian aesthetic regime.[47]

Even a cursory glance at early Christian authors betrays the sophistication of such destruction. Faced with the Aphrodites of his time, Clement of Alexandria offered a deeply learned, proto-art historical deconstruction of images that was akin to Jeremiah's. He rightly points out that lust is the origin of the image of Aphrodite. The statue is *not* a goddess, he tells us—it is an image of the sculptor Praxiteles's lover.[48] He draws on classical literature to cite instances of people having sex with these images, akin to people doing so with their computer screens today. "*Technē* [art, technique] deceives you by another witchcraft, leading you on to honor and worship the images and paintings, if you do not fall in love with them."[49] "Let art be praised," Clement tells us, "but let it not deceive a person into thinking it is true."[50]

Clement then points to his readers, who are made in the image of God: "O former images, which all do not resemble [the model], I wish to restore you to the archetype, in order that you too may become similar to me."[51] I can think of no better illustration of this than the work of Jeremy Botts of Wheaton College. In his installation at Lombard Mennonite Church, he employed a series of strings tethered to a hand.[52] Like the early Christian tradition, Botts is appropriately iconoclastic. He only depicts the hand of the Father, not the face—for the Father cannot be directly imaged. The hand, inspired by Botts's grandfather, is connected through the strings of providence to both God and fellow parishioners (see figures 5 and 6). These strings "restore [us] to the archetype," as Clement put it, that we might better resemble Jesus.[53]

---

[47]This is not to suggest that Christian art before the Renaissance was opposed to nudity. See Sherry C. M. Lindquist, ed., *The Meanings of Nudity in Medieval Art* (Burlington, VT: Ashgate, 2012); Henry Maguire, *Other Icons: Art and Power in Byzantine Secular Culture* (Princeton: Princeton University Press, 2007); Myrto Hatzaki, *Beauty and the Male Body in Byzantium: Perceptions and Representations in Art and Text* (London: Palgrave Macmillan, 2009). Leo Steinberg's *The Sexuality of Christ in Renaissance Art and in Modern Oblivion*, 2nd rev. and exp. ed. (Chicago: University of Chicago Press, 1996), did not have the chance to take this more recent evidence into account.

[48]Laurea Salah Nasrallah, *Christian Reponses to Roman Art and Architecture: The Second-Century Church amid the Spaces of Empire* (Cambridge: Cambridge University Press, 2010), 280. I thank Chelsea Westra for this reference.

[49]Ibid., 283.

[50]Ibid.

[51]Ibid., 293.

[52]The process is depicted in Joonhee Park's film "Passage," made to accompany this volume: www .youtube.com/watch?v=PoWot6ZLktY.

[53]Ibid., 293.

And yet, a level of destruction is necessary to be so restored. Asked to choose an image and replicate it in a creative way for a course in which I was

Figure 5. Jeremy Botts's installation *Bee in Hand.* Photo by Matthew Milliner.

Figure 6. The inspiration for *Bee in Hand,* Charles Bonner with his grandson Jesse Nathanael Botts. Photo by Jeremy Botts.

the instructor, Lanie Howard made a replication of the vandalized Aphrodite mentioned above. She interprets the cross on Aphrodite's forehead as baptism, or the sign of the cross etched into the foreheads of parishioners on Ash Wednesday, both of which are radical acts but not actual deaths. "You were not literally dead or buried or crucified or risen," wrote Cyril of Jerusalem regarding baptism. "Yet from the imitation of the realities salvation truly came to us. Christ was literally crucified and buried and literally rose from the dead; we symbolized in ourselves what he experienced and thus truly shared in his salvation."[54] There is an analogous death that happens to all of us who have been baptized— and in the Christian regime, there is a death that happens to all images as well. The Christian tradition does not mature beyond this initial act of image destruction. Rather, it is founded upon it. "Christ kills the image on the Cross," writes Jean-Luc Marion. "Thus he fulfills the Old Testament prohibition: 'You shall not make for yourself any idol, nor any likeness.'"[55] Flirting with both iconoclasm and the cult of glamour, Lanie Howard's replication truly transcends the ISIS/Cover Girl alternative (see figure 7).

[54]Cyril of Jerusalem, *Mystagogical Catecheses,* quoted in Maxwell E. Johnson, ed., *Benedictine Daily Prayer: A Short Breviary* (Collegeville, MN: Liturgical Press, 2005), 219.

[55]Jean-Luc Marion, *The Crossing of the Visible,* trans. James K. A. Smith (Redwood City, CA: Stanford University Press, 2004), 72.

As mentioned above, evangelical Christians in particular have been embarrassed by their iconoclastic heritage, apologizing for it so that they might become culture makers themselves. This is, to be sure, a necessary correction, but it risks neglecting the iconoclastic foundation that should underlie any Christian approach to art. As theologian Natalie Carnes put it, "To love images, iconophilia, may even require iconoclasm."[56] Jacques Ellul rightly asserts that iconoclasm is "the first act of the Christian life."[57] But this is not just an evangelical heritage. There is a shared ecumenical heritage of iconoclasm across Christian traditions that art historians for the last decade have been uncovering, a "deep-rooted distrust of the duplicitous in image-making [that] runs through the Christian tradition."[58] A brief survey of some of these developments will help substantiate this claim.

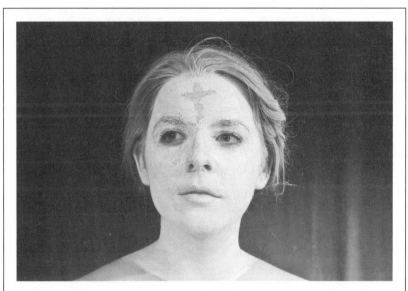

Figure 7. Lanie Howard's replication of an Aphrodite vandalized by early Christians

To begin with the Orthodox tradition, iconophile theology won the day not so much by opposing the iconoclasts but by assimilating their insights. One of the more sophisticated iconoclastic arguments ever offered is attributed to the

---

[56]Natalie Carnes, "Making, Breaking, Loving, and Hating Images: Prelude to a Theology of Iconoclasm," *Logos: A Journal of Catholic Thought and Culture* 16.2 (2013): 26.
[57]Ellul, *Humiliation of the Word*, 96.
[58]Michael Camille, *The Gothic Idol* (Cambridge: Cambridge University Press, 1991), xxvi.

Byzantine Emperor Constantine V. The emperor claimed that icons of Christ were not permissible because they claimed to be *alive*—that is, to mediate the divine or human natures of Jesus. Both of these options he deemed heretical. Should one claim that an icon mediates the divine nature of Jesus, one become Nestorian, separating the divine from the human nature. In addition, divine nature is beyond depiction. If one claims, on the other hand, to only depict the human nature, one again falls into the Nestorian trap, separating the human from the divine nature. Christ without a divine nature, furthermore, is Arian. Finally, if one attempts a middle ground by mixing the divine and human natures in the icon's depiction, one falls into the Miaphysite position.

Rather than opposing these insights, the iconophiles Theodore the Studite and Patriarch Nicephoros *conceded* all of these points.[59] They argued instead that the icon mediates no nature, divine or human. Images are not alive. Images merely signal, through name and likeness, the persons they depict, whose nature (or in Christ's case, *natures*) remain beyond depiction. I have argued elsewhere that this is perfectly compatible with John Calvin's theory of images.[60] But for our purposes, it shows a deeply and properly limited view of what an icon can accomplish.

It is, furthermore, beautifully illustrated by photographer Greg Halvorsen Schreck. Roland Barthes pointed out that the bewitchment of photography arises from the conflation of image and prototype: "In short, the referent adheres."[61] However, through his invention of what he calls Lambertian photographs, Schreck has managed to separate image and prototype again.[62] By creating a "photograph" that only casts an image when light is cast upon it, Schreck has managed to make an image without any positive presence apart from light. If one considers the light of the original referents in heaven, as

---

[59]Second-generation Byzantine iconophile theory is nicely explored by Ian McFarland in chapter seven of this volume.

[60]Matthew J. Milliner, "Iconoclastic Immunity: Possibilities for Reformed/Orthodox Convergence in Theological Aesthetics Based on the Contributions of Theodore of Studios," *Theology Today* 62 (2006): 501-14.

[61]Roland Barthes, *Camera Lucida: Reflections on Photography* (New York: Hill and Want, 1981), 5.

[62]As Schreck puts it in his artist's statement: "The science of the images is based on Lambert's Law, from 1760. The equation calculates the diffuse reflection intensity of a surface based upon the angle of illumination and the angle of observation. . . . Mark Woodworth, a friend, an industrial physicist, coded Lambert's equation into a software program that translates grayscale pixel densities into angular surface changes that can be milled on to a wood surface." Greg Halvorsen Schreck, "Lambertian Portrait Photograph: On the Art of Fixing a Shadow" (October 2011).

there is Byzantine warrant to do,[63] Schreck's technique—especially in the form of the Shroud of Turin—precisely illustrates advanced Byzantine iconophile theory (see figure 8).[64]

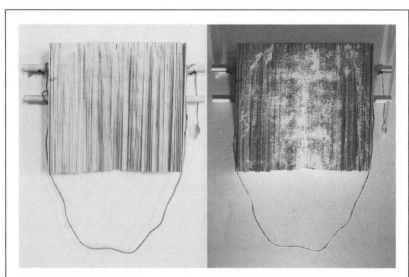

Figure 8. Greg Halvorsen Shreck's Lambertian photograph, *The Shroud.* Photo by Greg Halvorsen Schreck.

It might seem more difficult to make a case for an iconoclastic impulse in Catholicism. The art historian Mia Mochizuki, however, has pointed out that whitewashing churches—an act frequently associated with the Protestant Reformation in Amsterdam—happened a century and a half before the outbreaks of Protestant iconoclasm.[65] Considering the famously white interiors of Cistercian monasteries or Brunelleschi's Florence interiors, this insight should not be surprising. Amy Knight Powell has argued that Catholic churches before the Reformation were already places of iconoclasm: "Before

---

[63]Matthew J. Milliner, "Man or Metaphor? Manuel Panselinos and the Protaton Frescoes," in *Approaches to Byzantine Architecture and Its Decoration: Studies in Honor of Slobodan Ćurčić*, ed. Mark J. Johnson, Robert Ousterhout and Amy Papalexandrou (Burlington, VT: Ashgate, 2011).

[64]When Byzantium neglected this emphasis on the prototype, they had later outbreaks of iconoclasm. For an overview of such "Komnenian Iconoclasm," see Bissera Pentcheva, *The Sensual Icon* (State College: Pennsylvania State University Press, 2010), 190-208.

[65]Mia Mochizuki, *The Netherlandish Image After Iconoclasm 1566-1672: Material Religion in the Dutch Golden Age* (Burlington, VT: Ashgate, 2008), 1. Mochizuki asks us to "acknowledge iconoclasm not only for its destructive force, but also for its generative power and the remarkable creativity it unleashed" (7), and to consider "a methodology of generative absence, one that does not equate void with nihilism" (323).

any iconoclasts attacked them, these images and rituals were already self-reflexive allegories of their own *suspended undoing*."[66] Some sculptures of Christ were taken down and placed in replicas of the Holy Sepulcher at Good Friday services. This ritual reminded worshipers to focus their attention not on images but on the heavenly realities to which images refer.[67] "Over the past few decades," writes Alexander Nagel, "historians of religion in sixteenth-century Italy have revealed a world of reforming activity in this period, some of it very sympathetic to Protestant positions."[68] Nagel has shown that church officials at the Siena Cathedral removed Duccio's famous Maestà altarpiece even before the Reformation, in 1506.[69] What is more, they depicted scenes from the Old Testament on the floor in order to remind the worshipers to be wary of idolatry. Michelangelo was at the forefront of this reform movement. Arguably, his artistic career culminated not in his more dazzling images but in acts of "soft iconoclasm."[70]

Protestant acts of iconoclasm, furthermore, were patterned upon earlier mandated removal, frequently occurring—as at Wittenberg in 1522—on the day of ritual church cleansing known as Green Thursday.[71] Eamon Duffy is no doubt correct that "the Reformation was a stripping away of familiar and beloved observances, the destruction of a vast and resonant world of symbols."[72] In many instances it surely went too far. Yet, "Reformation iconoclasm was not a monolithic phenomenon, nor simply a philistine movement of religious vandalism. It was a multi-dimensional phenomenon with an enormous religious, political and social impact."[73] Its principles were "at bottom

---

[66]Amy Knight Powell, *Depositions: Scenes from the Late Medieval Church and the Modern Museum* (Brooklyn, NY: Zone Books, 2012), 26.

[67]Ibid., 81.

[68]Alexander Nagel, *The Controversy of Renaissance Art* (Chicago: University of Chicago Press, 2011), 198.

[69]Ibid., 207.

[70]Alexander Nagel, *Michelangelo and the Reform of Art* (Cambridge: Cambridge Univerity Press, 2000). See also Anna M. Kim, "Creative Iconoclasms in Renaissance Italy," in *Striking Images, Iconoclasms Past and Present*, ed. Stacy Boldrick, Leslie Brubaker and Richard Clay (Burlington, VT: Ashgate, 2013), 65-80.

[71]Joseph Koerner, "The Icon as Iconoclash," in *ICONOCLASH: Beyond the Image Wars in Science, Religion and Art*, ed. Bruno Latour and Peter Weibel (Cambridge, MA: MIT Press, 2002), 189.

[72]Eamon Duffy, *The Stripping of the Altars: Traditional Religion in England, c.1400–c.1580* (New Haven: Yale University Press, 2005), 591. Duffy's history has been complemented by an account that shows the richness of Protestant England's image culture: Tara Hamling, *Decorating the "Godly" Household: Religious Art in Post-Reformation Britain* (New Haven: Yale University Press, 2011).

[73]Willem J. Van Asselt, "The Prohibition of Images and Protestant Identity," in *Iconoclasm and*

theological."[74] Iconoclasts were not necessarily rabid mobs illegally entering other people's churches. Instead, these were people with legal sanction, "going into what was once their own space . . . [in] an act of corporate and visible repentance for the mistaken ways they had sought to understand God's presence."[75]

In short, the Protestant, Catholic and Orthodox traditions share an iconoclastic heritage, each assimilating it in different ways. The early Protestant tradition, moreover, *reminded* the wider church of this image-breaking heritage when it was at risk of being neglected, and a similar reminder may be necessary in the present day. The Art Department at Wheaton College affords one example of such remembrance.

FORTRESS OF RESISTANCE

Why, however, would artists at an evangelical Christian college be any different from the macro-art world? Why would the attempts of these artists to critique the dominant image culture not also be immediately absorbed? My contention is that a genuine prospect of resistance arises from the sincerity of their Christian faith.

After all, according to art historian James Elkins, sincere religious status downright guarantees the status of being different. The art world "can accept a wide range of 'religious' art by people who hate religion, by people who are deeply uncertain about it, by the disgruntled and the disaffected and the skeptical, but there is no place for artists who express straightforward, ordinary religious faith."[76] Elkins has since shown some hesitation about his position, first articulated more than a decade ago. Meeting intelligent people of faith has caused him to see a "different way of reading art history."[77] Other theorists

---

Iconoclash: Struggle for Religious Identity, ed. Willem van Asselt, Paul van Geest, Daniela Müller and Theo Salemink (Leiden: Brill, 2007), 308.

[74]Carlos Eire, *War Against the Idols: The Reformation of Worship from Erasmus to Calvin* (Cambridge: Cambridge University Press, 1989), 7.

[75]William Dyrness, *Reformed Theology and Visual Culture: The Protestant Imagination from Calvin to Edwards* (Cambridge: Cambridge University Press, 2004), 48.

[76]James Elkins, *On the Strange Place of Religion in Contemporary Art* (Abington, UK: Psychology Press, 2004), 47.

[77]James Elkins, "Iconoclasm and the Sublime: Two Implicit Religious Discourses in Art History," in *Idol Anxiety*, ed. Josh Ellenbogen and Aaron Tugendhaft (Redwood City, CA: Stanford University Press, 2011), 117.

have also lately seen a need for more religious vocabulary among art critics.[78] Nevertheless, secularism prevails in the art world, such that Sarah Thornton flatly asserts, "Contemporary art has become an alternate religion for atheists."[79] Insofar as this condition endures, the artists of Wheaton College have attained an elusive otherhood by virtue of their faith. Elkins laments that his fellow secular academics cannot step outside of secular modernity into religious practices,[80] but the artists of Wheaton College's Adams Hall have done precisely that.

I am not suggesting that all religious artists function in this way; many self-consciously religious artists only endorse the status quo. Nevertheless, theological tools may be indispensible in the task of prying oneself free from the dominant culture. Most contemporary art, claims Jacques Ellul, "is intrinsic to the system . . . [and so] immediately [is] reintegrated into the system."[81] The "technical establishment" that has mutated the visual domain in order to create our image-driven age is far too powerful.[82] Ellul's metaphor for this condition is a glacial desert of "rich and superabundant images that have invaded everything."[83] But as a Christian he finds hope, for the Wholly Other comes from God. "He is incommensurable and cannot be assimilated or utilized—can produce an opening, a breaking up of the iceberg."[84] The artists of Adams Hall—cleaving as they do to the Wholly Other—offer examples of the kind of iconoclastic artists Ellul hoped for.[85]

Consider a filmmaker, Joonhee Park, who offers the very thing Koons refuses: restraint. It is beyond the scope of this chapter to comment on each of the films created in concert with this publication, nor is this necessary since

---

[78]"In denying themselves recourse to religious vocabulary or theological conceptuality, modern art critics give up what would be advantageous to a profound encounter with the works in question." Jeffrey Kosky, *Arts of Wonder: Enchanting Secularity* (Chicago: University of Chicago Press, 2012), 173.

[79]Thornton, *Seven Days*, xvi.

[80]James Elkins, *What Is an Image?* (State College: Pennsylvania State University Press, 2011), 9.

[81]Ellul, *Humiliation of the Word*, 110.

[82]Ibid., 199.

[83]Ibid., 258. "A screen of images is placed between me and my world—a circle of images that become so much truer than my own life I cannot rid myself of them" (120).

[84]Ibid., 110.

[85]His more extensive remarks on modern art seem to suggest he did not find such artists himself. Jacques Ellul, *The Empire of Non-Sense: Art in the Technological Society* (Berkshire, UK: Papadakis, 2014).

they speak for themselves.[86] But in "Messages," Park conveys the theme of the fall—the image distorted. He begins with a sparing clip of people made in the image of God leaving a record of romance on top of a lookout tower in Seoul. Park then chronicles an opposite feature of Seoul's topography—a suicide bridge. A suicide occurred when Park was on site, and he might have gotten footage. But Park chose instead to stay his hand. In contrast to Park's restraint, the artist Sarah Charlesworth combed through images of suicide and blew them up into near life-sized images. To walk through her exhibition at the Art Institute of Chicago was to be confronted with life-size placards of death.[87] As a former film producer for a commercial enterprise, Park knows how to create slick images, but he chooses not to. Perhaps this is part of what art education involves today: rather than mastering technologies in order to merely deploy them, we might master them in order to hold them back. This is a constant feature of Park's documentary work, even while in other works he refuses to spare his viewers difficult moments, such as watching the disembowelment of a Mongolian yak.[88]

Or consider Leah Samuelson, whose field is community art. This enterprise defetishizes the created art object and its maker to place the focus back on the viewing community, which is decidedly not a cultured elite.[89] Community art ensures the "art world" is connected to daily life and human services, and vice versa. Compared to the celebrity culture of Abramović and Koons, this paradigm can only be described as iconoclastic.

On the cover of this book is David Hooker's *Corpus* (see figure 9). Like Schreck's Lambertian Shroud of Turin, *Corpus* is anything but the straightforward image of Jesus often found in evangelicalism[90]—and therein is its power. To create a piece far more daring than Jeff Koons's enshrined vacuum cleaners, Hooker collaborated with Wheaton's custodial staff to collect vacuum

---

[86]Joonhee Park, "Messages," YouTube video posted by Wheaton Art, March 30, 2015, www.youtube .com/watch?v=4I_hyZxfVKc.

[87]"Sarah Charlesworth: Stills," www.artic.edu/exhibition/sarah-charlesworth-stills. The Art Institute show ran September 2014–January 2015.

[88]Joonhee Park, "Seeds of the Desert," YouTube video posted September 29, 2011, www.youtube .com/watch?v=4iD3ElZ_2gI.

[89]Kate Crehan, *Community Art: An Anthropological Perspective* (Oxford: Oxford University Press, 2011). I thank Erin McCord for this reference.

[90]One bestseller concedes that evangelical bookstores and churches are places "where there are lots of drawings and paintings of Christ." Todd Burpo with Lynn Vincent, *Heaven Is for Real: A Little Boy's Astounding Story of His Trip to Heaven and Back* (Nashville: Thomas Nelson, 2010), 93.

dust that he used to cover the body of Jesus. Vacuum dust is filth, but Hooker, inspired by Martin Luther's Heidelberg Disputation, deigned to imitate the

Figure 9. David J. P. Hooker's *Corpus*. Photo by Matthew Milliner.

love of God by making lovely that which is unlovely.[91] In so doing, Hooker deftly commented both on the theological truth that Jesus takes on the sin of the world (our filth), and—because the skin cells of the Wheaton community are in those vacuum bags—that we are the body of Christ. Hooker's work thereby keeps pace with major theological conversations. His sculpture highlights the third, neglected element of the *corpus mysticum*—the church[92]—and it also encapsulates the scandal of Jesus' taking sinners into his body, as explored by Ephraim Radner.[93] Hooker's image of Jesus defies standard depictions, and can therefore be considered an iconoclastic as much as an iconophile act—not just culture making, but culture breaking as well. Nevertheless, Hooker's goal is not destruction but the restoration of power to images that are at risk of becoming religious clichés.[94] Such restoration is most evident each year on the morning of the autumnal equinox when, serendipitously, Jesus is spotlighted by the rising sun (see figure 10).

Hooker is not alone in tinkering with traditional images of Jesus. From Serrano's *Piss Christ* to Cavallaro's *My Sweet Lord,* such alterations are a staple of art-world practice. The similarity to such approaches has caused some to interpret Hooker's sculptures as acts of irreverence. But what such critics miss

---

[91]"The love of God does not find, but creates, that which is pleasing to it. The love of man comes into being through that which is pleasing to it." Heidelberg Disputation, thesis 28, http://bookof concord.org/heidelberg.php.

[92]Henri de Lubac, *Corpus Mysticum: The Eucharist and the Church in the Middle Ages* (South Bend, IN: University of Notre Dame Press, 2006).

[93]Pushing against overly sanitized visions of our union with Christ, Radner writes, "The Church's unity is established in and because of her sins, not in themselves, but as they stand in relation to God as creator and redeemer in Christ Jesus. The oneness of God is just *this* oneness with the sinful Church." Ephraim Radner, *A Brutal Unity: The Spiritual Politics of the Christian Church* (Waco, TX: Baylor University Press, 2012), 460.

[94]More of Hooker's work substantiates this observation. In an image that hangs in our Art Department building, he has placed the same dust on Francis's San Damiano cross, outlining Jesus without filling in the space. As a response to cheap images of Jesus, one of his drinking vessels offers an outline of the image of Christ but with a void in place of recognizable features.

is that Hooker's sculptures arise from sincere Christian faith—one that (unlike most artists who tinker with Jesus) is ensconced in community. Hooker's acts of iconoclasm succeed every week in a genuine liturgical setting because his fellow congregants trust him. They know that his Jesuses are not attacking Christ—instead, they are attacking us. They attack our lazy eyes, reminding us, as Hooker put it, that "any way of defining beauty we come up with that does not include the ugliness of the Cross of Christ is insufficient."[95]

Hooker's most hideous Jesus is the one that is most liturgically active; it is a crucifix used every Lent at All Souls Anglican Church in Wheaton (see figure 11). It was created in collaboration with rector Martin Johnson, who was formerly a celebrated set designer for the Vancouver opera. Covered in wax, Hooker's crucifix calls to mind another Chicago-area sculptor, John Kearney, who took a cross that was burned on a black man's lawn in an act of racism and transformed it into a sculpture of Jesus as a lynched black man.[96]

Figure 10. David J. P. Hooker's *Corpus* on the morning of the fall equinox. Photo by Greg Halvorsen Schreck.

Figure 11. David J. P. Hooker's crucifix juxtaposed with Joel Sheesley's Good Shepherd. Photo by Matthew Milliner.

Should one wish to escape Hooker's disturbing image of Jesus at All Souls, leaving the church requires

---

[95]David Hooker, "Corpus," Wheaton College Chapel address, March 30, 2015, www.youtube.com /watch?v=Ci3WB2CE0Vg.

[96]Deanese Williams-Harris, "Artwork wrought from burned cross is donated to Chicago church," *The Chicago Tribune*, October 6, 2008, http://articles.chicagotribune.com/2008-10-06/news /0810050272_1_chicago-church-cross-burned.

a confrontation with Joel Sheesley's surrealist painting of camels on a suburban lawn that hangs in the narthex (see figure 12). The image suggests that Jesus' teachings about wealth and poverty fit about as comfortably into the suburban lifestyle as the camels do in the painting. This warning against the comforts of wealth pierces the suburban congregants who need to hear it

Figure 12. Joel Sheesley's *Camels* (53x58), in the narthex of All Souls Church, Wheaton, Illinois. Photo by Matthew Milliner.

most. This also is an iconoclasm of sorts—the pleasant patterns of suburban acquisition unsettled by the inconvenient teachings of Jesus.[97]

In another of his photographs, Greg Halvorsen Schreck pursues a similar iconoclastic line of attack (see figure 13). Sadly, Andrei Rublev's famous icon of the Old Testament Trinity has become "so well known and overused as to have lost some of its initial impact."[98] But like Hooker, Schreck took a risk to keep this image from descending into a cliché. With the same kind of reverent iconoclasm, he subverted it to illustrate a different kind of trinity: "Dagon or Ishatar or Melkart," claimed Jacques Ellul, "are now Money State and Technique,"[99] or Power, Prestige and Possessions, as Martin Johnson puts it in a homiletical refrain.[100] Whatever you want to call this impostor trinity, it is not holy, and it is not God. Schreck thereby combats the driving forces of our image-driven age by exposing them.

Though easily misconstrued as flippant, Schreck's alarming visual move stems from his deep love of the Russian tradition, especially as mediated by

---

[97]Compare the rationale of Christie's employees for the art market: "After you have a fourth home and a G5 jet, what else is there? Art is extremely enriching." Sarah Thornton, *Seven Days*, xvi.

[98]Sarah Coakley, *God, Sexuality, and the Self: An Essay 'On the Trinity'* (Cambridge: Cambridge University Press, 2013), 253.

[99]Ellul, *Humiliation of the Word*, 95.

[100]Johnson echoes the trope from Richard Rohr, *Radical Grace* (Cincinnati: St. Anthony Messenger Press, 1995), 18.

filmmaker Andrei Tarkovsky. The move is anything but unprecedented; consider the anti-Madonna depicting Satan with the antichrist on his lap in the Torcello Cathedral or the Victorian painter George Frederic Watts's painting of worshipers of Mammon.[101] Schreck fuses both approaches into his Rublev reversal. Like Watts, Schreck shocks us into the worship of the true God by bringing our idolatries to the foreground. He shows us a glimmer of Sarah and

Figure 13. Greg Halvorsen Schreck's triptych *American Trinity and the Cry of the Deer.*

Abraham hosting the meal below; in their pioneer garb they seem emblems of a simpler American approach to consumption that has been lately eclipsed. But Schreck also offers his viewers hope. On retreat at a Benedictine monastery, Schreck saw deer, which he interpreted as a gesture of grace. Like the deer on the ancient templon at St. Catherine's Monastery at Sinai, evoking Psalm 18:33, these deer offer a way into God's reality—out of our perversions of it and back into our status as humble creatures.

In addition to the iconoclastic images described above, there is one beautiful image of Jesus in the rear of All Souls Church, painted by Sheesley (see figure 14). Are straightforward, beautiful images of Jesus permissible for artists seeking to be iconoclastic? Is not this the very thing that Hooker, Botts

---

[101]Watts's goal is precisely the same as Schreck's—to expose our idolatries. As Watts put it, "Material prosperity has become our real god, but we are surprised to find that the worship of this visible deity does not make us happy." G. F. Watts, "The Present Conditions of Art." He even had plans to set up a statue of Mammon in Hyde Park, "where he hoped his worshippers would be at least honest enough to bow the knee publicly to him." M. S. Watts, *George Frederic Watts: Annals of an Artist's Life*, vol. 2 (London: Macmillan, 1912), 149; cited by the Tate Museum, www.tate.org.uk /art/artworks/watts-mammon-n01630.

and Schreck deliberately avoid? Ellul critiques the Orthodox theology of icons but concedes, "Everything in the theology of the icon is acceptable from an eschatological perspective, as long as it is a present affirmation of what will ultimately take place."[102] Sheesley offers what Ellul was seeking: his Christ is

Figure 14. Joel Sheesley's Good Shepherd mural at All Souls Church, Wheaton, Illinois. Photo by Matthew Milliner.

framed in an eschatological context where the Chicagoland area has been grafted into the New Jerusalem. The golden sky evokes the coming eschaton. The waters of Ezekiel 47 burst forth under the heavenly temple foreshadowed in the church. Here are the baptismal waters that have put us to death, even as we are remade and grafted back into the tree of life. And Sheesley's image is deliberately unreachable, such that one could not venerate it even if one wanted to. Together, Sheesley's and Hooker's images of Jesus offer one last aspect of iconoclastic critique. All Souls, under the authority of a Hispanic Anglican bishop, presents its congregants with a black and Middle Eastern Jesus week after week. Perhaps this is just the thing that Willie Jennings hopes for when he calls for an "artistic ecclesiology" where called artists in community dispatch a "creative critique of the white aesthetic regime."[103]

---

[102]Ellul, *Humiliation of the Word,* 241.

[103]Willie Jennings, presentation at the Wheaton Theology Conference (April 2015).

CONCLUSION

One objection to the entire thrust of this chapter is this: What if God endorses the patterns of our consumerist culture? Didn't God say as much to Katy Perry? It is unclear where this daughter of an evangelist stands today in regard to Christianity. There are reports of her rejecting her faith, yet she still appears to worship a general Moralistic Therapeutic God.[104] In an interview before the Grammy Awards, Perry claimed divine approval for her Super Bowl performance:

> I was praying and I got a word from God and he says, "You got this and I got you."
> . . . And then I was on top of the lion and a random guy looked at me with a headset
> that I'd never communicated with before, he looked me straight in the eyes and
> said "You got this." And I was like, "Oh, that's God confirming I can do this!"[105]

Having whimsically associated Katy Perry with the whore of Babylon to begin this chapter, let me conclude on a more positive note. Perhaps her word from the Lord *was* genuine. But every word requires interpretation, and Perry seems to be putting the accent on the *got*: "You *got* this." But what if the accent was on the *this*? As in, "You got *this*, Katy"—power, prestige, possessions— "and I got *you.*" God's people are called to resist our image-driven age because God loves the images—us—who are caught up within it. He calls us to break free of all counterfeit images and be restored to his own *true* image.

If this is our task, then the artists of Wheaton's Art Department, in contrast to the mainstream art world, offer strategies for resisting the least-edifying aspects of our image-driven age. Their Christian faith is what enables them to occupy the optocracy with some degree of success. I hope they can inspire similar culture-breaking strategies in other churches and micro-art worlds, all of which might look very different. But if the Limelight Shops are any indication, churches that choose *not* to resist the present regime of images will soon look very much the same.

---

[104]"I'm not Buddhist, I'm not Hindu, I'm not Christian, but I still feel like I have a deep connection with God," she said. "I pray all the time—for self-control, for humility. There's a lot of gratitude in it. Just saying 'thank you' sometimes is better than asking for things." Cheryl Chumley, *Washington Times*, February 9, 2015, www.washingtontimes.com/news/2015/feb/9/katy-perry-who -renounced-faith-god-was-with-me-for.

[105]Jon Blistein, "Katy Perry on Super Bowl: 'God Said, "You Got This,"'" *Rolling Stone*, February 8, 2015, www.rollingstone.com/music/news/katy-perry-on-super-bowl-god-said-you-got-this -20150208.

6

CARRYING THE FIRE, BEARING THE IMAGE

Theological Reflections on Cormac McCarthy's The Road

Christina Bieber Lake

*God comes before everything. He goes before us on
the road, and is always there before us.*

HENRI DE LUBAC, *THE DISCOVERY OF GOD*

INTRODUCTION

One of my colleagues once noted that *The Road* is the one novel for which everyone who spoke to him about it also reported where they were when they read it. Like hearing about John F. Kennedy's assassination, the experience of reading this hauntingly beautiful tale of trauma burns itself into the reader's brain. My own experience is similar. I read the book right after it was published, less than six months after the birth of my son Donovan. It was February, I was in bed with a sinus infection and I wept over almost every page. I could not stop until I got to the end.

The Road packs a tremendous punch. The plot is simple, and the story moves forward briskly with little adornment. A man and his young son have been surviving on their own after some incident has blighted the landscape, killed most people on the planet and obliterated social structures. We watch as they move south toward the coast, not sure of what they will find. The man knows only that his life is now being given to keeping his son alive. If ever a novel seemed devoted to depicting how far humanity can stray from the image of God, this is it. The man and boy see the worst of everything: cannibalism, slavery and other cold-blooded acts of violence. This stark narrative may be McCarthy's most convincing articulation of his belief that art must engage matters of life and death if it is to have any significance.

The bleakness of this novel (and many of his other novels) has spurred discussion not only of McCarthy's beliefs about God and the fate of humanity but also of the place of faith in American fiction. Paul Elie fueled this debate when he argued in the *New York Times* that there are, in contemporary literature, no defenders of Christian theology to rival Flannery O'Connor and Walker Percy in their day. Cormac McCarthy and Don DeLillo "are seen as prophets, but Christianity in their work is a country for old men."[1] Amy Hungerford, in her book *Postmodern Belief*, has also argued that American fiction has lost its faith. She treats *The Road* only briefly in her epilogue, but early in the book she presents McCarthy's *Blood Meridian* as a prime example of a trend in American fiction of drawing on biblical language as a way of giving a book the feeling of Scripture's moral authority when the book's actual authority is merely aesthetic. "We are left," says Hungerford, "with the presumptuous creation of a prose that sounds like scripture, tempts one to read (for metaphysical structures) as if one were reading scripture, and yet withholds all but the aesthetic and sentimental effects of scripture. In this sense, McCarthy has written, in *Blood Meridian*, a sentimental novel of the highest order."[2] *The Road* fares no better. Through its beautiful language, McCarthy transforms "biblical authority into literary authority re-conceived as supernatural authorship or rhetorical power."[3]

No matter how one reads our so-called postsecular moment, Hungerford's argument about contemporary American literature is powerful and difficult to refute. Allen Ginsberg wanted his openly irreligious and scandalous poems to be chanted. Don DeLillo's novels self-consciously offer fully immanent, rhetorical substitutes for religious transcendence even while many of his characters

---

[1] Paul Elie, "Has Fiction Lost Its Faith?," *New York Times*, December 19, 2012, www.nytimes.com/2012/12/23/books/review/has-fiction-lost-its-faith.html.

[2] Amy Hungerford, *Postmodern Belief: American Literature and Religion Since 1960* (Princeton, NJ: Princeton University Press, 2010), 95.

[3] Ibid., 136–37.

seem to suspect that such substitutes are not enough. But I will argue that Mc-Carthy's interaction with the Bible and its role in American religious consciousness is of an entirely different order than that of either Ginsberg or DeLillo. Though McCarthy professes no belief, engagement with metaphysics and theology is foundational to his fiction. To borrow Flannery O'Connor's description of the South, his landscapes are "Christ-haunted."[4] Intentionally or not, his narratives push against what Charles Taylor calls a "closed immanent frame": the modern conviction that humanity must bring its own meaning to an otherwise meaningless world.[5]

I make my argument in two parts. First, I show that, far from the Bible being a borrowed and merely aesthetic authority for McCarthy, his work evokes it in a way that forces the astute reader to return to it. In *The Road*, the book of Job and its metaphysical questions regarding personhood and suffering is placed in the foreground. Second, this novel's beauty is not best explained by an effort on McCarthy's part to replace God's authority with beautiful prose. Instead, like the book of Job itself, the novel must be beautiful to the extent that it is answerable to the goodness of human persons as made in the image of God. *The Road* exists under what Hans Urs von Balthasar has called the "demand of the beautiful," and it pulls its readers—however unwittingly—to respond to that demand.

ECHOES OF JOB

Hungerford's argument that McCarthy's texts borrow the authority of the Bible without engaging its content relies on her positioning him in a long line of writers who conceive of themselves as playing God in assigning fates. But in the case of *The Road*, comparing the author (or even the narrator) to God is a confusion. McCarthy is better likened to the storyteller of the book of Job, and the narrator of *The Road*, particularly when he is taking on the man's perspective, is less like God than he is like Job himself. The novel's situation and

---

[4]Flannery O'Connor, *Mystery and Manners: Occasional Prose*, ed. Sally Fitzgerald and Robert Fitzgerald (New York: Farrar, Straus and Giroux, 1969). O'Connor writes, "From the standpoint of the writer, it is safe to say that while the South is hardly Christ-centered, it is most certainly Christ-haunted. The Southerner, who isn't convinced of it, is very much afraid that he may have been formed in the image and likeness of God. Ghosts can be very fierce and instructive. They cast strange shadows, particularly in our literature" (44-45).

[5]Charles Taylor, *A Secular Age* (Cambridge, MA: Belknap, 2007), 539-93.

subsequent soul-searching thus evoke the biblical book most known for asking why the world is full of suffering and evil.

The book of Job is initially narrated like any conventional story. It begins, "There was once a man in the land of Uz whose name was Job. That man was blameless and upright, one who feared God and turned away from evil" (Job 1:1). Outside of the prologue and epilogue, the narrator of Job (similar to McCarthy in *The Road*) does not intervene to tell us how to interpret the story. The rest of the book of Job is composed, almost completely, of dialogue between Job and his counselors, and later between Job and God. While *The Road* is also written in the third person, it features a stronger and more active narrator who is separate from McCarthy (all of the time, since this is a work of fiction) and from the man (some of the time). The narrator of *The Road* sometimes renders judgment on the man and boy's situation, judgment that appears to be largely separate from the characters' point of view. That this is the case is undeniable at the end of the novel, where narration continues after the man's death. In spite of this separation, it is more frequently the case that the narrator delivers the man's perspective through free indirect discourse and similar means.

This matters because I contend that when the narrator's perspective aligns closely with the man's perspective, it mirrors Job's point of view and echoes biblical language. We are being asked to compare their situations and their attitudes and to see their words in the mode of lament. Recall that Job has no idea why his world has suddenly fallen apart. He receives messengers, one after the other, who inform him that his livestock, servants and entire family have been struck down and destroyed. He rips his clothes, shaves his head and drops to his knees in despair. He has boils on his skin. He declares that he loathes his own life (Job 7:16). He says he speaks with bitterness in his soul (Job 10:1). Although he does not curse God or charge him with wrongdoing, he laments his birth with intensity and poetic beauty:

> Let the day perish in which I was born,
> and the night that said,
> "A man-child is conceived."
> Let that day be darkness!
> May God above not seek it,
> or light shine on it.
> Let gloom and deep darkness claim it.

Let clouds settle upon it;

let the blackness of the day terrify it.

That night—let thick darkness seize it!

let it not rejoice among the days of the year;

let it not come into the number of the months.

Yes, let that night be barren;

let no joyful cry be heard in it.

Let those curse it who curse the Sea,

those who are skilled to rouse up Leviathan.

Let the stars of its dawn be dark;

let it hope for light, but have none;

may it not see the eyelids of the morning—

because it did not shut the doors of my mother's womb,

and hide trouble from my eyes. (Job 3:3-10)

The emphasis on darkness reveals the metaphysical weight of the passage. George Steiner argues that Job's lament over his own birth echoes Jeremiah 20:14-18, but "in *Job* it is no individual, it is the cosmos which is cursed. The day is to be made darkness, 'let the stars of the twilight thereof be dark,' let light go out undoing, un-creating God's primordial *fiat*."[6] When Job asks why he was born, comparing himself to the "infant that never sees the light" (Job 3:16), he is not lamenting his individual situation as much as declaring the "suffocating blackness" of extinction, the anxiety over why anyone should be born only to face suffering and death.

The man's situation in *The Road* is as dire—and as weirdly severe—as Job's. His lament also takes on cosmic proportions. At 1:17 on the day his wife would give birth to his only son, the clocks stop and the world as they had known it comes to an end, leaving them in a barren landscape that grows increasingly cold and dark. Ash is everywhere. There is a blackness that is so impenetrable the narrator insists it would "hurt your ears with listening."[7] They walk in a "cold autistic dark" where the only voices with any human feeling are their own. The narrator's tone, especially when clearly aligned with the man's, is as metaphysical as Job's: "On this road there are

---

[6]George Steiner, *Grammars of Creation Originating in the Gifford Lectures 1990* (London: Faber & Faber London, 2001), 45.

[7]Cormac McCarthy, *The Road* (New York: Alfred A. Knopf, 2006), 15. Following citations from *The Road* are parenthetical in text.

no godspoke men. They are gone and I am left and they have taken with them the world. Query: how does the never to be differ from what never was?" (32). Another passage, ambiguous as to whether it is the narrator or the man's perspective, reads, "Perhaps in the world's destruction it would be possible at last to see how it was made. Oceans, mountains. The ponderous counterspectacle of things ceasing to be. The sweeping waste, hydropic and coldly secular. The silence" (274). The man and his son have long been abandoned by the suicide of their wife and mother, a woman whose only answer, like that of Job's wife, had been to curse God and die. Their isolation is near total. To read their story is to follow a small, flickering flame moving slowly in a field of utter darkness.

The silence surrounding the man and the boy is of pivotal importance. Are we to read it as the silence of God? If so, then the parallel with the book of Job is even more striking. For although the main part of Job consists entirely of dialogue, it is the dialogue of the false counselors who are trying to tell Job that his situation is his fault. Eliphaz is Job's first false counselor, and he talks a lot. He tries to tell Job that he is blessed because God has disciplined him. He counsels Job to trust that God is taking care of him, to know that all of this is for his own good. But Job is not persuaded. After Eliphaz stops talking, Job continues to speak for two chapters more, saying among other things, "For the arrows of the Almighty are in me; my spirit drinks their poison; the terrors of God are arrayed against me" (Job 6:4). When he addresses God, he questions him, very much like the man does in *The Road*: "Why have you made me your target? Why have I become a burden to you?" (Job 7:20).

In a scenario without sense, the false counselors try to explain God's actions. Job maintains his innocence throughout his lament, and the tension builds. Will God ever show up? Indeed, the best explanation for the fact that the book of Job is composed as a dialogue is because its primary issue is whether an absent God will appear and put Job's questions to rest. Job's cries and complaints "are best viewed as calls on the seemingly absent God to become present," and Job longs to be in a relationship "in which God would call and Job would answer."[8] Job wants to hear from God, but he wants

---

[8]Lindsay Wilson, "Job, Book of," in Kevin J. Vanhoozer, Craig G. Bartholomew, Daniel J. Treier and N. T. Wright, eds., *Dictionary for Theological Interpretation of the Bible* (Grand Rapids: Baker Academic, 2005), 386.

speech with the full authority of God's presence, not the rationalizing of the counselors. This helps us understand his famous monologue:

> O that my words were written down!
> O that they were inscribed in a book!
> O that with an iron pen and with lead
> they were engraved on a rock forever!
> For I know that my Redeemer lives,
> and at the last he will stand upon the earth;
> and after my skin has been thus destroyed,
> then in my flesh I shall see God,
> whom I shall see on my side,
> and my eyes shall behold, and not another.
> My heart faints within me! (Job 19:23-27)

Job's desire to have his life recorded in a book corresponds with his desire to see God, to know that God is there and not silent. In short, Job wants to know that God sees him. Job's "friends" can never explain God's actions, and their presence cannot take God's place.

The dialogue is evoked and inverted in *The Road*, but the silence serves the same end. It centers around the same question: We are here; we are suffering; where is God in all of this? When the man addresses God, he also shakes his fist and pleads with God to show himself:

> He descended into a gryke in the stone and there he crouched coughing and he coughed for a long time. Then he just knelt in the ashes. He raised his face to the paling day. Are you there? he whispered. Will I see you at last? Have you a neck by which to throttle you? Have you a heart? Damn you eternally have you a soul? Oh God, he whispered. Oh God. (11)

The man's thoughts here are very different in tone from those of the four men in the naturalistic story "The Open Boat" by Stephen Crane. In that story, the men are in peril, and once it occurs to each that the universe has no regard for him, "he at first wishes to throw bricks at the temple, and he hates deeply the fact that there are no bricks and no temples."[9]

The longest conversation in the book is between the man and an old man they meet on the road who calls himself Ely. Like Eliphaz, he talks a lot, but his

---

[9]Stephen Crane, *The Open Boat and Other Stories* (W. Heinemann, 1898), 28.

message is more like that of Job's wife—to curse God and die. Although he says that words are useless, he uses a lot of them: "I think in times like these the less said the better. If something had happened and we were survivors and we met on the road then we'd have something to talk about. But we're not. So we don't" (171-72). But he does keep talking, telling them that he has known for a long time that there are no gods, and that it will be better when all the people are gone as well because "we'll all breathe easier." The man says with a sarcastic edge, "That's good to know." Ely replies earnestly, "Yes it is. When we're all gone at last then there'll be nobody here but death and his days will be numbered too. He'll be out in the road there with nothing to do and nobody to do it to. He'll say: Where did everybody go? And that's how it will be. What's wrong with that?" (173).

These evocations of Job's situation make it impossible to side with James Wood when he argues that McCarthy's text is only theological at the end, not throughout.[10] Instead, the best explanation of McCarthy's choice to put the man and boy in a stripped-down, postapocalyptic scenario is so that he could exaggerate the greatest metaphysical and theological questions that face us all. We are all confronted with the brutal facts of our imperfect existence. We are all confronted with the fact that things fall apart. We are all confronted with the fact that we have the power to kill others and to destroy the earth. Why are things this way? Both Job and the man in *The Road* see themselves as cursed by God. But neither one of them chooses to curse God in return, either by behaving like an animal or by taking his own life.

THE DEMAND OF THE BEAUTIFUL

If I am correct that McCarthy is evoking the book of Job in order to draw readers into a metaphysical dialogue with it and not, as Hungerford would have it, to draw an ersatz authority from it, then there are several implications. The first, as I have already suggested, is that metaphysical questions regarding suffering, violence and evil are engaged. But it also means that the question of whether God will show up in the end is more than just a matter of flipping a coin. It is a question written into the structure of the narrative itself, a point I will develop later.

A second implication, perhaps not as readily apparent, involves the beauty of the language of the novel. Job is one of the most poetic books of the Bible,

---

[10]James Wood, *The Fun Stuff: And Other Essays* (New York: Farrar, Straus and Giroux, 2012), 64.

and most scholars would agree that its beauty serves a greater purpose than mere ornament. But beauty has a contested status: Does beauty reside in the thing itself, or is it merely a matter of subjective taste? Is it universal, or is it a culturally constructed, fungible category? While I do not have the space to enter into those debates here, my argument depends on an understanding of beauty that contains both objective and subjective aspects. I believe that when a narrative contains beautiful language, the most likely (but not necessary) explanation is that at least part of what we recognize as beautiful reflects an intersection with what we recognize as goodness and truth—categories that necessarily have theological resonances. I believe the beauty of *The Road* is of this type.

I will make my case in conversation with Hans Urs von Balthasar's theological aesthetics. In the first volume of *The Glory of the Lord*, von Balthasar argues that beauty should not be considered apart from the other two non-Platonic transcendentals (truth and goodness).[11] For von Balthasar, art for art's sake is thus a meaningless and destructive concept. When humanity no longer believes in truth and goodness, we sever beauty from them and make it into a mere mask, a surface thing with no capabilities greater than giving a few sensual delights. Thus "we no longer dare to believe in beauty and we make of it a mere appearance in order the more easily to dispose of it."[12] Since beauty is an inherent part of the truth and goodness of the world God has created, disposing of it in this manner is a human effort to reject the mystery of being. In so doing, we reject the Creator of that mystery.

To make matters worse, when beauty is treated as mere appearance, the good of creation and in creation begins to lose its attractiveness to humanity. "Man stands before the good and asks himself why *it* must be done and not rather its alternative, evil."[13] Being gets translated into a mere "lump of existence," and humanity is no longer able to read its language, which is beauty. Beauty, when it is severed from goodness and truth, points only to itself and not to another being. Von Balthasar calls this aestheticism.

---

[11]Hans Urs von Balthasar, *The Glory of the Lord: A Theological Aesthetics I: Seeing the Form*, ed. Joseph Fessio and John Kenneth Riches, trans. Erasmo Leiva-Merikakis (San Francisco: Ignatius Press, 2009). The non-Platonic part is important because the incarnation of Christ moves the issue from the abstract and universal to the concrete and particular. Beauty is not a Platonic universal.
[12]Ibid., 18.
[13]Ibid., 19.

For von Balthasar, it is possible to separate beauty from goodness and truth. When we make beauty into a mask that we can manipulate in the service of our own interests, we go against our best God-given instincts. Primary among these instincts is the desire to go outside ourselves to connect with an other, including the ultimate other, God. Art mirrors the choice to be in the world and act in the world as a choice made in freedom, a choice that has the additional effect of deepening self-understanding, deepening the self as a person in communication with others.[14] At this point von Balthasar writes:

> Through his body, man is in the world. As he expresses himself, he acts and intervenes responsibly in the general situation. *He inscribes his deeds indelibly upon the book of history, which, whether he likes it or not, henceforth bears his imprint permanently.* Here, at the very latest, man must realize that he is not lord over himself. Neither does he rule his own being in freedom so as to confer form upon himself, nor is he free in his communication. *As body, man is a being whose condition it is always to be communicated;* indeed, he regains himself only on account of having been communicated. For this reason, man as a whole is not an archetype of Being and of Spirit, rather their image; he is not the primal word, but a response; he is not a speaker, *but an expression governed by the laws of beauty, laws which man cannot impose on himself.* As a totality of spirit and body, man must make himself into God's mirror and seek to attain to that *transcendence and radiance that must be found in the world's substance if it is indeed God's image and likeness—his word and gesture, action and drama.*[15]

Thus, human being in its origin (being created in the image of God) is already "form"—a picture, an image, in some way, of God—and it cannot cease to be so.

My point is that McCarthy's prose is not beautiful because he wants his art to take the place of scripture. Instead, it is beautiful because it is Christ-haunted. Von Balthasar's passage best explains how that beauty operates. Note that the man's actions in the world of the novel do indeed make marks upon it: some good, some bad. And McCarthy, of course, is the one who records all of these actions in a book. As Job lamented, "Oh that my deeds were written down," McCarthy attends to the man and the son by telling their tale in a dignified way, a way that values their experience and calls it beautiful. As a storyteller he is a witness, and as readers so are we.

---

[14]Ibid., 21.
[15]Ibid., 21-22 (my emphasis).

McCarthy has explored this view of storytelling as witness in numerous other places, notably in the novel *The Crossing*. In it, a lapsed priest tells the protagonist the story of an embittered old man he once ministered to. The old man had been through a Job-like experience, catastrophically losing his entire family while he was away. In deep grief, he went on a mad rant against God. What the priest claims he learned from the old man's story boils down to the fact that the story itself is the most important thing. When that story is told to another—and now retold to the protagonist of *The Crossing* and to us—it reveals its value. Our stories provide, however unwittingly, a witness. It is a complicated interchange, but it ends with the priest affirming not the goodness of God (the priest had behaved toward the old man the way Job's counselors behaved toward him, trying to convince him of God's goodness) but the fact of God. All is fated by God; nothing escapes God's reach. Here the priest, referring to himself in the third person, makes a conclusion about what he learned:

> What the priest saw at last was that the lesson of a life can never be its own. Only the witness has power to take its measure. It is lived for the other only. The priest therefore saw what the anchorite could not. That God needs no witness. Neither to Himself nor against. The truth is rather that if there were no God then there could be no witness for there could be no identity to the world but only each man's opinion of it.... Bear closely with me now. There is another who will hear what you never spoke. Stones themselves are made of air. What they have power to crush never lived. In the end we shall all of us be only what we have made of God. For nothing is real save his grace.[16]

Although we cannot be sure that McCarthy's opinion matches that of the priest, McCarthy's storytelling itself performs this kind of witness. It gives witness to the other, implying the existence of an ultimate Other who has validated that act of giving witness. Indeed, the ultimate Other is what has enabled the act of witness, for "if there were no God then there could be no witness for there could be no identity to the world."

Novels like *The Road*, along with many other works of fiction, tacitly assent to von Balthasar's argument that the human being is not lord over himself; he cannot "confer form upon himself." Von Balthasar's argument is very similar

---

[16]Cormac McCarthy, *The Crossing* (New York: Vintage, 1995), 158.

to that made by Mikhail Bakhtin, who compares the author's consciousness to God's only in that it reveals that aesthetic vision is something that by definition a person cannot have of one's self.[17] No matter how he may try to deflect us by never naming the man or the boy in *The Road*, McCarthy has set us up to see this man and his son's life as significant. McCarthy has drawn us to the beauty of this man's life and his struggle—and to the importance of his moral choices, his witness to the readers who will "hear what you never spoke."

In the next part of his argument, von Balthasar insists that a person is not free in communication. A person is instead a being "whose condition it always is to be communicated," and the self is regained by this communication. The man and his story are communicated here; thus they participate in a kind of being, a fictional being that nonetheless relates analogically to the larger idea that all persons' lives are communicated to someone, somewhere, all the time. We are seen by God, and have been so from the beginning. By writing the story of this man and this boy, McCarthy participates in this idea—indeed, witnesses to it—intentionally or not.

In *The Road*, there are several places of open assent to this idea. In the first two pages of the book, we are introduced to the man, who awakens from a bad dream and reaches out for the boy to make sure he is there. From the first, this novel is about human connection. Before the boy wakes up, the man surveys the area, and we read that he "sat there holding the binoculars and watching the ashen daylight congeal over the land. He knew only that the child was his warrant. He said: If he is not the word of God God never spoke" (5). The man, who speaks very little throughout the novel, says these words aloud. Mc-Carthy emphasizes this with the words "he said," which are often excised from the trimmed-down dialogue of the book. Thus, the man literally communicates the boy while also indicating that the boy is a communication of God. The man is not drawing a parallel between the boy and Jesus as the Word of God, but the boy is a word spoken by God into existence. Aesthetic vision is, in this case, like divine speech-act theory; it requires one person looking at another, speaking the other into existence or acknowledging the other by speech. The boy turns and opens his eyes, and we read the first dialogue:

---

[17] M. Bakhtin, Michael Holquist and Vadim Liapunov, *Art and Answerability: Early Philosophical Essays*, trans. Kenneth Brostrom (Austin: University of Texas Press, 1990).

Hi, Papa, he said.

I'm right here.

I know. (5)

The fact that we are spoken into existence, as the word of God in creation, is for von Balthasar the reason humankind is not an archetype of Being and Spirit, as if competing with God. We are instead made in the image of God. Humankind "is not a primal word," he argues, "but a response; he is not a speaker, but an expression governed by the laws of beauty, laws which man cannot impose on himself."

It is because of this that Jens Zimmermann argues, along with von Balthasar, that theology "establishes aesthetics as integral to self-knowledge." Zimmermann provides his own translation of von Balthasar: "All our acts of self-expression are embedded in history and leave traces we cannot alter. We are not original in being and spirit but copy, not original word but answering word, not freely speaking but expressed meaning, and therefore completely under the demand of the beautiful which we ourselves cannot control."[18] Following von Balthasar, Zimmerman argues that recognition of the beautiful in the mystery of being has the inherent power to draw viewers into the contemplation of something deeper. Humanity, made in the image of God, is beautiful and shows the beauty of all being. Jacques Maritain similarly argues that when something is beautiful, it "belongs to the kingdom of the spirit and plunges deep into the transcendence and the infinity of being."[19]

When aesthetics are properly bound up with the true and the good centered on the mystery of being, it is no longer possible to dismiss the ugliness of the postapocalyptic world McCarthy presents as theologically irrelevant or as hostile to theism. Nor is it possible to argue that McCarthy's theological passages are tacked on in an attempt to make a materialistic and naturalistic novel appear metaphysical. Instead, the entire novel reveals that when humankind walks away from God and turns the world into an ash heap, we make it harder, but not impossible, to recognize the beauty and goodness of creation. This partly explains why the novel is concerned so parabolically, archetypally,

---

[18]Jens Zimmermann, "'Quo Vadis'? Literary Theory Beyond Postmodernism," *Christianity & Literature* 53, no. 4 (Summer 2004): 515.

[19]Maritain in Mario O. D'Souza CSB and Jonathan R. Seiling, eds., *Being in the World: A Quotable Maritain Reader* (Notre Dame, IN: University of Notre Dame Press, 2014), 25.

metaphysically and theologically with darkness and light. The man and the boy face a world growing increasingly dim; indeed, the apocalyptic blight, whatever it was, is described as a "cold glaucoma dimming the world" (3) and leaving them bereft of warmth and direction.

Seen this way, the expression "carrying the fire" has core significance. The man made up this expression to encourage the boy. It stands for, among other things, the fact that they are trying to be the "good guys"—to not give up, to not eat people, to not kill anyone except when their lives are in danger. In short, "carrying the fire" is retaining their humanity. In these actions they become a beacon of light in utter blackness evocative of John 1:5: "The light shines in the darkness, and the darkness did not overcome it." Indeed, every time the man looks at the boy he sees him as a light so beautiful that he cannot bring himself to take the boy's life to prevent others from hurting him:

> There were times when he sat watching the boy sleep that he would begin to sob uncontrollably but it wasn't about death. He wasn't sure what it was about but he thought it was about beauty or about goodness. Things that he'd no longer any way to think about at all. (129-30)

Of course, the man *is* thinking about beauty and goodness, though the passage emphasizes that the structures that make these thoughts possible are quickly dissipating. This is due in large part to the man and boy's increasing isolation in this world. But the structures for these thoughts exist for us as readers, and they are in this novel, which touches beauty and goodness in multiple ways and invites us to do the same.

To put it simply, this is not an ugly novel. It appreciates and depends upon our recognition of the difference between light and dark, between goodness and evil.[20] Furthermore, the drama of the novel, like the book of Job, surrounds the question of whether the man will curse God and die precisely because he and his son are losing any way of thinking about beauty or goodness—anything, in other words, that makes life worth living. This loss, not death, is what the man is sobbing about, and it is a powerfully theological moment.

---

[20]Whatever delight he may find in depicting corruption, McCarthy's conception of evil is thoroughly Augustinian. Evil is the absence of good. There is no point in *The Road* where the reader is led to celebrate or glory in evil, though we are led to contemplate the possible dissolving of good, the uncreation of creation as humankind descends into the worst version of itself.

Finally, von Balthasar's insight that the human being is a communicated word helps us to understand the significance of the isolation the man and the boy experience in *The Road*. Though able to live on their own for some time, the novel begins with them being forced out of their isolation and onto the road. The man is rightly suspicious of most people they meet—people who have turned to evil ways to survive, who have abandoned loving cooperation for slavery and cannibalism. By the time we are introduced to the father and son, they have already become "each other's world entire" (6), which is not, of course, a sustainable long-term situation. The boy instinctively knows this and is always trying to find others.

The power and logic of a plot forcing a man out of isolation to save his family becomes clear when we reflect on the doctrine of the *imago Dei*. Following the lead of Karl Barth, many theologians insist that loving dialogical relationships with others is where the image of God is primarily seen. For example, Alistair McFadyen writes, "Humanity is fully in the image of God only where it is a lived dialogical encounter."[21] Emmanuel Mounier makes a similar point, noting that the person as a created being exists only in relation to others; this is especially revealed in communication.[22] Whether or not the image of God depends on personal relationship, the man and boy's isolation is a problem because it increasingly removes them from seeing the created goodness of others. They have each become the other's only means of seeing the image of God in the human world. This explains why the man and boy are so desperate to continue speaking to one another, though their dialogue becomes clipped and self-imitative in their isolation.

The isolation in *The Road* also helps to explain why the narrator and the man lament that language itself is dissolving along with the general de-creation of the world. As they camped,

> The man tried to think of something to say but could not. He'd had this feeling before, beyond the numbness and the dull despair. The world shrinking down about a raw core of parsible entities. The names of things slowly following those things into oblivion. Colors. The names of birds. Things to eat. Finally the names of things one believed to be true. More fragile than he would have thought. How much was

---

[21]Alistair I. McFadyen, *The Call to Personhood: A Christian Theory of the Individual in Social Relationships* (Cambridge: Cambridge University Press, 1990), 32.

[22]Emmanuel Mounier, *Personalism* (Notre Dame, IN: University of Notre Dame Press, 1989), 23.

gone already? The sacred idiom shorn of its referents and so of its reality. Drawing down like something trying to preserve heat. In time to wink out forever. (89)

The worry is that the world of things is shrinking, and with it the names of those things. Because the world is de-creating all around the man and the boy, eventually language itself is going to disappear, leaving a gray world with no distinctions whatsoever.

So how are we to explain beautiful language in a book that is describing the decay of things and of language? We have three options. First, as Hungerford might argue, the novel's beautiful language could be an effort to shore up against these ruins, with the artist taking God's place in creating the world through language. Second, the novel itself and its beautiful language could be simply a nostalgic remembering of a former beauty that is disintegrating. Or, third, the beautiful language could be insisting that as long as there are persons carrying the fire of goodness and truth, beauty is never really lost.

While I do not believe the first thesis for reasons I have described, the second remains compelling. The narrator provides numerous descriptions of the dissolving world that suggest in time the "sacred idiom" will "wink out forever." But if we read these laments over the dissolving world in light of their echo of the book of Job, the second thesis is harder to sustain. And the clearest bit of evidence against this thesis is the novel's ending: the discovery of the boy, after his father's death, by what is unquestionably a trustworthy community—with children. The father's sacrifice and refusal to curse God and die has not been in vain. As if that fact were not enough, McCarthy provides this penultimate paragraph:

> The woman when she saw him put her arms around him and held him. Oh, she said, I am so glad to see you. She would talk to him sometimes about God. He tried to talk to God but the best thing was to talk to his father and he did talk to him and he didnt forget. The woman said that was all right. She said that the breath of God was his breath yet though it pass from man to man through all of time. (286)

Against the silent waste of suicide and abdication, and specifically in the name of God, the boy talks to and does not forget his father. Of course there is nothing necessarily Christian about this conception of God, and it is not my purpose to argue as such. But it is certainly possible to read this passage as an example of God showing up in the primary way he does today: in people who name him as God and who love others in his name. This idea is consistent with von Balthasar's insistence that the human is an image of God and a response, not an archetype and a primal speaker. Simply put, the passage is overtly theological in a way that McCarthy could have easily avoided. Consider the similarity of this passage to a quotation from Theophilus of Antioch:

> God has given to the earth the breath which feeds it. It is his breath that gives life to all things. And if he were to withhold his breath, everything would be annihilated. His breath vibrates in yours, in your voice. It is the breath of God that you breathe— and you are unaware of it.[23]

God answers Job's queries not with explanations but with himself—his voice, his breath. Here, God answers the man's queries through this family that continues to talk about God and to God. What the boy finds in the end is not luck. It is goodness in the form of other persons who are also "carrying the fire." Luck is as impersonal as the flip of the coin; goodness, in our world, requires a human face. With this passage McCarthy reveals, intentionally or not, his great love for the father and the son, love that is too deep to either leave them in despair or to leave their story untold. He is their witness to us, and "if there were no God then there could be no witness for there could be no identity to the world but only each man's opinion of it."[24]

If McCarthy's landscape is as Christ-haunted as I have argued that it is, we are left with the third explanation for the beauty of the novel. If the good, the beautiful and the true are the imprint of God in the world, then these things will reveal him. If human persons are made in the image of God and are under the "demand of the beautiful" in the way that von Balthasar describes, if persons are beautiful according to laws of being that they neither make nor control, then McCarthy is participating in this logic by making the language of *The Road* sing and hum. This is what Jacques Maritain suggests when he argues that "the artist, whether he knows it or not, consults God in looking at things."[25] This is also why, in his book on beauty, Roger Scruton argues that beauty cannot be considered a property that can be ascribed to some things to the exclusion of others. Beauty is more like a posture toward things seen.

---

[23]Quoted in Martin Laird, *Into the Silent Land: A Guide to the Christian Practice of Contemplation* (Oxford: Oxford University Press, 2006), 37.

[24]McCarthy, *The Crossing*, 158.

[25]D'Souza and Seiling, *Being in the World*, 30.

Beauty "demands an act of attention. And it may be expressed in many different ways. Less important than the final verdict is the attempt to show what is right, fitting, worthwhile, attractive or expressive in the object: in other words, to identify the aspect of the thing that claims our attention."[26]

This leads us to consider the immense, lamenting beauty of the last paragraph of the novel, clearly now from the narrator's point of view:

> Once there were brook trout in the streams in the mountains. You could see them standing in the amber current where the white edges of their fins wimpled softly in the flow. They smelled of moss in your hand. Polished and muscular and torsional. On their backs were vermiculate patterns that were maps of the world in its becoming. Maps and mazes. Of a thing which could not be put back. Not be made right again. In the deep glens where they lived all things were older than man and they hummed of mystery. (286-87)

Hungerford argues that "it is the words," not the carrying of the fire, "that hold out hope—that put the speckled trout back into the river and the river back into the valley and make things right again even as the words say these things cannot be done."[27] Hungerford reads the passage as McCarthy reveling in his God-like power. But to believe this requires readers to forget that, before this passage appears, we have spent 250 pages attentively following a man who loves his son and refuses to give in to evil. We have cheered on the father and son as they carry the fire, believing against their circumstances, as Job did, that a light still shines in the world and the darkness has not overcome it. What has greater power than a well-told story to draw our attention to the essential beauty of being that humanity is always and everywhere in danger of ignoring or desecrating? For we, like Job and like the man, have the choice of life or death before us all the time. If we choose to let it, the light of goodness and love in the world can indeed flicker and grow dim. Maybe McCarthy is more of a prophet of the end times than he knows. When the Son of Man returns, bringing justice, will he find faith on the earth? (Lk 18:8).

Perhaps McCarthy's final paragraph, emerging after the appearance of God in the loving faces and voices of the good family, prophetically warns us of our peril. It warns us that when we destroy our world or blur it beyond recognition,

---

[26]Roger Scruton, *Beauty: A Very Short Introduction* (Oxford: Oxford University Press, 2011), 13.
[27]Hungerford, *Postmodern Belief,* 136.

we lose. What we lose is a map to the world in its creation and its becoming—
the whole story of why we are here at all. Words cannot replace the map of
creation. They also cannot replace living human beings if we decide to erase
the image of God in this world by annihilating each other. The created world
is old, and everything in it still hums of mystery. The question is—as it always
has been—whether we can hear it.

Part Three

VISION

7

WHAT DOES IT MEAN
TO SEE SOMEONE?

Icons and Identity

Ian A. McFarland

*For it is the God who said, "Let the light shine out of
darkness," who has shone in our hearts to give the light of the
knowledge of the glory of God in the face of Jesus Christ.*

2 CORINTHIANS 4:6

INTRODUCTION

This chapter explores the significance of icons for the claim that human beings
are made in God's image. This is not a task I undertake lightly. Especially
among Westerners like myself, for whom they are not a native part of the liturgical landscape, icons can easily give rise to misunderstanding. But I do not
think this is the main theological problem posed by icons today. Since World
War II, there has been among Western Christians—Catholic and Protestant,
liberal and evangelical—a wide-ranging effort to mine the theological, devotional and liturgical insights of the Orthodox tradition. This effort—prompted
in part by the writings of Orthodox theologians, especially Vladimir Lossky,
John Meyendorff and John Zizioulas, who have sought to address Western as
well as Eastern audiences in their work—has had significant impact on a
number of areas of theological reflection. These include trinitarian doctrine

and, through a reappraisal of the Orthodox category of deification or *theosis,* anthropology and eschatology. While icons have not commanded the same level of attention in Western academic theology, something of their popular appeal can be gauged from their use on book covers, in church bulletins and in Sunday school curricula.

And this is where the problem lies: icons, though often received with enthusiasm in the Christian West, are regarded as having a decorative rather than theological significance. In short, they are not viewed as prompting us to *think* differently about God or the world that God creates and redeems. When they are discussed in theological terms, reference is usually made to their role in depicting human beings as transfigured in glory. While this understanding of icons is correct as far as it goes, it is too prone to be interpreted in terms of an otherworldly spirituality that does not accurately reflect the dogmatic grounding of icons in Orthodox theology. Icons received their theological justification in Orthodoxy as a necessary implication of the *this*-worldly reality of the incarnation. With this in mind, I want to suggest that the chief significance of icons is missed if the emphasis on their depiction of glorified humanity eclipses their role in helping us to see each other here and now. Specifically, icons clarify what it means to speak of human beings as created in the image of God.

This idea that icons help us to see people on earth may seem startling given the way icons look. It does not take much exposure to Orthodox iconography to recognize that the genre is highly stylized, with conventions—high foreheads, large eyes, small mouths—that do not suggest realistic portraiture.[1] And yet, there are other iconographic conventions, less immediately obvious, that speak more directly to the role of icons in training our sight. For example, the subjects of icons are never shown in profile but always in full or three-quarter face. More significantly, while icons are never signed by the artist, all icons are *named.* Indeed, the icon is not complete until it is named. These two ideas—that seeing a person involves looking them in the *face* and acknowledging that a face belongs to a particular *someone*—point to the

---

[1] Leonid Ouspensky says, "The Fathers of the Seventh Ecumenical Council . . . had to distinguish carefully between an icon and a portrait. The latter represents an ordinary human being, the former a man united to God." *Theology of the Icon,* 2 vols., trans. Anthony Gythiel and Elizabeth Meyendorff (Crestwood, NY: St. Vladimir's Seminary Press, 1992), 1:162.

anthropological significance of icons as liturgical primers for interpersonal encounters in the here and now.[2] Before I develop this claim, it is necessary to give some historical background on the development of icon veneration in the Eastern churches.

ICON AS CHRISTOLOGICAL PROBLEM

The history of how icons emerged as a defining feature of Eastern Christianity is far from clear. Although the catacombs provide evidence of Christian sacred painting dating back to the second century, there is not much evidence for icons prior to the time of Constantine. During the early Byzantine period, however, they became an established part of devotion in the Eastern church, to the extent that the Quinisext Council (sometimes called the Council in Trullo) of 692 explicitly directed that portraits of Jesus in human form should replace symbolic depictions of him as a lamb.[3] Soon afterward, however, an iconoclastic reaction set in. This was initiated by Emperor Leo III, who issued decrees banning icons in 726 and 730, and by his successor, Constantine V, who intensified iconoclastic policies and gave theological depth to the icono-clast position, culminating in the decrees of the iconoclastic Council of Hiereia in 754.

From a Western perspective, one striking feature of the debates is the rela-tively minor role played by the Ten Commandments. Initially, defenders of icons like John of Damascus did feel the need to address the charge that icons were an idolatrous violation of the Mosaic proscription on crafting images of God. John did so by drawing a distinction between worship (*latreia* in Greek), which was properly offered to God alone, and veneration (*proskynēsis*), which referred to public expressions of respect or deference, ranging from bowing before the emperor to reverencing an altar. Icons, he argued, were objects of veneration only. Since they were not made to be worshiped, their production did not violate the proscriptions of the Decalogue.[4]

---

[2] One might also note in this context iconographers' practice of using reverse perspective, which, rather than drawing the observer into the world of the painting (as in the linear perspective typical of modern Western painting), brings the subject of the icon into the real space occupied by the observer (see Ouspensky, *Theology*, 2:495-98).

[3] Canon 82, cited in St. Theodore the Studite, *On the Holy Icons*, trans. Catherine P. Roth (Crest-wood, NY: St. Vladimir's Seminary Press, 2001), II.38.

[4] See St. John of Damascus, *Three Treatises on the Divine Images*, trans. Andrew Louth (Crestwood, NY: St Vladimir's Seminary Press, 2003), I.5-6, 14.

This distinction seems to have been accepted, for though the debate over icons seesawed back and forth for nearly a century after John's death until the definitive vindication of the pro-icon iconodule (from *dulia*, the Latin term for veneration) position in 843, the Ten Commandments do not figure prominently in the later stages of the debate.[5] Instead, the arguments for and against icons turned on the christological question of whether the fact of the incarnation—God's taking flesh in the person of Jesus—justified the production of images for liturgical use.

In order to understand this latter set of arguments, it is necessary to take a brief detour into the conceptual and terminological technicalities of the christological principles shared by both sides in the debate. These principles were rooted in the decrees of the Council of Chalcedon (451), further refined at the Second (553) and Third (681) Councils of Constantinople. Crucial to all three councils was the use of the distinction between *nature* and *person* (Greek *hypostasis*) to parse the relationship between humanity and divinity in Jesus. Although this distinction has roots extending back to fourth-century trinitarian debates, it was only in the course of the christological controversies that wracked the empire in the fifth and sixth centuries that it achieved fully developed form. Whereas earlier Christian writers tended to understand nature as referring to a general category of entity ("dog") and hypostasis to a concrete instantiation of that nature ("Lassie"), by the end of the sixth century nature was taken to refer to the "whatness" of a thing, or the kind of entity it is, and hypostasis to "whoness," or personal identity. This shift represented an important, if subtle, modification of earlier usage: any reality can be analyzed in terms of general and concrete, but only certain entities—God, angels and human beings—could be described in terms of *what* and *who*. A single plant may contain a number of separate rose blossoms and an anthill thousands of individual ants, but people are not simply a series of individual instantiations of the genus "human." In other words, people are not only a series of concrete some*things*, but also identifiable as particular some*ones*.

As already noted, this understanding of the distinction between nature and hypostasis was developed in the process of Christians trying to speak clearly

---

[5]Ouspensky comments that when Pope Hadrian I defended icon veneration against the charge of idolatry in his message to the Second Council of Nicaea in 787, "For the Eastern Church . . . this was a subject which had been left behind long ago, almost an anachronism" (*Theology*, 1:132).

and consistently about the uniqueness of Jesus. According to the christo-logical definition promulgated at Chalcedon, Jesus, though just one hypostasis (or "person"), has two natures, one divine and one human, such that "one and the same Lord Jesus Christ, the only-begotten Son, must be acknowledged in two natures, without confusion or change, without division or separation."[6] In other words, Jesus is a single some*one*—the Son of God—but he lives out that identity through two some*things*, such that as God's Son he leads at once both a fully divine and a fully human life.

This basic christological definition carried with it a number of interesting implications. For example, because Jesus of Nazareth was understood to be hypostatically identical with the Son of God (again, *who* he is), it was both possible and necessary to say things like "the Son of God suffered on the cross" and "Jesus of Nazareth is the Creator of the universe." Both propositions follow from the confession that the one Word who was with God in the be-ginning lived simultaneously and without any qualification both a fully human and a fully divine life.

John of Damascus, the most influential iconodule theologian during the first generation of the iconoclast controversy, pioneered the use of christo-logical arguments derived from this Chalcedonian conceptual frame to defend the production and veneration of icons. Unlike his use of the worship-veneration distinction, this defense of icons did not forestall further debate. John argued that while the Mosaic proscription of images made sense prior to the incarnation, the situation has changed now that God has assumed human flesh.[7] In line with Chalcedon's insistence that the integrity of both of Christ's natures is preserved in the incarnation "without confusion or change," John stressed that although the *divine* nature remains invisible even after the incarnation, because the *human* nature preserves its distinctive properties in being assumed by the second person of the Trinity, and because the properties of that nature include possession of a definite shape and size, Jesus could be depicted iconographically. As John put it, "The nature of the flesh did not

---

[6]*Compendium of Creeds, Definitions, and Declarations on Matters of Faith and Morals*, 43rd ed., ed. Heinrich Denzinger, Peter Hünermann et al. (San Francisco: Ignatius Press, 2012), §302.

[7]John points out that even in the Old Testament, proscription of liturgical images was not absolute, given the role of images of cherubim and other creatures in the temple furnishings, for example. But he adds that there was no question here of producing images of *God*, which became possible only after the incarnation. See John, *Three Treatises*, I.20.

become divinity, but as the Word became flesh immutably, remaining what it was, so also the flesh became the Word without losing what it was."[8] This deployment of the Chalcedonian distinction between the divine *nature* that remains ever beyond depiction and the divine *person* of the Word encountered in the flesh would become crucial in later stages of the debate. John insisted, "I do not depict the invisible divinity [*theotēta*, the divine nature], but I depict God [*theon*, that is, the person of the Son] made visible in the flesh."[9]

In 754, Constantine V summoned the Council of Hiereia to offer formal rebuttal to John's arguments and confirm the orthodoxy of iconoclasm. Ingeniously, he attacked icon veneration by drawing on the same distinction between person and nature that John had used to defend it. Constantine contended that the Chalcedonian definition of Christ as one person with two complete natures, joined unconfusedly and inseparably, put the iconodules on the horns of a dilemma. What, he asked, did the iconodules imagine they were depicting in their pictures of Jesus? Was it the divinity together with the humanity? In that case, they had clearly confused the natures, contrary to the Chalcedonian definition, since the divine nature, being invisible, was incapable of physical depiction. Or was it only the human nature of Christ that was painted? In that case, the natures were being divided from each other (by portraying one without the other), also contrary to the teaching of Chalcedon. It followed that the production of icons was illicit, since no icon could possibly capture Christ's being as both fully divine *and* fully human.

Faced by this argument, the iconodules needed to respond in kind. Although the Second Council of Nicaea in 787 is recognized as providing authorization for the production and veneration of liturgical images, it was only a generation after this council that Theodore the Studite, a monk of Constantinople responding to a resurgence of imperial iconoclasm, offered a comprehensive theological rejoinder to the iconoclast position. Following the lead of John of Damascus, Theodore maintained that insofar as depictability was an intrinsic property of human nature, to deny that Christ could be portrayed in icons was to deny his humanity. More significantly, against the iconoclasts' charge that any visual depiction of Christ could not possibly include the divine nature, Theodore argued that it was a category error to assume that

---

[8] Ibid., III.6.
[9] Ibid., I.4.

either of Christ's natures was depicted in an icon. Natures are conceptual abstractions, and abstractions cannot be depicted. It is part of the nature of human beings to have hair and eyes, for example, but one cannot depict hair or eyes in general, but only as a given particular instantiation in an individual. He concluded that what is portrayed in an icon is not the nature of the subject but rather the individual person or hypostasis:

> For how could a nature be portrayed unless it were contemplated in a hypostasis? For example, Peter is not portrayed insofar as he is animate, rational, mortal, and capable of thought and understanding; for this does not define Peter only, but also Paul and John, and all those of the same nature. But [he is portrayed] insofar as he adds along with the common definition certain [particular] properties, such as a long or short nose, curly hair, a good complexion, bright eyes, or whatever else characterizes his particular appearance.[10]

Note the terms of Theodore's argument. What we normally think of as the higher features of humanity—reason, consciousness, will and so forth—are not capable of depiction at all. Rather, we know a person through material particularities—nose, hair, eyes and the like—or what Theodore terms "hypostatic properties." The implication of this claim will be the subject of the balance of this chapter, but I will state it briefly here: although *what* we see when we look at other human beings is just various bits of matter, in seeing them we see a person—a particular *who.*

According to the Chalcedonian Christology accepted by both sides of the iconoclast controversy, the hypostasis of Christ—*who* he is—is none other than the eternal Word, the second person of the Trinity. It follows that in seeing Jesus we see God the Son, in shaking Jesus' hand we shake God's hand, and so forth. In his debates with the iconoclasts, Theodore argued that in the same way that Jesus' human body—like any human body—manifests his personal identity, so a picture of Jesus—like a picture of any human being—is able to depict that identity.

Furthermore, although an icon always depicts a particular person, Theodore insists that an icon's ability to manifest the hypostasis of the one depicted is not dependent on the artist's skill in producing an accurate likeness.

---

[10]Theodore, *On the Holy Icons,* III.A.34. Cf. John of Damascus: "Nature does not subsist in itself [*kath'heautēn ouch hyphistatai*], but is visible in hypostases" (*On the Orthodox Faith,* chap. 6, Patrologia Graeca 94:1004A).

Rather, even as the diverse appearance of crosses made for devotional use ("small and large, wider and narrower, with blunt or sharp ends, with or without inscription"), none of which corresponds to the dimensions and textures of the historical wood on which Jesus was executed, does not preclude their all being recognized as the cross, so the presence of variations in iconographic depictions of Jesus does not prevent us from recognizing them all as pictures of Jesus.[11] And, Theodore concludes, the same goes for icons of Mary and the other saints, for "veneration is given to the image not insofar as it falls short of similarity, but insofar as it resembles its prototype."[12]

ICON AS AN ANTHROPOLOGICAL STATEMENT

At this point it is possible to see how christological justification for the production of icons has significant entailments for a Christian understanding of human beings as created in the image of God. Before we explore that question in detail, however, it is necessary to explain how the arguments for the veneration of images of *Christ* (who was confessed to be truly God) could be used to justify the veneration of *saints* (who were in no way thought to be divine). John of Damascus argued that veneration of the saints was justifiable in that Christ's incarnation allowed human beings to share by grace the divine status Christ possessed by nature as God's Son.[13] Though he does not put it in quite these terms, John's point is that our status as *human* persons—beings God recognizes and claims as someones to be loved—is secured by the fact that in Christ a *divine* person lives as a human being. Insofar as Christ, as God's Son, is a person who claims solidarity with us by identifying his Father with ours (see Jn 20:17; Heb 2:11), he establishes us as persons, too. He makes us some*ones* as well as some*things*. For this reason, John concludes, "Through the images of the saints," no less than through images of Christ, "I offer veneration and honor to God, for whose sake I reverence his friends also."[14]

---

[11]Theodore, *On the Holy Icons*, III.C.5. Cf. Ouspensky's distinction between icon and portrait in note 1 above.

[12]Ibid.

[13]"For from the time when God the Word became flesh, and was made like us in every respect . . . and was united without confusion with what is ours, and unchangingly deified the flesh through the unconfused coinherence of his divinity and his flesh with one another, we have been truly sanctified" (John, *Three Treatises*, I.21; cf. I.19).

[14]Ibid., III.26. As with John's argument against the charge of idolatry, this line of argument appears to have been persuasive: once it was conceded that icons of Christ are licit, there does not seem to

In short, insofar as icons are understood to depict persons (rather than natures), and insofar as God in assuming human flesh addresses all human beings as persons called to share in the eternal communion of the divine persons, there can be no objection to making icons of saints. The saints are just those human beings who, having answered God's call, remind us of our status as persons who are likewise summoned to communion with other persons, divine and human.[15] Indeed, according to the principles of orthodox iconography, the depiction of Christ properly includes the depiction of other human beings, since the subject of the icon can be identified *as* Christ in the first place only if he can be recognized as the one whose life is portrayed in the Gospels.[16] Thus because Christ is the son of Mary it is appropriate for him to be shown with his mother; because Christ is the one whose glory was revealed to Peter, James and John, it is appropriate to depict him on the Mount of Transfiguration; and so on.[17] Even as we are images of God by virtue of our relationship to the one image who is the eternal Son, so the incarnate Son's identity as the image of God is inseparable from *his* relationships to other people—relationships that are grounded in and mediated by the materiality of the body that allows both him and us to be depicted on icons.[18]

The production of icons is thus rooted in the fleshly materiality of Jesus, the same materiality that constitutes and mediates his relationships with other human beings. And because this materiality identifies Jesus as the person he is (even as it identifies us as the persons we are), the production of icons

---

have been any serious objection raised to icons of the saints. Theodore the Studite makes only one brief reference to arguments against veneration of the saints in the first of his three refutations; see *On the Holy Icons*, I.17-18.

[15]"The icon does not represent the divinity. Rather, it indicates man's participation in the divine life" (Ouspensky, *Theology*, 1:166).

[16]In the words of Patriarch Tarasius of Constantinople, "It is appropriate to accept the precious icons of Jesus Christ . . . provided such icons are painted with historic exactness [*historikōs*], in conformity with the Gospel narrative." J. D. Mansi, *Sacrorum Conciliorum nova et amplissima collection*, 31 vols. (Florence and Venice, 1758–98), XIII.404D; cited in Ouspensky, *Theology*, 1:167 (translation slightly altered). Cf. Cyril Mango, *Byzantium: The Empire of New Rome* (New York: Charles Scribner's Sons, 1980), 264: "To regard . . . Byzantine religious art as symbolic reveals a grave misunderstanding: on the contrary, it sought to be explicit, literal, even realistic."

[17]"Christ is never alone. He is always the head of His Body. In Orthodox theology and devotion alike, Christ is never separated from His Mother . . . and His 'friends,' the saints. The Redeemer and the redeemed belong together inseparably." Georges Florovsky, "The Ethos of the Orthodox Church," *The Ecumenical Review* 12, no. 2 (1960): 195; cited in Ouspensky, *Theology*, 2:279.

[18]"The grace that sanctifies both the humanity of Christ and the body of a deified [hu]man is the same. That is why in Orthodox art their representations are done in the same manner" (Ouspensky, *Theology*, 2:456).

testifies to the belief that the human body discloses the person whose body it is. In other words, icons remind us that in seeing a human body, I see a person. When I look at a human being, what I see—in terms of the biophysics of vision—is a body. And yet, a body is not all that I see. This may not seem like a remarkable claim at first glance, but it cuts against some entrenched presuppositions about the relationship between ourselves and our bodies that mark modern Western culture.

However one comes down on the mind-body problem that has stalked Western philosophy since Descartes, it is fair to say that we tend to decouple persons from bodies, treating the person as a reality that lies beneath or behind what we see—and for this reason, ultimately separable from it. From this perspective—notwithstanding Christian belief in bodily resurrection—the body is assumed to be a kind of barrier behind which we need to penetrate in order to apprehend the person within. It follows that the body does not manifest the person directly; rather, the presence of a person must be inferred from various bodily movements (speech, intentional action and the like). Instead of being identified with the person, the body is viewed as the person's instrument. We may obsess over how our bodies look, but the fact that we view them as objects to be sculpted, enhanced, reduced, punctured, polished and otherwise modified in order to project a particular image suggests we see the body's value as more instrumental than intrinsic.[19]

Something very like this view was also a part of the Greco-Roman intellectual world in which Christianity took root. The Platonic vision of the immortal and indestructible soul lodged or trapped in a frail mortal body was a powerful influence on early Christian anthropology, even as the church consistently rejected the idea that the body was an accidental or dispensable feature of human being. This kind of thinking is visible even in John of Damascus's writings in defense of icons. For John, icons have an auxiliary function in the life of faith. As "books for the illiterate,"[20] they provide a material bridge

---

[19]My position here has affinities with Ludwig Wittgenstein's famous remark, "The human body is the best picture of the human soul" (*Philosophical Investigations*, II.iv, 3rd ed., trans. G. E. M. Anscombe [New York: Macmillan, 1958], 178). While the parallels are real, it is important to note that the hypostasis is not the same as the soul (according to Chalcedonian Christology Jesus had a human soul but, as the eternal Word, was not a human hypostasis). Indeed, one merit of an anthropology developed in Chalcedonian terms is that it is equally compatible with dualist (body-soul) anthropologies and physicalist approaches that deny that human being includes any metaphysical element irreducible to material interactions.

[20]John, *Three Treatises*, I.47; cf. II.10, III.9.

to the invisible: "holy things made by hand that lead us through matter to the immaterial God."[21] Christologically, this understanding of icons suggests a troublesome division between Jesus' body and the eternal Word, with the icon—as an image of the body—serving like a ladder that, once scaled, may comfortably be left behind. Indeed, an icon's value is arguably even more equivocal for John insofar as he also describes it as "a mirror and a puzzle, suitable to the body."[22] Again, the body appears as something we have to look behind or beyond to grasp the truth of Christ's divinity.

In short, John casts the materiality of the icon—and, by implication, the body it depicts—as something of a crutch: a deficient though serviceable means of drawing the intellect to apprehension of higher, fundamentally immaterial reality.[23] Understood this way, icons are liturgical adiaphora, matters of Christian practice that are not strictly necessary, though potentially useful. Such a view of icons suggests a theology in which the material, whether identified with the body or its image, is similarly construed as a means to an end rather than having any intrinsic theological significance.

To be sure, because it is true that what we see when we look at a human being (or her icon) is always matter and not the hypostasis as such (which is not material), there can be no objection to speaking of icons portraying an invisible reality. It is vital to recognize that it is characteristic of human beings, including Jesus, that the hypostasis subsists and is revealed *in* the material, not above or behind it. On this point, Theodore the Studite is much clearer than his more famous predecessor. He explicitly rejects the idea that seeing pictures of Jesus based on the biblical narratives is in any way inferior to hearing or reading the words of the Gospels.[24] For Theodore, icons are not an

---

[21]Ibid., II.23.

[22]Ibid., II.5; cf. III.2. The language of "mirror" (*esoptron*) and "puzzle" (*ainigma*) is taken from 1 Cor 13:12, but John, unlike Paul, applies it explicitly to the incarnation (i.e., it is not our understanding of God and God's ways, broadly conceived, that is the puzzle for John, but specifically God enfleshed).

[23]This sense that the body is less than a perfect vehicle for revealing the Son is also found in John's *Exposition of the Orthodox Faith*, III.6, which combines a clear affirmation that the Word "was united to the whole [of human nature] that he might in His grace bestow salvation on the whole man" with the claim that this union took place "through the medium of the mind which is intermediate between the purity of God and the grossness of the flesh." John of Damascus, "An Exact Exposition of the Orthodox Faith," in *Hilary of Poitiers, John of Damascus*, ed. Philip Schaff and Henry Wace, trans. S. D. F. Salmond, vol. 9 of Nicene and Post-Nicene Fathers, 2nd series (Peabody, MA: Hendrickson, 1995 [1899]), 50.

[24]"For hearing is equal to sight, and it is necessary to use both senses. Whoever takes away one

accommodation for the illiterate permitted in light of the incarnation but a necessary feature of Christian witness demanded by the confession of the Word's having taken flesh. Comparing the relationship between Christ and his icon to that between a seal and its imprint, he reasons as follows:

> A seal is one thing, and its imprint another. Nevertheless, even before the impression is made, the imprint is [virtually present] in the seal. There could not be an effective seal which was not impressed on some material. Therefore Christ also, unless he appears in an artificial image, is in this respect idle and ineffective.[25]

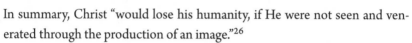

In summary, Christ "would lose his humanity, if He were not seen and venerated through the production of an image."[26]

One may demur on the question of whether images are as necessary for faithful Christian confession as both Theodore and subsequent Orthodox tradition maintain while still recognizing that this understanding of icons is linked to a compelling anthropological vision. A crucial implication of Theodore's position is that insofar as God is revealed to us personally solely by the Word's assumption of human flesh, it is impossible to encounter a human person apart from a human body. It does not follow that a person is reducible to his or her body, for a body changes over time in ways that can—and generally do— include the loss or destruction of parts, ranging from relatively benign phenomena like baldness, through the gradual degradation of neurons leading to diminished mental capacity, to sudden traumatic events resulting in amputation and disfigurement. A human being does not become any less a person through such developments. As already noted, Theodore insists that variations in the quality of the painting do not vitiate the icon's ability to render the hypostasis: even as physical disfigurement does not diminish an individual's personhood, so a poorly executed icon is still an icon—a depiction of someone.

The point remains, however, that there is no encounter with the person apart from the body, and it is for this reason that for Theodore pictures

---

would have to remove the other also" (Theodore, *On the Holy Icons*, I.17). The parity of hearing and sight had been defended at Second Nicaea as well; see Ouspensky, *Theology*, 1:138. By contrast, although John views icons as doing the same work as books and can even call sight "the first of the senses" (*Three Treatises*, I.17), the association of icons with illiteracy gives them a secondary character.

[25]Theodore, *On the Holy Icons*, III.D.9.

[26]Ibid., III.D.8. Cf. Ouspensky, *Theology*, 2:481-82: "Being one of the basic truths of revelation, the image is therefore one of the components of the doctrinal fullness of the church."

are needed when, as in the case of Jesus and the saints, the body is no longer present to view. In short, if you want to meet a human person, you need to have a body. The idea that the former could be present apart from the latter fails to reckon with the basic character of human beings as embodied persons.

Icons thus remind us that as much as it is true that a person is never to be identified with the presence or absence of any particular bits of matter that make up her body, there is no encountering a person apart from her body.[27] This claim takes its most startling form in Jesus, who is a divine person: the only-begotten Son and true God. The theology of icons implies that to presume to know God as other than incarnate is to presume to know God other than God in fact is, and thus to fail to know God at all. And because there is no knowing Jesus, the one true image of the invisible God, in abstraction from the body he assumed from Mary, we must confess that there is no knowledge of *any* human being, as one created in that image, apart from his body. For if human beings are only persons—children of God and brothers and sisters of Christ—because God has come among us and called us to communion with the divine persons in Jesus, then it stands to reason that even as we are naturally embodied, we are not persons apart from our bodies. It follows that the body is not a mere container from which the person might in principle be separated; rather, the (human) body manifests the (human) person, just as the (human) body of Jesus reveals the (divine) person of the Son. Take away the body, and the person goes with it.

CONCLUSION

There is a paradox in icons. On the one hand, they are supposed to be based in historical reality: they are identifiable as particular people with clearly defined roles in specific historical situations. On the other hand, in an icon a person is represented "not according to the appearance of his corruptible flesh but according to the glorified body of Christ."[28] So to portray a person is to depict a body in a particular historical context (Jesus at the Last Supper,

---

[27]Theodore notes that because a human body and its image are correlative realities in the same way that a human body and person are, it follows that "the image of Peter appears in Peter, just as Peter appears in his own image" (*On the Holy Icons*, III.C.8). He continues, "Therefore the image of Christ is not differently venerated from Christ Himself, but is venerated in the same way."

[28]Ouspensky, *Theology*, 2:486.

John the Baptist disheveled and clothed in camel's hair, Mary Magdalene with a jar of ointment), but the body is not portrayed literalistically—it is transfigured.

This paradox is necessary as a means of affirming both the inseparability and nonidentity of the person and her body. Inseparability because to see a human person—as well as a divine person—requires looking at a body: there is neither seeing nor knowing a person apart from his body. At the same time, the person is not reducible to the body we see now, not only because the body changes and is subject to alteration without the integrity of the person being diminished, but also because we confess that all bodies will undergo a final, definitive transformation that will disclose the person in unforeseeable majesty. This point reminds us of the sin of idolizing particular types of human bodies—white bodies, able bodies, thin bodies, young bodies and so on. Icons thus echo the testimony of John that "we are God's children"—persons—"now; what we will be has not yet been revealed. What we do know is this: when [Jesus] is revealed, we will be like him, for we will see him as he is" (1 Jn 3:2).

Icons thus train us to see persons in two ways. First, they protest against the materialist reduction of the person to the body, as though the body were nothing more than an object for our manipulation and consumption. Second, they challenge the dualist view of the body as a more-or-less accidental container for the person, as though the existence of another person could be known only through a process of deduction. The anthropology reflected in icons is not consistent with the idea that persons are inferred from bodies. Even Jesus' divine personhood is not something we infer from his actions (after all, in Jn 14:12 Jesus himself teaches that his disciples will perform greater works than he does, but it would be a mistake to infer their divinity on that basis). Rather, his person simply confronts us in his actions, so that as Jesus addresses us we encounter him as a person.[29] Icons function as a sign of this

---

[29]"There is no point in the works of Jesus to which one can unambiguously refer and say that here Jesus can truly be recognized, unambiguously and without doubt, as the Son of God on the basis of his works. . . . First, because it is never possible, in human terms to draw a conclusion about a person from his works, and second, because Jesus is God, and direct conclusions about God on the basis of history are never possible either. . . . Only through Christ's own revelation do I have opened to me his person and his works." Dietrich Bonhoeffer, "Lectures on Christology," in *Berlin: 1932-1933*, vol. 12 of *Dietrich Bonhoeffer Works*, ed. Larry L. Rasmussen, trans. Isabel Best and David Higgins (Minneapolis: Fortress Press, 2009), 309-10.

confrontation: we are summoned to engage Jesus and the saints, and thereby to acknowledge their and our personhood.[30]

While it might seem that confronting painted saints could be a distraction from the community of living human beings around us, it need not be so.[31] Icons summon us to remember that we are confronted by other persons as we confront other human bodies, and that their and our reality as children of God is given in that confrontation, as we seek to discern with one another the shape of the life to which we are called as persons in the body of Christ. Icons are not books for the illiterate but prompts for those who might otherwise be tempted to be indifferent to the community.

Of course, all this raises the question of why we would be inclined to separate a person from her body in the first place, given that our knowledge of persons is inseparable from bodily mediation. I suspect that a major reason for this temptation is our experience of death. The persons we know die, and we do not tend to identify dead bodies as persons. We say things like "that person is no longer with us." Even though the physical body of one who has died may look no different than it did when they were alive, something significant has happened. The person no longer responds to us when we speak. We seem no longer able to engage him as a person. We quite appropriately do not engage a corpse as a person—a someone—but rather as something to be buried or burned.

And yet, things are not quite that simple: we do not bury or burn human bodies as we do rubbish. When bodies are treated that way, as in the death camps of World War II, we take it as a sign that something has gone deeply wrong. Instead, we treat them precisely as dead *persons*. If we take seriously the Christian belief that human beings are by nature embodied, then I would argue that there is no basis for denying that a dead body *is* the person we knew—that it is none other than Peter, Mary or Fred lying there. The object of Christian hope for the vindication of our lives as persons before God and one another is the resurrection of the body. We must confess that we don't know much about

---

[30]"Only a personal image creates a way that leads to its prototype, whether the latter be the person of God become man or that of a human being deified by the uncreated grace of the Holy Spirit" (Ouspensky, *Theology,* 2:453).

[31]Robert Jenson argues that this temptation is realized in the Orthodox iconostasis, which constitutes a visual barrier between the congregation and clergy consecrating the eucharistic elements. *Systematic Theology,* vol. 2, *The Works of God* (New York: Oxford University Press, 1999), 288.

how that will look. But if we know that we will be like Jesus, then we know it will mean having a body, for Jesus is risen from the dead as an embodied person.

To be sure, to say that human beings are created in the image of God does not mean that they physically look like Jesus. On the contrary, icons emphasize that all human beings who are not Jesus look different from him and from each other: as persons, they are particular, unsubstitutable individuals. To say that they are in God's image is rather to say that, like Jesus—who is the visible image of the invisible God—they can *be* imaged. They have bodies that allow them to be depicted as persons and so encountered as persons. Again, this does not require us to look past their bodies, as though their hypostatic identity were some hidden "ghost in the machine," but rather we look at them in all their variable, physical particularity. We look at some*thing* (a human body with particular characteristics), and we see some*one* (Mary). At least, we should. That someone is not reducible to that particular something, for we know that "we will all be changed" (1 Cor 15:51); but she is inseparable from it, for there is no human life, now or in glory, without a human body.

The theology of icons tells us that at a very basic level to be made in the image of God means that we can be imaged like God. God, of course, is invisible, which is why the Israelites were prohibited from worshiping images: "You saw no form when the LORD spoke to you ... out of the fire" (Deut 4:15). And yet, in Jesus God has taken visible form as a human being, "born of a woman" (Gal 4:4) and like us "in every respect" (Heb 2:17). We know God because God has come to us in a body. We know him in that body. In the Eucharist we continue to commune with him through that body. And that body binds us to him; he lives and is recognizable only as he is related to other bodies, both in the past and in the present. We know him as the person he is only as we encounter him among those other bodies: his friends, the saints, both living and dead. Icons remind us of this.

But our knowledge of him and of the persons who are his friends—and thus of what it means to be made in God's image—is incomplete in the present. In their "unrealism," icons remind us of this, too. What that ultimate encounter will be like remains unknown to us now. But we move forward in confidence, taking our present bodies as tokens of the bodies—and thus of the persons—that we shall be, knowing that whatever the future holds, then as now "we will be like him, for we will see him as he is."

8

IMAGE, SPIRIT AND *THEOSIS*

Imaging God in an Image-Distorting World

Daniela C. Augustine

INTRODUCTION: FROM IMAGE TO LIKENESS

Many Eastern church fathers differentiate between the terms *image* and *likeness* with reference to humanity's ontology and vocation within the cosmos.[1] Their theological vision depicts these terms as reflective of the transfiguring movement from prototype to telos, from potentiality to actualization, while magnifying the redemptive tension between divine grace and human responsibility as an intended pedagogy on becoming like God. Therefore, *image* is the full God-given potentiality for attaining the likeness, while *likeness*, understood as *theosis* culminating in union with God, is the vocation and destiny of human existence.[2] In the ontological brokenness of the fallen world, spiritual ascent toward *theosis* is experienced as "a journey into God"[3] through the sanctifying work of the Holy Spirit who transfigures humanity from glory to glory (2 Cor 3:18), making it a partaker of the divine nature (2 Pet 1:4).

Indeed, *theosis* is Christlikeness, and since Christ is the visible image of the invisible God (Col 1:15), to be truly human is to be Christlike.[4] Yet, *theosis* is

---

[1] Timothy Ware, *The Orthodox Church* (New York: Penguin, 1997), 219-21; Vladimir Lossky, *The Mystical Theology of the Eastern Church* (Crestwood, NY: St. Vladimir's Seminary Press, 1976), 114-21.

[2] Christophoros Stavropoulos, "Partakers of Divine Nature," in *Eastern Orthodox Theology: A Contemporary Reader*, ed. Daniel B. Clendenin (Grand Rapids: Baker, 1995), 183-84.

[3] Sarah Coakley, *God, Sexuality, and the Self: An Essay 'On the Trinity'* (Cambridge: Cambridge University Press, 2013), 19.

[4] His All Holiness Ecumenical Patriarch Bartholomew I, *Encountering the Mystery* (New York: Doubleday, 2008), 132.

also experienced as renewal and healing that engulfs not only humanity but also all of creation in life-giving union with the Creator. This all-permeating cosmic healing involves free-willed, Christo-formed, Spirit-empowered human agency. Therefore, humanity's vocation is engraved from the beginning in its ontology. Indeed, the first Adam represents the communion of heaven and earth as the mystical union of matter and spirit, visible and invisible, created and uncreated.[5] Adam stands within the world as a microcosm that is to unite creation to the Creator until the entire world is transfigured into an ecclesial *macro-anthropos*: a destiny actualized in the cosmic Christ as the last Adam.[6]

The path toward attaining the likeness of God demands the cooperation and alignment of the free human will with the divine will. It is a continual Christic transfiguration through sanctification of personal will and desires, in fasting from self on behalf of the other as an expression of incarnated love toward God and neighbor. Because Christo-form love is a free and voluntary response to God's call to humanity, the freedom of human will in the image of God is a prerequisite for attaining the divine likeness. As Vladimir Lossky states:

> To be what one must in loving God, one must admit that one can be the opposite; one must admit that one can revolt. The resistance of freedom alone gives sense to the union. . . . This freedom comes from God: it is the seal of our divine participation, the masterpiece of the Creator.[7]

---

[5]Thus, according to Dimitru Staniloae, the human being appears last within the divine creative act "as a kind of natural link (*syndesmos*) between the extremities of the whole," so that on behalf of the cosmos he or she may maintain and fulfill "the all-encompassing mystery that is the union of God with creation" and may be "the conscious and willing means through which God maintains and fulfills this union." *The Experience of God: Orthodox Dogmatic Theology*, vol. 5, *The Sanctifying Mysteries* (Brookline, MA: Holy Cross Orthodox Press, 2012), 4.

[6]For Vladimir Lossky, the church (as the communal body of Christ) is destined to engulf the cosmos, reuniting it with God. Lossky states, "The church is the center of the Universe, the sphere in which its destinies are determined. All are called to enter into the church, for if man is a microcosm, the church is a *macro-anthropos*, as Maximus says" (Lossky, *Mystical Theology*, 178). Dimitru Staniloae, also using the language of St. Maximus the Confessor (*Mystagogy*, chap. 7, Patrologia Graeca 91.684C-685A), depicts the human being as a *microcosm* and the world as *macro-anthropos* and emphasizes human agency in the process of gathering all creation into union with God. *The Experience of God: Orthodox Dogmatic Theology*, vol. 1, *Revelation and Knowledge of the Triune God* (Brookline, MA: Holy Cross Orthodox Press, 2005), 4-6.

[7]Vladimir Lossky, *Orthodox Theology: An Introduction* (Crestwood, NY: St. Vladimir's Seminary Press), 72.

It takes one will to create humanity but two to sanctify it, or in Lossky's words, a "single will to rise up the image, but two to make the image into a likeness."[8]

Echoing Athanasius, Lossky asserts that God became flesh so that humanity might receive the Holy Spirit.[9] The Spirit is the One who applies what is objectively accomplished in Christ to the life of the individual believer and the community of faith, forming Christ's body on earth as the communal icon of God. Therefore, Pentecost is not merely a continuation of the Incarnation or its sequel. It is its result and purpose as the inaugural event of the Spirit's sanctifying work in humanity.[10] As Christophoros Stavropoulos states, "The Holy Spirit is the main and essential beginning of sanctification."[11]

In light of all this, I will offer a theological reflection on the Spirit's work in humanity's ontological renewal. I will start with a brief exegesis of the Eastern Orthodox icon of creation and its undergirding "theology of the face," explore ways in which humanity images the Trinity within the cosmos, and conclude by highlighting the significance of Pentecost in establishing the church as the icon of the Trinity on earth.

THE MEMORY OF A WORLD ILLUMINATED BY THE DIVINE FACE

Humanity is a restless, homesick creature, haunted by the memory of Eden as the lost home for which it has been created—the memory of shalom as harmonious wholeness in communion with God and neighbor, both human and nonhuman. This memory is the anamnesis of life shaped by seeing God's face and recognizing it in the face of the other as in the self—a tri-directional mirroring of the meaning and destiny of being human. As depicted in Christian worship (which is, among other things, an enactment of humanity's restored access to Eden), this is the memory of standing without fear before God in transparent openness toward the other—openness built into the very fiber of humanity's communal reality as sacramental imaging of the trinitarian life within the created cosmos.

In its creaturely essence, humanity is to exhibit the communion of matter and spirit in a perichoretic movement of love toward God and neighbor. Thus the human being does not image the Trinity on his or her own, nor just within

---

[8]Lossky, *Orthodox Theology*, 73.
[9]Lossky, *Mystical Theology*, 179.
[10]Lossky, *Orthodox Theology*, 85.
[11]Stavropoulos, "Partakers of Divine Nature," 188.

the parameters of relationships with fellow humans. God appears as the third—or rather, the first—person of the communal dynamic that sustains the essence of authentically human ontology. In the sacred meaning of cosmic time, relationship with the Creator precedes relationship with fellow humans and the rest of creation. As depicted by the Eastern Orthodox icon of creation, the very first face humanity sees when coming forth from the earth through divine creative agency is the face of its Maker.

Through the icon, the beholder sees the face of God, which we have come to recognize as the face of Christ, the only face of the Creator humanity has seen (1 Cor 15:45). As in a mirror, the first Adam sees his face in the last Adam. The theological point of the icon is that God and humanity have something in common, something expressed in the theological symbolism of the divine face. The uncreated, eternal God shares his face with the created, finite human being. God gives his face to Adam and Eve so that—individually and collectively—they may become his icon within the cosmos. Thus the depositing of the divine image within the human being becomes the mystical mark of his or her priming for communion and community with God and with one another. Through the agency of the Holy Spirit, this communion makes humans partakers in the divine life and nature.

Indeed, the tri-directional mirroring of the divine image depicted in the primordial life of Eden points to its relational nature. For humanity to be truly human, it has to stand in communion with both God and the fellow human. When one of these communicants is absent, when one of these fundamental relationships is broken, human identity threatens to become dehumanized. The theology of the face presents the possibility of sustainable humanness only through a continual standing face-to-face with God, for only then can one face the human other and the rest of the world in a way consistent with the meaning and vocation of being human. The icon depicts humanity's fall as a turning away from the face of the Creator toward the world, making the world an end in itself, substituting creation for the Creator (Rom 1:25). The icon asserts that all sin is, in a way, a form of idolatry.

Eastern Orthodox icons reflect the significance of the theology of the face. The faces of the saints, while different, are also all intentionally reminiscent of the face of Christ, the prototype and telos of humanity. Icons depict humanity transfigured in *theosis* together with all of creation. The recalling of the divine face in the faces of the saints articulates holiness as the visible and tangible presence of God in human lives that are transfigured by the Holy Spirit into Christlikeness. Therefore, the liturgical incorporation of the saints' icons could be understood not merely as recognizing the presence of the "great cloud of witnesses" (Heb 12:1) but also as a summons from the divine face to encounter our human telos and vocation. Standing face-to-face with the icon, we face our true, healed human ontology. Looking at the icon teaches us to discern the face of God in the fellow human, which in turn humanizes us. Therefore, believers are instructed to look at the face—especially of the icon of Christ during confession. We are to look neither from above nor from below, not from a posture of superiority or inferiority, for to do so would distort the image of God in the other and therefore in the self.

The icon is a depiction of the renewed creation summoned in the last Adam and made luminous with the beauty of restored communion between heaven and earth.[12] The halo around the heads of saints is "an iconographic device, an outward expression of holiness, a witness of the light"[13] of the world, Jesus Christ (Jn 8:12), taking residence in redeemed humanity. Through sanctified humanity, the entire cosmos is once again illuminated. Therefore, objects in icons "do not project shadows."[14] Light is the very background of the icon, permeating everything. Leonid Ouspensky points out that, in imaging sanctified humanity, "the icon represents the reality which was revealed in the transfiguration on Mount Tabor."[15] Thus the liturgy of the Feast of the Holy Face includes this proclamation: "Having illuminated the human image which had grown dark, O Creator, thou didst reveal it on Mount Tabor . . . and now bless and sanctify us, O Lord, who lovest mankind, by the brightness of thy most pure image."[16]

Finally, Pentecost could be viewed as Christ's incarnation within the community of faith through the agency of the Holy Spirit[17] and as the renewal of the image of God within the human community. The Spirit's kenosis

---

[12]Leonid Ouspensky, "The Meaning and Content of the Icon," in *Eastern Orthodox Theology: A Contemporary Reader*, 58.

[13]Ibid., 53.

[14]Ibid., 62.

[15]Ibid., 43-44.

[16]Ibid., 44.

[17]For more on the theological significance of Pentecost, see my work *Pentecost, Hospitality, and Transfiguration: Toward a Spirit-Inspired Vision of Social Transformation* (Cleveland, TN: CPT, 2012).

transforms the hundred and twenty in the upper room into Christ-bearers and living extensions of his resurrected body on earth. Sergius Bulgakov refers to Jesus' miraculous conception as "the Pentecost of the Virgin."[18] The Holy Spirit descends on Mary in response to her willingness and readiness for service (Lk 1:38) and transforms her into an instrument of God's Word becoming flesh (Jn 1:14). In a similar manner, as the Spirit descends on the disciples, Christ is conceived in them and they are empowered toward Christlikeness (Acts 1:8). Individually and corporately, they become *theophorous* (God-bearing), carrying forth the One who is the light and life of the world. Pentecost depicts the hope for the mending of the cosmos as incarnate in the sanctified human community—the community whose eyes have been illuminated by the Spirit to recognize God's face in the face of the fellow human and to mirror it back for all to see, until everything becomes illuminated.

MAKING THE DIVINE COMMUNITY VISIBLE IN THE COSMOS

Imaging God as a communion of otherness. John Meyendorff describes an Eastern Orthodox understanding of theology as "*internal* vision, which requires ascetic . . . communal effort, an effort made within the community of saints."[19] It depicts human existence as unceasing liturgical askesis expressed in striving toward tangibly depicting the trinitarian life in and through the life of the human community. This imaging starts with a vision of God as a communion of otherness, as a mystery of unity and difference, demanding humanity's reflective, perpetual self-respacing[20] on behalf of others so they may freely be and become. This is enacted in consecrated, sacramental fasting from the self as an expression of one's free choice to decrease in order for God to increase until the divine presence saturates the totality of one's life. Transfigured by this in-Spirit-ed askesis into a living home and sanctuary of the divine

---

[18]Sergius Bulgakov, "The Virgin and the Saints in Orthodoxy," in *Eastern Orthodox Theology: A Contemporary Reader*, 67.

[19]John Meyendorff, "Doing Theology in an Eastern Orthodox Perspective," in *Eastern Orthodox Theology: A Contemporary Reader*, 87 (emphasis original).

[20]I use the term *self-respacing* (or "respacing on behalf of the other") throughout this chapter to indicate the intentional effort to create conditions for the flourishing of the anthropic and non-anthropic other by fasting from self-indulging desires and even needs for the sake of meeting the needs of others and extending to them unconditional hospitality (e.g., through material resources, life and future). For more on the use of the term, see my work, *Pentecost, Hospitality, and Transfiguration*, especially chapters 2 and 3.

presence, the human being becomes a reflective, liturgical image of the Creator Trinity speaking forth the cosmos into existence and hosting it within its own—kenotic and ascetic—communal self as an act of generous, unconditional, divine hospitality. In the willingness to welcome God in the self, the human being is enlarged by the deifying Spirit and enabled to extend unconditional, loving hospitality to the entire cosmos. In thus becoming a living temple of the divine presence, humanity finds itself reflecting divine spaciousness and love for the other. In the sanctifying work of the Spirit, making humanity partake of the divine nature, love for God becomes love for God's entire world, and the creature experiences and manifests the likeness of the Creator as perfect love for the whole of creation. Thus embodying the life of the Spirit, one finds the self apprehended into the trinitarian communal life. Striving to recapture the image, one is instead captured by it.[21]

The Holy Spirit draws not only humanity but also the whole created realm into the life of God. Yet, while the Spirit strives to bring all the cosmos into life-giving communion with the triune God, the Spirit's love (in the words of Sarah Coakley) "presses not only outwards to include others, but also inwards (and protectively) to sustain difference between persons, thus preserving a perfect and harmonious balance between union and distinction."[22] Thus translating and incarnating the mystery of the triune life within the material cosmos, the Spirit fosters communal unity while cultivating and celebrating otherness. Each collapse of unity into uniformity, of conversational polyphony into a monologue that mutes the voice of the other, each flattening of polychromatic otherness into monochromatic homogeneity, grieves the Spirit and distorts the divine face imprinted on the human community. It defaces the image in a violent rejection of the other, a totalitarian imposition of the self upon the world. Along this line, the fall can be understood in terms of giving the self "ontological priority over the Other."[23]

Humanity's call to *theosis* is a call to otherness. This call, proceeding from the ultimate Other, is the foundational event of human existence, the

---

[21]As Sarah Coakley points out, the work of the Holy Spirit is "incorporative" and "reflexive." The Spirit works to incorporate humanity into the trinitarian communal life, as well as to work "reflexively" in believers, "in the circle of response to the Father's call"—the call to be transfigured in the divine likeness (Coakley, *God, Sexuality, and the Self,* 111).

[22]Ibid., 24.

[23]John D. Zizioulas, *Communion and Otherness* (New York: T&T Clark, 2006), 43.

constitution of what it means to be truly human.[24] It is a call to Christ's otherness engraved in human ontology as the potentiality to become like the other while retaining one's distinct otherness. The first Adam turns his face away from the Other into himself, resigning his vocation to love God in loving and caring for his world; the last Adam, in his redemptive embrace of the other, restores the ontological communion of otherness constituting the calling and telos of the first Adam.

The account of the tower of Babel rearticulates the communal dimension of humanity's drama that was first enacted in the Garden of Eden. It depicts humanity turning away from its vocation to the other and concentrating its creative energies into a homogenizing attempt at self-deification. Indeed, the image of Babel represents an antipode to the *imago Dei*. It depicts human creativity as a distorted imaging of divine creativity, contrasting the inclusion and exclusion of the other. By destroying the tower, God creates the conditions for authentic human community through securing the presence and voice of the other and establishing the communal necessity of diversity in unity (Gen 11:7-8). The accomplishment of human community after Babel demands accepting the other and making space for them in the self through learning their language.

Unconditional hospitality for the other. The creation of the world is an act of divine love expressed as radical re-spacing of the Trinity in welcoming and hosting the existence and conversational inclusion of the other. It can be understood as an internal act of the Trinity's loving askesis and kenosis. On the one hand, in an ascetic expression of self-giving love, God fasts from himself in order to create space and time for the existence of the other. In a gift of unconditional hospitality, God becomes the immediate dwelling place of the other as the very environment in which they live and move and have their being (Acts 17:28). On the other hand, God pours himself into the other through the kenosis of the Word and the Spirit so that the creature may come to be. In the act of creation, we see the Trinity as an ascetic community of self-sharing with the other—this is the materialization of God as love. We see a communal life of radical hospitality (*philoxenia*) marked by unconditional love for the other, the different, the absolute stranger. As the fruit and cosmic

---

[24]Ibid., 42.

expression of the divine reality of love, humanity is created to be an icon of the Trinity on earth and to exhibit the same communal life marked by askesis (self-fasting) and kenosis (self-sharing) in relation to the fellow human and the rest of creation. Humanity is placed amid the cosmos as a priestly, eucharistic, communal reality in order to serve as an agent of the world's transfiguration into the likeness of God's communal life until the divine community becomes all in all.

Since humanity is created in the image and likeness of God, from the beginning the spirit of askesis is to be cultivated in the human being through abstaining from some of the fruit of the garden (Gen 3:2-3) for the sake of communion with God and nature. The priestly vocation of humanity involves the eucharistic discernment of the world as a divine gift of substance and beauty, a place for cultivating a community of shared life with the other.

In Genesis 1, God creates within the divine communal self an opening for the possibility and flourishing of others and also builds a home for them.[25] God creates within himself a home for humans so that, in turn, they may learn to image the trinitarian communal life by welcoming God within themselves and presenting their own beings as a home for the divine presence. Ultimately, the eucharistic nature and pedagogical goal of the cosmos is to transform all everyday work of world-making into a home-building for the other. Human creative labor becomes a priestly sacramental enactment of God's love for creation. The very love that hosts the cosmos in self-sacrificial nurture and care for all creatures demands the same of humans as faithful stewards of God's household.

The poetry of the fourth Gospel's prologue fuses together visions of the divine creative act as both unconditional hospitality for and a loving communal discourse with the other. It depicts the act of cosmic creation as proceeding from the Word that speaks it forth while being turned toward God (*pros ton theon*; Jn 1:1).[26] The creative speech is not directed outside the divine reality but remains in the inner communion of the Trinity. Thus, creation takes

---

[25]For an exposition on God as an architect building and furnishing a house, see John Dominic Crossan, *God and Empire: Jesus Against Rome, Then and Now* (New York: HarperOne, 2007), 51-52.

[26]On the significance of the preposition *pros*, see D. A. Carson, *The Gospel According to John*, Pillar New Testament Commentary (Grand Rapids: Eerdmans, 1991), 116; and Francis J. Moloney, *The Gospel of John, Sacra Pagina* 4, ed. Daniel J. Harrington (Collegeville, MN: Liturgical Press, 1998), 35.

place within the perichoretic intimacy of the Trinity. If the creation of the world is an outcome of a loving communal conversation made visible through the *poiēsis* of divine creativity, then its transformation into a sanctuary for the divine presence—via creative, in-Spirit-ed, human agency—cannot be accomplished by other means. The flourishing of all God's creatures requires an intentionally dialogical human community, bringing together its polyphonic diversity into a constructive conversational unity that images the divine life in active, creative consensus of world-making as home-building and sanctuary-carving for the other.

Conversational inclusion of the other in a dialogical community is essential for the possibility of building a common future. This conversational embrace opens the door to envisioning a world of multidimensional unity between self and other while preserving distinctiveness. Re-spacing one's right to speak for the sake of creating space for the voice of the other presents the possibility of shaping a future of harmonious diversity, of sociocultural unison within the challenging landscape of a pluralistic world. Indeed, nothing less would be sufficient to image within the cosmos the communal life of the Creator Trinity as multiplicity of consubstantial hypostases joined in harmonious, conversational oneness for world-making as liturgical askesis in unconditional hospitality for the other.

In light of this, if Babel is both a conversational exclusion of others and a refusal to welcome them in communion, Pentecost constitutes Babel's overturning by the kenosis of the Spirit upon the believers. Pentecost is the antidote to the age-old temptation to employ Babel's blueprint in human cultural world-making. It offers a paradigmatic vision of the incarnation of God's self-giving hospitality in the community of the believers as an extension of Christ's body on earth. The outpouring of the Spirit manifests God's ascetic re-spacing and kenotic self-sharing in welcoming all nations under heaven through submitting his Word to the form and sound of their ethnic tongues (Acts 2:5-6). Therefore, the speech of the faith community on Pentecost embraces the language of the other in a gift of divine hospitality. The Spirit invites all humanity to make its habitat in the sociality of the Trinity. It is an initiation of dialogue by re-spacing oneself and creating conditions for the conversational inclusion of the other. It is a gesture of welcoming all foreigners, aliens and strangers in their own terms.

Imaging God in prayer and human world-making.[27] The divine act of creation unfolds before heaven, its enthralled witness. Heaven hears and sees the materialization of the trinitarian discourse as harmonious "visible words"[28] within the *poiēsis* of the cosmos. Thus creation unfolds as a divine liturgy performed by God himself before heaven's worshiping host in the cathedral of the universe. Within the liturgical choreography of the perichoretic movement, each creature comes forth as a "word of obedience and worship,"[29] as a response to the summoning self-proclamation of the uncreated, eternal Word.

In this divine liturgy, humanity is the special creature made to hear the Word's calling and respond to it in prayer, the creature whose ontological actualization is to be attained through partaking of God's communal discourse, the conversational communion of the divine nature (2 Pet 1:4). This resonates with Jenson's interpretation of the image of God in humanity as "consisting in the action of prayer."[30] For Jenson, "God's ritual word to us" is sacrament, but sacrifice as "embodied prayer" is our ritual word to God.[31] Therefore, human life before the Creator is "an antiphony of God's word to us and our word to God; and the whole antiphony is both audible and 'visible.'"[32]

In its priestly and liturgical essence, humanity is to offer unceasing intercession on behalf of the world, taking it in prayer before its Creator. Therefore, the act of intercessory prayer mirrors, in a way, the Trinity's sustaining, providential work in creation, the work of the Word and the Spirit for the life of the world according to the will of the Father. Intercession is an act of re-spacing on behalf of the other, a form of fasting from self and exercising hospitality. Intercession is caring for the other's well-being and striving to provide the other with what is needed in order to flourish. Intercession embraces the pain, brokenness, struggles and hopes of the other, making place for them in one's words, thoughts and embodied life in the world and carrying the other before the face of the Creator. Intercessory prayer is making time and space for the other within one's life and being.

---

[27]A version of this section of the essay was presented at the American Association of Religion's 2014 meeting and will be included in a volume on the theology of Robert Jenson.

[28]See Augustine, *Tractates on the Gospel of John* 80.3.

[29]Robert W. Jenson, *Systematic Theology*, vol. 2, *The Works of God* (New York: Oxford University Press, 1999), 8.

[30]Jenson, *Works of God*, 68.

[31]Ibid., 59-60.

[32]Ibid., 59.

Further, to pray for others is to bring them within the trinitarian communal conversation that is extended to the creature called to become *theoumenon*.[33] Therefore, prayer could be seen as imaging the askesis and kenosis constituting God's creative act, yet it is also reflective of the Trinity's ongoing providential care for creation. This understanding asserts prayer as a divinely ordained means of communion with the Creator and a way of partaking in the divine nature. It teaches humanity how to image the life of the Trinity by acquiring a "eucharistic spirit" and an "ascetic ethos."[34] To be capable of prayer means, in the words of His All Holiness Bartholomew I, that we "have the capacity to offer the world back to God in thanksgiving, and it is only in this act of offering that we become genuinely human and truly free."[35]

Humanity's being created to partake in the divine communal discourse of world-making as "intertrinitarian love"[36] implies our creative capacity as well as a sense of open-endedness, spontaneity and creative freedom within the teleology of the world's becoming. According to Jenson, who is echoing Augustine of Hippo, "the freedom by which we as persons participate in the divine life is the very Spirit that evokes all life, all the dynamic processes of creation."[37] Therefore, the universe is "an omnipotent conversation that is open to us."[38] This openness makes prayer meaningful, for the Spirit's hospitality extends to us the freedom to speak up, discuss, plead and even argue, confronting the world's condition and addressing the communal Creator in "faith and trust" for its mending.[39] Prayer responds to the openness of possibilities sustained within the Spirit's spontaneity and freedom. Therefore, Paul instructs the believers to pray without ceasing (1 Thess 5:17). This is to take place "at all times in the Spirit" (Eph 6:18 WEB).

In this reality, humanity's *theo-formation* is the ultimate goal of the freedom nurtured by the Spirit. Prayer does not change God and the telos of creation;

---

[33]St. Gregory of Nazianzus spoke of humanity as *zōon thoumenon*, "an animal that is being deified" (*Oration* 38.11).

[34]Bartholomew, *Encountering the Mystery*, 118.

[35]Ibid., 132.

[36]Dimitru Staniloae, *The Experience of God: Orthodox Dogmatic Theology*, vol. 2, *The World: Creation and Deification* (Brookline, MA: Holy Cross Orthodox Press, 2005), 18.

[37]Jenson, *Works of God*, 42.

[38]Ibid., 44.

[39]One can recall, for example, the passage in Gen 18:17-33 depicting Abraham's inclusion in the divine discourse and his pleading on behalf of Sodom and Gomorrah.

it changes us into the divine likeness. Prayer is joining the Spirit's intercession for the healing of the cosmos and partaking in the Spirit's "sighs too deep for words." "We do not know how to pray," but we can enter into and entrust ourselves to the intercessory movement of the Spirit who "helps us in our weakness" (Rom 8:26).

Indeed, prayer as world-mending becomes a divine-human partnership; we breathe, speak, groan and move with, in and through the Spirit. Yet, prayer is more than laboring alongside God in world-mending. In the freedom of the Spirit, prayer becomes creative world-making, speaking forth beauty and hope within the cosmos. It is a consecrated, cultic creativity that mirrors the divine discourse back toward the Creator, thus transforming the "Let there be" into "Lord, let there be," fully conscious of its dependence on the divine creativity. Since prayer is more primordial than belief,[40] human world-making could be understood as an antiphony, a responsive prayer of the paradise-haunted, homesick creature who longs for the beauty and harmony of its origin within the divine presence. As His All Holiness Bartholomew I points out, "Beauty is a call, beyond the here and now, to the original principle and purpose of the world."[41] Therefore, human creativity is a means of communion with the Creator—it is a prayer, an offering to God, an act of worship. In the post-fall world, human creativity is marked by the tension between a deep-seated memory of paradise and the struggle to forget God and compensate for his absence by the gratification found in human civilization itself. Reflecting, therefore, on Genesis 4:22 and the life of the descendants of Cain as "the first citizens, the inventors of arts and techniques," Lossky states that the "arts here appear as cultural, not cult, values; they are a prayer that is lost since it is not addressed to God."[42]

The first creative human act recorded in the biblical narrative—Adam's naming of the animals—required speech. As divine speech brings forth all creation, so human speech inaugurates humanity's inspired, liturgical imaging of the divine creativity within the cosmos. Yet, this creativity remains located in the dynamics of collaborative dialogue between humanity and God. Adam speaks as an act of completing what God has created. The human adds its *logoi*

---

[40]Harvey Cox, *The Future of Faith* (New York: HarperOne, 2010), 5-6.
[41]Bartholomew, *Encountering the Mystery*, 28.
[42]Lossky, *Orthodox Theology*, 87.

to the *logoi* spoken by the eternal *Logos*. Thus, human language, as creation, "coincides with the very being of things."[43] Adam can name the animals because of the deep organic connection between humanity and the rest of God's creatures. Thus, as Lossky points out, Adam knows the animals "from within; he specifies their secret. . . . [He is] poet as he is priest, poet for God."[44]

If human prayer and cultural productivity are to mirror the divine creative act and facilitate the transfiguration of humanity into the likeness of the Creator, then language is essential. Alongside the entire created cosmos, language presents itself as a means of communion between humanity and God and among human beings in the process of theo-formation. Its essence is communal, for language can only be shared with the other. Therefore, language is introduced as the means of bonding all of humanity into one polyphonic speech community,[45] into a creative discourse cultivating the cosmos toward its eschatological gathering into the one incarnate Word—a vision actualized by the Spirit in the event of Pentecost.

INSTEAD OF A CONCLUSION: PENTECOST AND THE CHURCH AS ICON OF THE TRINITY ON EARTH

The iconostasis of the church at the Theological School of Halki holds among its treasures an icon that articulates the foundation of Orthodox ecclesiology—an intricate piece devoted to the Trinity. The upper portion of the icon narrates the story of the three divine guests visiting Abraham at Mamre (Gen 18:1-15). Since no one has seen God (Jn 1:18), this is the only visual representation of the Trinity that is considered canonical in the Eastern Orthodox tradition. The lower portion is a triptych depicting three theophanic scenes in the New Testament. On the left is the icon of Jesus' baptism in water: the public trinitarian witness to the identity of the Son through the voice of the Father and the Spirit descending as a dove. On the right is the icon of the transfiguration on Mount Tabor, an articulation of "the humanity of the Son, manifesting forth that deity which is common to the Father and the Spirit."[46]

---

[43]Ibid., 69.
[44]Ibid.
[45]As Jean-François Lyotard reminds us, the translatability of language points to the fact that all human beings are called to one speech community. "The Other's Rights," in *On Human Rights*, ed. S. Shute and S. Hurley (New York: Basic Books, 1993), 140-41.
[46]Lossky, *Mystical Theology*, 243.

This icon depicts the inner circle of disciples joining the Old Testament witness of the Law and the Prophets symbolized by Moses and Elijah (Mt 17:2). They see the uncreated divine energies piercing through the veil of the Son's humanity and illuminating the cosmos while they hear the voice of the Father and are immersed in the cloud of the Spirit. In the center of the triptych is the icon of Pentecost—the transfiguration of the community of faith into Christ's communal body on earth, empowered by the Spirit to do the will of the Father. In this event, the church is established as the image of the Trinity on earth. Little wonder that the Orthodox tradition celebrates the day of Pentecost as the festival of the Trinity.[47]

If the church is an image of the Trinity, she is also an image of the Holy Spirit. Yet, the Spirit bears witness not to himself but to the Son (Jn 15:26). He comes in the name of the Son the way the Son comes in the name of the Father. This is why John of Damascus states, "The Son is the Father's image, and the Spirit the Son's."[48] The Holy Spirit, however, does not have an image that is made visible in another divine person. Instead, Pentecost made the invisible Spirit visible in the community of faith. If the Old Testament "proclaimed the Father openly, and the Son more obscurely," and the Gospels reveal the Son plainly, but the Spirit dimly,[49] Pentecost presents the church animated and empowered by the Spirit as his image on earth. The church makes the invisible Spirit visible and tangibly communicated in the unity of the saints' diversity. They have been empowered to live together the life of the triune God as their own life. The two distinct dimensions of the Spirit's presence, the communal and the eschatological,[50] both become clearly visible in the Pentecost inauguration of the church as his image on earth: Pentecost unfolds the *eschata,* evoking the prophetic fusion of time and eternity as the "last days" erupt into

---

[47]Ibid., 239.

[48]St. John of Damascus, "An Exact Exposition of the Orthodox Faith" 1.13, in *St. Hilary of Poitiers, John of Damascus,* ed. Philip Schaff and Henry Wace, trans. S. D. F. Salmond, vol. 9b of Nicene and Post-Nicene Fathers, 2nd Series (New York: Christian Literature Company, 1899), 16. As Lossky states, "The divine Persons do not themselves assert themselves, but one bears witness to another" (*Mystical Theology,* 160).

[49]Gregory Nazianzen, "Oration 31, *The Fifth Theological Oration: On the Holy Spirit,*" in *S. Cyril of Jerusalem, S. Gregory Nazianzen,* ed. Philip Schaff and Henry Wace, trans. Charles Gordon Browne and James Edward Swallow, vol. 7 of Nicene and Post-Nicene Fathers, 2nd Series (New York: Christian Literature Company, 1894), 326.

[50]John D. Zizioulas, *Being as Communion: Studies in Personhood and the Church* (Crestwood, NY: St. Vladimir's Seminary Press, 1995), 131.

the present and become its time-transcending substance. Yet, this eschato-logical vision also unveils the Spirit-saturated community with its radical egalitarian catholicity and democratized polyphony of prophetic utterance.

The "likeness of God" is not a distant mirroring of the divine image but the fullness of a communion and community with the Creator through the incor-porating and transfiguring work of the Holy Spirit. A community that images the Trinity in the cosmos is marked by the recognition of and commitment to humanity's irreducible consubstantiality and equality; it depicts the divine life in perichoresis as the unceasing movement of covenantal love between all members of the community. This love is manifested in justice for the other as unconditional access to life and human flourishing. Rabbi Jonathan Sacks states that society is faceless, but community "is society with a human face"—the face of God made visible in the covenantal lovingkindness between its members. Only when we discover God's image in ourselves by learning to discern it in others are we capable of building a "human and humanizing" society.[51]

God abides amid his people—the new human community—within re-deemed relationships between fellow humans. There, in the tri-directional mirroring of the divine face, heaven descends on earth. Thus, according to the Decalogue, redemption takes place in the sacred space between one human being and another—God and neighbor—and is experienced as the healing of relationships that re-humanize society and mend the broken world.

On Pentecost the church was established as the visible, embodied com-munal theophany of the invisible divine proto-community. Thus, in her mys-tical union with God in the Spirit-saturated human community, the church becomes the telos of creation and stands in the present as the embodiment of the world's future in which God will be all in all (1 Cor 15:28). Pentecost's kenosis of the Spirit transforms the corporate body of Christ into the com-munally embodied temple of the divine presence within the cosmos (2 Cor 6:16; Eph 2:19-22), destined to be the vehicle through which God extends his redemptive hospitality to all of creation. The Spirit brings forth the church so that the entire cosmos may become a church—a eucharistic communion of heaven and earth in the union of God and his world. This is the breathtaking, glorious future of humanity in the likeness of God.

---

[51]Jonathan Sacks, *To Heal a Fractured World: The Ethics of Responsibility* (New York: Schocken, 2005), 54.

9

THE GOD OF CREATIVE ADDRESS

Creation, Christology and Ethics

Janet Soskice

INTRODUCTION

Does God have an image problem in our image-driven world? Not, perhaps, for readers of this volume, but more widely the Christian God is seen as a joyless figure who lingers around the corners of the world, vanishing but not quite forgotten. A theologian acquaintance was seated on a flight next to an astrophysicist who said that he could not believe in God because the universe was just too complex. But what kind of God could he not believe in? A universal fixer who occupied his unending days keeping the planets in orbit? If we believe that God created everything that is, including space and time, then God can be no small, twiddling-around sort of God. We must suspect that the physicist's image of God was just too small.

But where should we look for a better image of God? An alarming but wholly biblical answer is "the mirror." If Genesis is to be believed, then God has over seven billion image problems walking around today. Calvin began his *Institutes of the Christian Religion* by pointing out, as others had done before him, that true wisdom consists in two parts: knowledge of God and of ourselves. Then he adds, "Which one precedes and brings forth the other is not easy to discern."[1] In Christian theology, the doctrines of God and of anthropology are bound inextricably; nowhere is this more evident than when the topic is, as for this collection, "the image of God in an image driven age."

---

[1] John Calvin, *Institutes of the Christian Religion*, ed. John T. McNeill, trans. Ford Lewis Battles (Louisville: Westminster John Knox, 2011), 1.1.

Explicit biblical mentions of the *imago Dei* fall in two places. The first set, from the book of Genesis, has been widely used in Christian ethics. The second set, from the Pauline writings, is usually reserved for high christological purposes and is almost never used in ethical debate. In this essay, I suggest that the two sets have profound points of unity having to do with the doctrine of creation. Further, if we attend to the way God creates, we may open up a new understanding of what it might mean for human beings to be in the image of the God of creative address.

SCRIPTURAL PRESENCE

Explicit scriptural mentions of the image of God are both strikingly didactic and frustratingly unclear. In Genesis 1, God makes humankind according to the divine likeness, granting them dominion over other living creatures, or at least over other animals. This image is not wholly lost when the first couple is expelled from the garden, as the instruction to Noah makes clear.[2] But after these few pronouncements, freighted with ethical implication, the Hebrew Bible says nothing positive about imaging God. Subsequent talk of images is, for the most part, of carved or graven images, cast images and alien gods until (for Christians) we get to the New Testament.

The Pauline writings resurrect the motif of the *imago Dei* and place it christologically center stage.[3] Christ is not only the second Adam but the "image of the invisible God, the firstborn of all creation" (Col 1:15). We find the cosmic Christ as agent of creation not only in Paul but also in John's Gospel and the book of Revelation. There, too, the incarnate Lord is the one through whom all things were made, the Alpha and the Omega, the first and the last (Rev 22:13), and the becoming visible of the invisible God. The prologue to John's Gospel brings the themes of creation, incarnation and visible glory together:

> He was in the beginning with God. All things came into being through him, and
> without him not one thing came into being. . . . And the Word became flesh and
> lived among us and we have seen his glory, the glory as of a father's only son, full of

---

[2]The covenant with Noah implies that while the blood of all animals is sacred, shedding the blood of a human being is of lethal import. The rationale is that the human being, alone of all creatures (and we must assume this includes angels), is made in the image of God (Gen 9:6).
[3]For my purposes, I am including Ephesians and Colossians as Pauline.

grace and truth. . . . No one has ever seen God. It is God the only Son, who is close to the Father's heart, who has made him known. (Jn 1:2-3, 14, 18)

Later in John, Philip's request to see the Father is met by Jesus' reply: "Have I been with you all this time, Philip, and you still do not know me? Whoever has seen me has seen the Father. How can you say, 'Show us the Father'? Do you not believe that I am in the Father and the Father is in me?" (Jn 14:9-10). Jesus is the fullness of the image, the visible representation of the invisible God. In seeing Jesus, Philip is told that he has seen the Father. Somehow it is not only Jesus but also other people who bear this likeness to God. This is how many generations of Christians have understood Jesus' teaching on feeding the hungry, tending the sick or visiting the prisoner. Insofar as we fail to tend to the needs of the least, we fail to attend to Christ himself (Mt 25). Christian actions and charitable works are based on the conviction that every human being bears the image of God and that in every human face, but especially in those of the poor and helpless, we see the face of Christ.

If, on the basis of Genesis, it was difficult to look in the mirror and see the image of God, then it might seem even more embarrassingly absurd to see the image of the firstborn of all creation in our own fallen countenances. Paul, however, is alarmingly positive about our hopes: "Just as we have borne the image of the man of dust, we will also bear the image of the man of heaven" (1 Cor 15:49). Not only are we made in the image of God but, as we grow in Christ, we become more so: "And all of us, with unveiled faces, seeing the glory of God as though reflected in a mirror, are being transformed into the same image from one degree to another; for this comes from the Lord, the Spirit" (2 Cor 3:18). Paul's references here are to Moses at Sinai. Moses, whose face shone after speaking with God, had to veil his face before speaking to the Israelites lest they be dazzled or destroyed by the reflection of divine glory. But those whom Paul addresses can gaze on the glory with no need for the veil, reflecting like mirrors the brightness of the Lord. Christians can somehow not only withstand divine glory but are being transformed into this glory. This not only brings anthropology into conjunction with theology but does so in an exalted way. We may well think that Paul has done a service in recovering the Genesis language of the *imago Dei*, but we may also worry that, in aligning it with Christ, he makes it difficult to see how we mere mortals can lay claim to be part of it.

Outside the New Testament, the notion of the *imago Dei* was also current among Jewish thinkers of Paul's day. Philo of Alexandria, in his *On the Creation of the Cosmos According to Moses*, suggests that human beings are made the image (*eikōn*) of God by virtue of their rationality. He also suggests that the agent of creation is the *Logos*, who is the image of God, and that humanity is made in the image of this image.[4] The connection between creation, creative Word and redemption is, as we shall see, entirely relevant.

From this brief survey we can see that the centrality of the motif of the image of God to Christian ethics and practice does not so much rely on explicit biblical preponderance as on a dense latticework of citations and associations across both testaments and in reception history. The *imago Dei*, then, is deeply anchored in biblical teaching but without fully resolved clarity.[5]

THE INADEQUACY OF IMAGE AS RATIONALITY FOR ETHICS

In what way can human beings be said to be in the divine image? Christian theologians have from early on opted for the reading that it was in virtue of their rationality that humans—or sometimes only males—were made in the image of God. This seemed an obvious place at which human beings differed from animals, but it has never been an entirely satisfactory reading. Despite august Christian and Jewish tradition—as we have seen, Philo also takes this tack—it is not mandated by Scripture. Contemporary Jewish exegete Tikva Frymer-Kensky argues that the Hebrew of Genesis indicates that physicality is somehow important to humanity imaging God. She draws attention to Genesis 5, where, in listing the descendants of Adam, the text repeats the language of created likeness in male and female:

> When God created humankind, he made them in the likeness of God [*dəmût ĕlōhîm*]. Male and female he created them, and he blessed them and named them "Humankind" when they were created. (Gen 5:1-2)

The text goes on to say that Adam "became the father of a son in his likeness, according to his image, and named him Seth" (Gen 5:3). Frymer-Kensky

---

[4] Philo, *On the Creation of the Cosmos According to Moses*, trans. David T. Runia (Leiden: Brill, 2001), especially §24-25 and §69-71.

[5] Ian McFarland has dealt with much of this with great clarity in his *The Divine Image: Envisioning the Invisible God* (Minneapolis: Fortress Press, 2005).

points out the implication that image-bearing has to do with physicality: "We create children who look like us, and we, and they, look like God."[6]

Moving quickly and almost exclusively, as the Christian fathers did, to the idea that it is by virtue of our rationality that we are in the image of God risks collapsing into a quasi-gnosticism, or at least a devaluing of the body. Frymer-Kensky says that, as "Christianity became more Hellenized, it began to adopt the Greek mind/body dichotomy, distinguishing between the 'lower' and 'higher' aspects of human being." At its worst, Christian theology imagined a mind that reflects God's glory and a body that just trudges along. By contrast, Rabbi Hillel taught that he honored God's commandments in going to the bathhouse, for it was his obligation to the body in the image of God.[7]

The shortcomings of this emphasis on mind or rationality have become more evident in modern times as we ask new questions: What is the difference between the mind and the brain? If none, is the mind then not also the body? If rationality is the criterion for being in the image of God, cannot the inference be drawn that those who are less than rational do not fully have the *imago Dei*? This line of argument has been invoked to defend discrimination on the basis of sex, race and disability. While there are some Christians who hold to female subordination, few do so today on the basis that women are not fully rational, yet this was classically considered the corollary of 1 Corinthians 11:7: "A man ought not to have his head veiled, since he is the image and reflection of God; but woman is the reflection of man."

Some critics of religion have suggested that the doctrine of the *imago Dei*—with its attendant convictions about the sanctity of *human* life—represents an obstacle to social progress. "Why, apart from an outmoded religion," this argument goes, "should we think *human* life is sacred? And if human beings deserve respect by virtue of their rationality as bearers of the divine image, should those who are subrational or even prerational (as in the case of babies) deserve equal respect or protection?" Peter Singer, author of the influential

---

[6]The use of the word *dəmût*, she argues, "in these two sentences, makes the physicality of God apparent," a relationship of image to source. Tikva Frymer-Kensky, "The Image: Religious Anthropology in Judaism and Christianity," in *Studies in Biblical Feminist Criticism* (Philadelphia: Jewish Publication Society, 2006), 92.

[7]Ibid., 97.

Animal Liberation,[8] and Helga Kuhse argued this way in their book *Should the Baby Live?*[9] In it, they made the case for infanticide, even of healthy babies, should the baby not be wanted. Why, people like Singer and Kuhse argue, should a seriously disabled baby be more "in the image of God" than a healthy and intelligent pig?[10] Is this not religiously sanctioned speciesism?

Apart from the invocation of speciesism, such arguments are not new. The late nineteenth and early twentieth centuries saw extensive eugenics debates in Britain, the United States and Germany. Many champions of the modern— including Christians—were eugenicists. Writing before the First World War, Hans-Walther Schmuhl, a leading German apologist for eugenics, argued, "By giving up the conception of the divine image of humans under the influence of the Darwinian theory, human life became a piece of property, which—in contrast to the idea of a natural right to life—could be weighed against other pieces of property."[11] Human bodies have become commodities to be trafficked for sex, raided for organs and bred for genetic materials.

While some of these positions are extreme, they cannot be ignored. If rationality is the ruling criterion, why should the lives of the mentally infirm— be they very young or very old or just mentally challenged—deserve respect? Here Christian ethical practice has usually exceeded its stated rationale, with an overwhelming consensus that humans bear the image of God not just as type (all humanity) but also as tokens (each individual). However, if the doctrine of the *imago Dei* is to carry the weight it traditionally has done, there is a need for theologians and ethicists to return to the biblical texts again.

As I have suggested, discussions of the *imago Dei* in Christian ethics overwhelmingly reference Genesis rather than the complex *imago* Christology of Paul. There are ready explanations: the *imago Dei* in Genesis is universal and explicitly tied to respect accorded to human beings. The Pauline *imago* teachings, by contrast, are directed toward cosmology, eschatology and

---

[8]Peter Singer, *Animal Liberation: The Definitive Classic of the Animal Movement*, 40th Anniversary Edition (New York: Open Road Media, 2015).

[9]Helga Kuhse and Peter Singer, *Should the Baby Live? Studies in Bioethics* (Oxford: Oxford University Press, 1986).

[10]On this, see the chapter *"Imago Dei"* in Janet Soskice, *The Kindness of God: Metaphor, Gender, and Religious Language* (Oxford: Oxford University Press, 2007); see also chapter 7, "The Kindness of God: Trinity and the Image of God in Julian of Norwich and Augustine."

[11]Cited in Richard Weikart, *From Darwin to Hitler: Evolutionary Ethics, Eugenics and Racism in Germany* (London: Palgrave Macmillan, 2004), 146.

spirituality. They may seem doctrinally remote from one another. But Paul must have had reasons for invoking Genesis and its language of the *imago Dei* when unfolding his Christology; while it may not be possible to fully fathom them, we can posit some links.[12] What Paul and Genesis share is, I suggest, a connection between the doctrine of creation and teaching about human dignity that becomes, in the case of Paul, also the question of human destiny. In the remainder of this chapter, I sketch the relationship between Genesis and Paul, between ethics and Christology.

SPEAKING BEINGS IMAGING THE CREATING WORD

In a Genesis narrative that makes much of fecundity and variety, the imaging of the Creator God in humanity seems to require at least more than one being. Thus, "In the image of God he created them; male and female he created them" (Gen 1:27). It may be that each one of us is in the *imago Dei*, but only insofar as we, each one, belong to one another. This is a biological fact about human beings: each of us, even the most austere hermit, was born and sustained over early months and even years by other human beings. Human beings, we find in Genesis 5, bring forth human beings "according to their image." This is an endorsement of the physicality of the *imago*.

Sexual difference also seems important to the Genesis narrative. Several notable twentieth-century theologians, including Karl Barth and Hans Urs von Balthasar, picked this up, folding the woman within the fullness of *imago* but also reinforcing a binarism wherein the woman exists for the man but seemingly not the reverse.[13] Sexual difference is not, however, the only kind of difference in the Genesis narrative, and neither are all differences simple binaries: there is night and day but also evening and morning, waters and dry land but also sky. Also, not only the humans but also the swarming multitudes of fish, birds and animals are told to be fruitful and multiply. What, then, is distinctive to the woman and the man? Or better, what is distinctive to the male and female together—what we might call the human "more-than-one"— that configures them as in the *imago Dei*?

---

[12]We may need to know more than we know or perhaps ever will know about first-century Judaism to piece this together.

[13]See Gerard Loughlin, "Nuptial Mysteries," in *Faithful Reading: New Essays in Theology in Honour of Fergus Kerr, OP*, ed. Simon Oliver, Karen Kilby and Thomas O'Loughlin (London: T&T Clark, 2012), 173-92.

I want to draw attention to Genesis 2:18-25, specifically to a remarkable
reading Friedrich Schleiermacher provides of Adam's naming the animals and
the emergence of Eve:

> Let me disclose to you a secret that lies concealed in one of the most ancient sources
> of poetry and religion. As long as the first man was alone with himself and nature,
> *the deity did indeed rule over him; it addressed the man in various ways, but he did not*
> *understand it, for he did not answer it;* his paradise was beautiful and the stars shone
> down on him from a beautiful heaven, *but the sense for the world did not open within*
> *him; he did not even develop within his soul* but his heart was moved by a longing *for*
> *a world,* and so he gathered before him the animal creation to see if one might
> perhaps be formed from it. Since the deity recognized that his [the deity's] world
> would be nothing so long as man was alone, it created for him a partner, and now,
> for the first time, living and spiritual tones stirred within him; now, for the first time,
> *the world rose before his eyes.* In the flesh and bone of his bone he discovered humanity,
> *and in humanity the world; from this moment on he became capable of hearing the voice*
> *of the deity and of answering it,* and the most sacrilegious transgressions of its laws
> from now on no longer precluded him from association with the eternal being.[14]

In Schleiermacher's day, as before and subsequently, the narrative of the
naming of the animals was typically read as Adam showing his mastery over
brute creation. Yet, in this midrash, Schleiermacher notes that Adam's naming
of the animals is in fact the story of a failure. At the end of the naming, whose
stated purpose was that he should not be alone, the man is still alone.

Schleiermacher (surely deliberately) never identifies the partner of Adam
as female. His point is not about sex but about speech. Adam, alone in the
garden, does not speak, for speaking is a social possession. We do not invent
speech for ourselves. We receive it from others; we are inducted into speaking
by those who care for us as infants. Through speaking, we are introduced into
the world. While the first chapters of Genesis are full of speaking, calling,
separating and commanding, we have no report of human conversation until
Adam says, "This at last is bone of my bones and flesh of my flesh" (Gen 2:23).[15]

Augustine, another great theological theorist of language, was acutely
aware that without other people we would not speak at all. In the prologue to

---

[14]Friedrich Schleiermacher, *On Religion: Speeches to Its Cultured Despisers* (1799), trans. Richard
Crouter (Cambridge: Cambridge University Press, 1996), 37 (my emphasis).

[15]Certainly prior to this there is no reflective human speech. The implication is that Adam's naming
could be mere list-making, not conversational engagement.

Teaching Christianity, a work set out as rules for dealing with Scripture, he tweaks those who "rejoice over their knowing the holy scriptures without human guidance; and, if that is the case, it is a genuine good they are rejoicing over, one quite out of the ordinary." He continues, "Let them grant me that each one of us, from earliest childhood, has had to learn our own language by constantly hearing it spoken, and has acquired a knowledge of any other language, whether of Hebrew or Greek, or any of the rest, either in the same way by hearing it spoken, or from a human teacher."[16] Speaking, like reading and writing, is a distinctive human attribute and also a social gift—something we learn from others rather than invent ourselves.

The early chapters of Genesis present God as a speaking being. God is throughout presented as summoning, calling, admonishing, commanding and creating by his word. This imagery is recurrent in the Hebrew Bible and the New Testament. We might say that the Genesis image of God is of a *God of creative address*. What might it mean, then, to consider that it might be as "speaking beings" that we are in the image of God?

Speaking is both a personal and collective accomplishment. While not everyone can speak at all times, and some will never speak, the human race would not be what it is without speech. While speaking is closely aligned with rationality, we tend to think of rationality as something each individual either possesses or lacks. Not so with language. As Schleiermacher and Augustine point out, we would not even speak to praise God had we not first learned to speak from other human beings. And as Ludwig Wittgenstein would demonstrate in the twentieth century, there is no such thing as a private language. Speech is a social possession and, moreover, speech involves the reciprocity of love. We see this especially when parents charm their babies into language, and when the other is old and frail and beyond speaking or unable to speak through illness or disability. These people, though voiceless, are also part of the community of speech. Here we have something that singles out our species, for while dolphins may vocalize and even sign, they do not write ballads or novels, use the future conditional or make promises. It may be that the elephants, like us, are stakeholders in environmental policy, but however intelligent they are, they cannot debate legislation.

---

[16]Augustine, *Teaching Christianity (De doctrina Christiana)*, prologue 4-5, trans. Edmund Hill, OP (Hyde Park, NY: New City Press, 1996), 102.

Yet, as speaking creatures human beings are still entirely creaturely and material. Speaking is physical, involving the tightening of vocal chords, the expulsion of air, the creation of sound waves. Speaking is as physical as rowing a boat, and humans as speaking beings are not at a distance from other creatures.[17] We are indeed made of dust but so is everything around us—all the trees, the birds, sea creatures and land animals. The earth itself, so astrophysicists tell us, is billion-year-old stardust. But human beings are dust that can promise, plan, call and respond—as does the biblical God.

The prologue of the Gospel of John also presents God as creating by speaking. With its "in the beginning was the Word" (Jn 1:1), it makes clear reference to Genesis. Yet, the prologue goes on to tell of a Word incarnate who, as man, speaks our human language while at the same time summoning and calling to new creation and a second birth. This incarnate Word is also the God of creative address. The identification of Jesus as the very visibility (and audibility) of the Creator God is not just a curiosity of John's prologue. Throughout the Gospel, Jesus repeatedly identifies himself with the "I AM" who spoke to Moses, the very God who made heaven and earth. These "I AM" sayings hearken back not only to Exodus but also to the "I AM" sayings of Isaiah. There, in a striking sequence of divine self-designations, YHWH declares that he *alone* is God, the Creator:

> For thus says YHWH,
> who created the heavens
> (he is God!),
> who formed the earth and made it
> (he established it;
> he did not create a chaos,
> he formed it to be inhabited!):
> "I AM YHWH, and there is no other." (Is 45:18, modified)

The Pauline writings similarly invoke Christ's participation in creation, identifying him with God's Word or Wisdom. This is famously so in Corinthians: "For us there is one God, the Father, from whom are all things and for whom we exist, and one Lord, Jesus Christ, through whom are all things and through whom we exist" (1 Cor 8:6). In Colossians we read:

---

[17]Rowan Williams discusses the physicality of speaking and its possible theological importance, among other themes, in his Gifford Lectures, *The Edge of Words: God and the Habits of Language* (London: Bloomsbury, 2014).

> He is the image of the invisible God, the firstborn of all creation; for in him all things in heaven and on earth were created, things visible and invisible, whether thrones or dominions or rulers or powers—all things have been created through him and for him. (Col 1:15-16)

The author of the epistle to the Hebrews brings together speaking, *imago* and Word in painting a picture of the Son as creative agent:

> In these last days [God] *has spoken to us* by a Son, whom he appointed heir of all things, through *whom he also created* the worlds. He is the reflection of God's glory and the *exact imprint of God's* very being, and he sustains all things by his powerful *word*. (Heb 1:2-3, my emphasis)

Yet, perhaps the most striking identification of Christ with the creative Word, the "I AM" of the Hebrew Bible, comes in the book of Revelation: "'I AM the Alpha and the Omega,' says the Lord God, who is and who was and who is to come, the Almighty" (Rev 1:8, modified).[18] In the resounding sequence of divine self-designations that follow this opening theophany, God and Christ are both named "Alpha and Omega" and "First and the Last," names that are themselves interpretative glosses on *the* Name: YHWH (Rev 1:17; 2:8; 21:6; 22:13).[19] The distinctive name "First and Last" is not of New Testament coinage but appears as a divine self-designation in Isaiah, where YHWH is the one God who creates and summons all into being:

> Thus says YHWH, the King of Israel,
> and his Redeemer, YHWH of hosts:
> "I am the first and I am the last;
> besides me there is no god." (Is 44:6, modified; see also Is 41:4)

And in Isaiah 48, we see creation as a summoning:

> I am He; I am the first,
> and I am the last.
> My hand laid the foundation of the earth,
> and my right hand spread out the heavens;
> when I summon them,
> they stand at attention. (Is 48:12-13)

---

[18]Here I am drawing on Richard Bauckham's excellent *The Theology of the Book of Revelation* (Cambridge: Cambridge University Press, 1993).

[19]See Bauckham, *Revelation*, 27.

The language is of a summoning, calling, creating and redeeming God. The "First and Last" is the one who will redeem all things because he has created all things. So the cosmic Christology of the New Testament holds Christ to be a living, visible and audible Word made flesh.

CONCLUSION

To summarize, the language of the *imago Dei* in Genesis has typically been mined for ethical purposes while Paul's elevated *imago* language is given a remote christological eminence. I have proposed, however, that Genesis and the Pauline texts share a concern with God's creative agency and human dignity and destiny, and further speak of human participation in that agency in terms of speech. Creating in Genesis does not rely on images of sexual generation; God does not "father" the world. Instead, the God of the Hebrew Bible creates through his Word: summoning ("Let there be light," Gen 1:3), separating (light from darkness), blessing, commanding and naming ("God called the light Day," Gen 1:5). This is a semiotic God whose very Word is the power to create. In Paul's understanding, too, God is one who summons, speaks and names.

This is why it is as speaking beings that we most image the God who is "living Word" in reciprocal, convivial and truthful speech. "Speaking beings" is something we are collectively, as there is a time when each of us did not and will not speak—and some will never speak. We speak to others and, in acts of love, for others. The perfection of human beings comes not despite others but with them in loving God and neighbor. We cannot, as Augustine observed, love our neighbors if we do not love ourselves. And we cannot love ourselves if we do not know ourselves as loved by God, as the image of God and the temple of God (1 Cor 3:17).

Augustine was deeply influenced by the story of Paul's conversion. It affected his preaching and what he did as a bishop. In particular, he was struck by the fact that the voice from heaven did not say, "Saul, Saul, why do you persecute my followers?" but "Saul, Saul, why do you persecute *me*?" (Acts 9:4, my emphasis).[20] Augustine came to see that his mixed, ragtag bunch of North African Christians were not just followers of Christ but the body of Christ, the

---

[20]In his sermons especially; see Augustine, *Expositions on the Psalms* 30.[2.]3; 38.5; 40.5; 53.1; 55.3; 89.30.

body of which Paul spoke. Each one was a temple of the living God, as Jesus claimed he was, and each was a stone in that speaking, summoning temple. The living presences of Christ among us are those Christians who preach, teach and, by works of love, are "being transformed into the same image from one degree of glory to another; for this comes from the Lord, the Spirit" (2 Cor 3:18).

I have argued that the historical emphasis on rationality as the locus of the image, while not entirely wrong, is sadly abbreviated. It neglects what appears to be Genesis's emphasis on the body and physicality. It individualizes what both testaments present as requiring the more-than-one.[21] More recent attempts, including my own, to anchor the *imago Dei* in sexual difference and fecundity, while moving away from the stress on the solitary individual, run the risk of collapsing into a gendered binarism just as static as the monism it intended to replace.

I have ventured a thought experiment in which we consider that the *imago Dei* resides in human beings as speaking beings. This is an entirely physical process: it is both individual and collective, and it anchors the *imago Dei* language in Genesis and Paul in the doctrine of creation. Moreover, it displays a humanity that images the one God who, now as always, speaks the world into being—calling, addressing, summoning—and, as Word incarnate, summons us into new life: a God of creative address.

---

[21]Even Augustine's attempt in *On the Trinity* to invoke the *imago* as memory, understanding and will seems to lock the image into the individual. See Soskice, *The Kindness of God*, chapter 7.

Part Four

WITNESS

10

THE SIN OF RACISM

Racialization of the Image of God[1]

Soong-Chan Rah

INTRODUCTION

In the St. Louis suburb of Ferguson, Missouri, the dead body of an eighteen-year-old named Michael Brown lay roasting in the heat of an August day. An encounter between a white police officer and a black youth resulted in the death and desecration of a black body and the ignition of a national conversation about the worth of black people's lives in American society. Over the waning months of 2014 and into 2015, on the heels of two nonindictments in the slaying of black men, protesters asserted that black lives matter. Rodney King, Oscar Grant, Michael Brown, Eric Garner, Tamir Rice and Walter Scott—some of the names on a long list of black victims of violence at the hands of law enforcement—are victims of an American narrative that devalues black bodies, black minds and black lives.

According to Willie Jennings, theology is the "imaginative capacity to redefine the social."[2] In other words, the power of theology is the power to expand imagination. William Cavanaugh defines the imagination of a society as "the sense of what is real and what is not; it includes a memory of how the society got where it is, a sense of who it is, and hopes and projects for the future."[3] Walter Brueggemann believes that "the task of prophetic ministry

---

[1]Portions of this essay appear in my *Prophetic Lament: A Call for Justice in Troubled Times* (Downers Grove, IL: InterVarsity Press, 2015).
[2]Willie Jennings, *The Christian Imagination* (New Haven: Yale University Press, 2010), 6.
[3]William Cavanaugh, *Torture and Eucharist* (Malden, MA: Blackwell, 1998), 57.

is to nurture, nourish, and evoke a consciousness and perception alternative to the consciousness and perception of the dominant culture around us."[4] Theology offers the possibility of a prophetic imagination that can transform individuals and society.

While Christian theology makes a transcendent imagination possible, this ability to see beyond the self in order to engage God and others can be distorted. The capacity for transcendent vision can lead to an arrogant sense of privilege for limited human beings. The capacity to connect with the divine can lead Christians to believe they hold a unique and preferred position before God. This sense of exceptionalism shapes the imagination of the dominant culture and informs engagement with those identified as other.

In a broken world, Christians often adopt a dysfunctional theological imagination. Jennings asserts, "Christianity in the Western world lives and moves within a diseased social imagination."[5] This imagination has resulted in a racialized identity that elevates the worth of the dominant culture over and against other cultures. In other words, a warped Christian imagination projects whiteness as normative and gives power to white Christianity to project a defining negative image of the other. When we engage the events of Ferguson and elsewhere in terms of the doctrine of the image of God, we must ask: How has a misreading of the image of God in the American evangelical narrative elevated the dominant race and culture over other races and cultures? How has a dysfunctional theological imagination contributed to a social reality that necessitates a campaign to make it clear that black lives matter? How has imagination gone wrong?

The Sin of the Racialization of the Image of God

The racialization of God's image in humanity is best understood as a sin that corrupts the doctrine of the image of God. Sin results when human beings attempt to take God's place. "To sin," John Stott states, "is, therefore, to take away from God what is his own, which means to steal from him and so to dishonor him."[6] The racialization of the *imago Dei* is a human attempt to elevate human standards above and in the place of God.

---

[4]Walter Brueggemann, *The Prophetic Imagination* (Minneapolis: Fortress Press, 2001), 3.
[5]Jennings, *Christian Imagination*, 6.
[6]John Stott, *The Cross of Christ* (Downers Grove, IL: InterVarsity Press, 1990), 188.

Every human being is made in the image of God. Racism declares, explicitly or implicitly, that the full expression of this image is found only in certain races. Racism thus usurps God's rightful position in creation. The main expression of racism in the United States is the theological distortion that elevates whiteness to a privileged position over other races. This racializes the image of God and links God's image to whiteness. Whiteness becomes universalized—the embodiment of all that is good, true and honorable. The racialization of the image of God—robbing some humans of their status as created in God's image—is a key factor in defining racism as sin.

Charles Hodge offers an expression of the classic Christian doctrine of the *imago Dei*: humanity "bears and reflects the divine likeness among the inhabitants of the earth, because he is a spirit, an intelligent, voluntary agent."[7] This means that "we could search the world over, but we could not find a man [or woman] so low, so degraded, or so far below the social, economic, and moral norms that we have established for ourselves that he had not been created in the image of God."[8] Western Christianity took this doctrine, which affirms the dignity of every human being, and warped it to elevate one people group over another.

Behind the sinful project of the racialization of the image of God there is an underlying assumption of white American Christian exceptionalism. The diseased theological imagination assumes that a superior expression of God's image exists in the white American, allowing the rejection of those who differ, particularly those of African descent. American exceptionalism, therefore, is a theological problem. The sin of setting up one's own image as the ultimate ideal results in an exaggerated self-perception. This assumption of superiority allows the white Christian American to take a position of final authority over others. The image of the white person becomes the norm by which other races are judged. Whiteness is elevated to the level of godliness. The person of color becomes the opposite of what is closest to God, and the biblical creation account is at the mercy of white supremacy. This reflects a fundamental violation of the image of God found in all people.

In this context, rather than confronting racist perspectives, theology became the tool of ongoing oppression. A warped understanding of the image

---

[7]Charles Hodge, *Systematic Theology*, vol. 2 (New York: Scribner, 1965), 99.
[8]Thomas Maston, *The Bible and Race* (Nashville: Broadman, 1959), 12.

of God became justification for white supremacy. Jennings explains:

> Whiteness was being held up as an aspect of creation with embedded facilitating
> powers. Whiteness from the moment of discovery and consumption was a social
> and theological way of imagining, an imaginary that evolved into a method of un-
> derstanding the world. It was a social imaginary in that it posited the existence of
> difference and collectivity for those in the Old World faced with the not easily ex-
> plainable peoples and phenomena of the New World. It was a theological imaginary
> because whiteness suggested that one may enter a true moment of creation gestalt.
> Whiteness transcended all peoples because it was a means of seeing all peoples at
> the very moment it realized itself. Whiteness was a global vision of Europeans and
> Africans but, more than that, a way of organizing bodies by proximity to and ap-
> proximation of white bodies.[9]

White bodies, not God, became normative in Christian anthropology. A dysfunctional theological imagination could not envision a world without the
primacy of white aesthetics.

The establishment of white superiority is not limited to the categories of
body and skin but extends to the mind as well. Assuming the superiority of
white bodies moves toward assuming the superiority of white minds and their
products—such as language and culture—with a corresponding deprecation
of black minds and their products. A notable example of the assumption of
the superiority of the white mind is found in the primacy of European languages. John Willinsky asserts that within the educational system, "English is
not taught as a second language but as the only medium of intelligible
communication."[10] He observes that "to acquire the English language is to
have a stake in its claim as a world language; it is to be a party to a history that
runs from the colonial past that first planted English across the globe."[11] In
evangelical missions and the Christian academy, English is the *lingua franca*
of theological discourse. European languages are considered central to theological study, and important works in evangelical theology are presumed to
be in English. A bias toward English is central for ministry. An Asian-American
pastor revealed to me that during an interview process, a denominational

---

[9]Jennings, *Christian Imagination*, 58-59.
[10]John Willinsky, *Learning to Divide the World* (Minneapolis: University of Minnesota Press, 2000),
208.
[11]Ibid., 193.

official mentioned that his knowledge of Mandarin could work against him as a pastoral candidate. To improve his job prospects, it was suggested that he state only his proficiency in English.

The assumption of the superiority of white minds can also be found in the elevation of white culture over nonwhite culture. Virginia Dominguez notes, "Any positive reference to culture almost always implies a European and Euro-centric culture."[12] For example, in an evangelical theology text, Ken Myers claims there are gradations of culture. He associates "high" culture—by impli-cation, culture that is closer to God—with Western forms of culture such as Rembrandt, Bach and Greek philosophy. He contrasts this with "low" or "pop" culture, represented by Bon Jovi, TV sitcoms and Andy Warhol. "High culture has its roots in antiquity, in an age of conviction about absolutes, about truth, about virtue," Myers asserts. "Its essential features make it capable of main-taining and transmitting more about human experiences in creation, and about God's redemptive intervention in history, than its alternatives."[13] Myers creates a third category, which he labels "folk" culture. His examples include Native American regalia, Korean drumming and African dancing. Myers claims that folk culture is "simpler in nature and less communicable from one folk to another."[14] In short, classical Western culture is superior to non-Western culture. Myers's bias in favor of Western white culture reveals the underlying assumption of the superiority of the white mind. For Dominguez, this assumption "buys too unproblematically into an elite Eurocentric view of culture that would ignore issues of language, public rhetoric, immigration policy, education, class, race, and ethnicity that provide both support and chal-lenges to that elite sense of culture as refinement and aesthetic achievement."[15]

In addition, Western Christians have often failed to see how non-Western expressions of Christianity could contribute to theology. White culture be-comes bound up with what it meant to be orthodox and to embody cul-turally acceptable Christianity. Christian identity, therefore, is tied to Western identity. What is assumed as normative in theology arises from the Western context. For example, while nonwhite, non-Western theology

---

[12]Virginia Dominguez, "Invoking Culture: The Messy Side of Cultural Politics," in *Eloquent Obses-sions*, ed. Marianna Torgovnick (Durham, NC: Duke University Press, 1994), 254.
[13]Kenneth A. Myers, *All God's Children and Blue Suede Shoes* (Irvine, CA: Crossway, 1989), 59.
[14]Ibid.
[15]Dominguez, "Invoking Culture," 247-48.

usually requires an adjectival marker—Black Theology, Liberation Theology, *Minjung* Theology—Western theology does not, since it is considered central and normative.

Warped theological assumptions about the image of God lead to a dysfunctional soteriology. Not even this essential topic has escaped the dysfunctional theological imagination of white supremacy. Jennings captures this theological failure:

> White indicates high salvific viability, rooted in the signs of movement toward God (for example, cleanliness, intelligence, obedience, social hierarchy, and advancement in civilization). Europeans reconfigured Christian social space around white and black bodies. If existence between Christian and non-Christian, saved and lost, elect and reprobate was a fluid reality that could be grasped only by detecting the spiritual and material marks, then the racial scale aided this complex optical operation.[16]

Salvation is linked to the capacity to approximate whiteness rather than the capacity to reflect the image of God. This link is built upon the faulty theological assumption of white superiority in all matters, including physical appearance, intellectual capacity, linguistic ability, cultural sophistication and spiritual possibility. All these assumptions are predicated upon white assumptions of superiority, rooted in a false belief in the unique endowment of God's image upon whites. Salvation for the African, therefore, became the process of moving toward approximation of the white world.

Those whose efforts toward approximating whiteness fall short are marginalized from mainstream American society. The diseased theological imagination is unable to prophetically confront the dysfunction of racial dynamics. Because this sinful imagination has accepted the racialized image of God, it contributes to the ongoing racialization of American society. Mass incarceration and failure to deal with the issue of immigration are salient examples of the inability of American Christian theology to address social failures. Instead, the ongoing racialization of the image of God and the elevation of white American expressions of Christianity furthers cultural captivity. In the remainder of this chapter, I will examine two historic snapshots that demonstrate the elevation of whiteness and the establishment of white supremacy in American evangelical theological discourse.

---

[16]Jennings, *Christian Imagination*, 35.

RACIALIZATION OF THE *IMAGO* IN AMERICAN CITIES

The first snapshot has to do with the perception of the American city through the lens of Anglo-American exceptionalism. American Christianity's relationship with the city is a shifting narrative that reveals assumptions about the superiority of white bodies and minds. In the early stages of US church history, Christians were optimistic about the exceptional future of the American continent and American cities. The governor of the Massachusetts Bay Colony, John Winthrop, believed his community was to be a "city set on a hill." "They would demonstrate before 'the eyes of the world' what the result would be when a whole people was brought into open covenant with God. . . . This was God's country with a mission to perform."[17] William Clebsch calls attention to "the vision of the new world as locus for a new city. . . . The new world prompted Christians from the sixteenth century through the nineteenth to think of America as the last and best of human societies following the westward course of empire."[18] Colonial American Christians anticipated that the cities of the New World would become cities set on a hill, New Jerusalems and Zions populated by Western European Protestant bodies.

This optimistic narrative changed over the course of the nineteenth and twentieth centuries as industrialization, urbanization, immigration and internal migration altered the face of the American city. Migration of African Americans from the former southern slave states coupled with an influx of non-Protestant and non-Western European immigrants into northern and East Coast cities resulted in the notable growth of these cities. These changes in population, however, meant that Anglo-Americans, who had previously seen cities as places of promise, now saw them as dangerous. Even before the Civil War, Robert Orsi writes, "In the feverish imaginations of antebellum anti-Catholic literary provocateurs, city neighborhoods appeared as caves of rum and Romanism, mysterious and forbidding, a threat to democracy, Protestantism, and virtue alike."[19] Randall Balmer adds, "Evangelicals suddenly felt their hegemonic hold over American society slipping away. . . . The teeming, squalid ghettoes, . . . festering with labor unrest, no longer resembled

[17]Winthrop S. Hudson, *Religion in America*, 3rd ed. (New York: Charles Scribner's Sons, 1981), 20-21.
[18]William A. Clebsch, *From Sacred to Profane America* (New York: Harper & Row, 1968), 39.
[19]Robert Orsi, *Gods of the City* (Bloomington, IN: Indiana University Press, 1999), 6.

the precincts of Zion that postmillennial evangelicals had envisioned earlier in the century."[20]

In the twentieth century, suburban communities offered an attractive alternative to evangelicals who saw the city in negative terms. Amanda Seligman notes, "In the years after World War II, a modern form of suburb, fostered by new tools, opened up around the country. Innovative financing techniques, subsidized by the federal government, enabled millions of white Americans to purchase property beyond city limits."[21] Many white urban dwellers took the opportunity to escape the city. The twentieth century witnessed the departure of whites and white churches from the city in significant numbers.

The suburbs became new outposts for white Christians fearful of changes in the city, and twentieth-century Christians adopted a strong sense of distinction and separation between cities and suburbs. The modern city was perceived as the center of all that was wrong with the world, while the suburb could be seen as a token of what was right. A narrative of decline now dominated Christian perception of the city, and those who participated in white flight could justify their actions. The white Christian could flee the city as a spiritual act, seeking to separate from evil. Suburbia became the New Jerusalem while cities became Babylon.

The movement of whites from cities to suburbs resulted in a shift of ministry emphasis toward suburban expressions of church life. Churches in the suburbs grew significantly in the latter half of the twentieth century. Winthrop Hudson notes that $26 million was spent on new church buildings in 1945, and that number increased to over $1 billion by 1960.[22] While church attendance increased in the suburbs, Herbert Gans's 1967 research on a quintessential suburban town revealed that moves from the city to suburbia involved no change in church or synagogue attendance.[23] Suburban church growth relied not on conversions but on the population shift of the white community into suburban outposts.[24] Harvie Conn summarizes studies conducted by

---

[20]Randall Balmer, *The Making of Evangelicalism* (Waco, TX: Baylor University Press, 2010).

[21]Amanda I. Seligman, *Block by Block: Neighborhoods and Public Policy on Chicago's West Side* (Chicago: University of Chicago Press, 2005), 210-11.

[22]Hudson, *Religion in America*, 384n45.

[23]Herbert Gans, *The Levittowners: Ways of Life and Politics in the New Suburban Community* (New York: Columbia University Press, 1967), 264.

[24]The homogenous unit principle (HUP) was one of the key magic formulas employed to grow suburban churches, and—intentionally or not—it affirmed the wisdom of white flight. The HUP

Dennison Nash and Peter Berger: "The impressive increases in church membership statistics in suburbia were only a reflection of the increased number of families with school-aged children in the country, the postwar 'baby boom' that had helped to produce the suburban migration itself."[25]

Recently, there has been a return of the white middle class to the city, including suburban Christians with a heart for urban ministry. However, these relocators may still cling to assumptions about the city rooted in the narrative of white flight. Even as whites relocate to help the city, they may still be living out a dysfunctional messianic narrative rooted in white middle-class identity. They may see themselves as saviors to the fallen city populated by sinful people of color. The white middle class that had successfully grown the church in the suburbs could now apply those ministry principles to the spiritually vacuous urban context and solve the problems of the city. Unfortunately, this narrative severely undermines the longstanding work of indigenous leadership in urban communities.

For example, many white evangelicals feel called to plant churches in poor black communities. They see this as a mission necessary to spread the gospel message, the best chance for poor neighborhoods in desperate need of salvation. Lance Lewis, an African American church planter from an evangelical denomination, comments on evangelical attempts to plant churches in poor black communities, noting white evangelical assumptions that "there are no 'good' churches in black neighborhoods that could possibly meet the spiritual needs of the community." He goes on to say, "It would be impossible for any evangelical denomination or ministry to plant a church in an all-black community that doesn't already have several active congregations serving that community. One must ask the question: why have we decided to plant here? The unspoken answer is: the existing black churches just aren't very good."[26] A warped perception of the city and assumptions about the success

---

allowed suburban churches to capture the migration of whites, which led to numerical growth. In turn, the growth of the suburban church justified the proliferation of church-growth principles that claimed to offer a method of growth applicable to all churches.

[25]Harvey M. Conn, *The American City and the Evangelical Church* (Grand Rapids: Baker, 1994), 98. See Dennison Nash and Peter Berger, "The Child, the Family and the Religious Revival in Suburbia," and Dennison Nash, "And a Little Child Shall Lead Them: A Test of an Hypothesis That Children Were the Source of the American 'Religious Revival.'"

[26]Lance Lewis, "Black Pastoral Leadership and Church Planting," in *Aliens in the Promised Land*, ed. Anthony Bradley (Phillipsburg, NJ: P&R, 2013), 27-28.

of suburban churches leads to a dysfunctional paternalistic narrative about saving the inner city through the magic formulas employed by white suburban churches.

The assumption about the city as Babylon justified white flight, and that same assumption later justified the return of white Christians to the city. These white Christians, who had built New Jerusalems in the suburbs, would help to save the fallen city and contribute to urban gentrification. The same places once envisioned as cities set on a hill meant to send out missionaries now became Babylons in desperate need of receiving missionaries from the Jerusalem outposts of the American suburbs.

Those who have served the city for decades do not determine perception of the city. The ministry of nonwhite Christians is not taken into account when determining that American cities are Babylon. Instead, the gaze of white Christians controls the imagination of American evangelicalism and forms the primary narrative for American Christianity. The image of God is imagined as expressed in the successful ministry of white suburban churches. The flourishing of God's image in the context of evangelical ministry is determined by approximation to whiteness. Urban churches are composed of nonwhite Christians and therefore are not understood as examples of the flourishing of the image of God. The urban Babylon is construed as a context where the image of God is largely absent.

AFRICAN AMERICAN EVANGELICALISM AND THE RACIALIZATION OF THE IMAGE OF GOD

Our second snapshot examines the emergence of African American evangelicalism in the latter part of the twentieth century. The organization of the National Black Evangelical Association (NBEA) and the rise and decline of African American evangelist Tom Skinner within the American evangelical subculture exemplify this narrative.

Nonwhite evangelicals have often had difficulty in finding acceptance in the dominant white evangelical culture. For example, for most of American evangelical history, the black church has been excluded from being called "evangelical." In 2006, journalist Ed Gilbreath pointed out that estimates of the number of evangelicals "usually separate out nearly all of the nation's African American Protestant population (roughly 8 or 9 percent of the US population), which . . . is typically pretty evangelical in theology and orientation. Indeed, 61 percent of blacks—the highest of any racial group, by far—described themselves as 'born again' in a 2001 Gallup poll."[27] In spite of similar theological stances, there is a lack of connection between white evangelicals and African American Christians. As church historian A. G. Miller notes, "Most scholars who study the evangelical phenomenon have had a difficult time situating black Evangelicalism historiographically and tracing its development as a movement."[28]

The development of a uniquely African American evangelical identity in the 1960s and 1970s reveals the racialization of the image of God among American evangelicals. The formation of this identity emerged from a strong black identity—connected to the black nationalist movement and civil rights movement—engaging with the larger context of the evangelical movement. African American evangelicals embraced the image of God in African American identity. The presence of African American evangelicals, therefore, had the potential for significant impact on the larger movement of evangelicalism in freeing the broader movement from cultural captivity to whiteness. However, numerous factors consistently undermined the influence of black evangelicals.

The limited impact of late twentieth-century African American evangelicals can be attributed in part to the failure of the larger movement to engage the black church as an expression of evangelical faith. That failure yielded an unnecessary gulf between white and black evangelicals. The black church, while holding to an evangelical theology, developed a particular expression that served the cultural context of African American Christianity. Douglas Sweeney explains, "African American Protestantism evolved as a special hybrid of black culture and international evangelicalism. Rooted deeply in the Bible and empowered by the Spirit, black faith was facilitated initially by evangelical witness."[29]

In the latter half of the twentieth century, exclusion of the traditional and historic black church from the larger evangelical movement meant that new

---

[27]Edward Gilbreath, *Reconciliation Blues* (Downers Grove, IL: InterVarsity Press, 2006), 40-41.
[28]A. G. Miller, "The Rise of African-American Evangelicalism in American Culture," in *Perspectives on American Religion and Culture*, ed. Peter W. Williams (Malden, MA: Blackwell, 1999), 261.
[29]Douglas A. Sweeney, *The American Evangelical Story* (Grand Rapids: Baker Academic, 2005), 127.

expressions were needed to intersect with white evangelicalism. One such expression can be found in the National Black Evangelical Association (NBEA), which facilitated the rise of a unique black evangelical identity. The NBEA held its first conference in 1963 in Los Angeles and was originally known as the National Negro Evangelical Association (NNEA). The narrative of the NBEA includes four overlapping formative threads, which provided four distinct influences on the association: a fundamentalist thread, a Pentecostal thread, a thread connected to African American graduates of evangelical schools and a thread from African American evangelists.

Three brothers—Whitfield, Talbot and Berlin Martin (B. M.) Nottage—helped to form the Plymouth Black Brethren, which would contribute to the fundamentalist thread of the NBEA. The Nottages converted to Christianity on their native island of Eluthera in the Bahamas. After immigrating to the United States, they planted a number of urban churches through proactive evangelism. These churches formed distinct clusters separate from the association of white Plymouth Brethren, partially due to a sense of unwelcome. B. M. Nottage said, "The 'all welcome' sign of the doors of most evangelical churches does not include the Negro. . . . Usually he isn't welcome and is not allowed to enjoy such fellowship."[30] While organizationally separate from the white denomination, the Black Brethren continued to reflect the conservative fundamentalism of their white counterparts.[31] The fundamentalist thread of the NBEA expressed a theological approximation of white fundamentalism. Theological affinity marked the relationship of the Black Brethren to their white counterparts, but this affinity existed alongside a mistrust of white power structures. Theological approximation of whiteness did not yield full insider status.

African American Pentecostals of the trinitarian pentecostal tradition[32] comprised the second thread. William H. Bentley and his wife, Ruth Bentley, emerged from this thread. William served as president of the NBEA from 1970

---

[30]The quotation is from a privately published sermon cited in Miller, "African-American Evangelicalism," 264.

[31]The fundamentalist thread, particularly through the influence of B. M. Nottage, is evident in NBEA leaders such as "Marvin Printis, the first president of the NBEA; William Pannell, professor of evangelism at Fuller Theological Seminary; and Howard Jones, the first black associate of Billy Graham" (Miller, "African-American Evangelicalism," 263).

[32]Such as the Church of God in Christ and the United Pentecostal Council of the Assemblies of God.

to 1976 and proved to be an important consensus-builder for the organization. Ruth would continue to uphold the work of the NBEA beyond her husband's passing, and she played an important role in the association's formation and establishment. The pentecostal thread differed from the fundamentalist thread in that many black Pentecostals emerged from traditionally black denominations free of white control. The pentecostal thread of the NBEA would occupy the ecclesial space between the fundamentalist thread of the NBEA and the traditional black churches.

These first two threads of the NBEA reveal expressions of evangelical faith in terms of a conservative theological orientation. But despite this proximity to the theological position of white evangelicals, many black evangelicals sought to operate under their own systems and structures. The NBEA would reflect the theological conservatism of mainstream evangelicalism while providing the space to express a uniquely African American identity.

The third thread emerged out of the growing number of African Americans graduating from evangelical institutions of higher education. Approximation of whiteness was achieved with educational credentials from schools such as Wheaton College, Moody Bible Institute, Trinity Evangelical Divinity School and Dallas Theological Seminary. While relatively small in number, these pioneering African Americans would serve as key leaders in the burgeoning black evangelical movement. The fact that they held credentials from evangelical colleges and seminaries led white evangelicals to assume these leaders would conform to evangelical orthodoxy. Their conservative theology would serve as a rallying cry for the NBEA. However, this theological orthodoxy would also encounter an increasing black nationalism evident in the culture at large. Part of the role of the NBEA was to develop a uniquely black theological reflection in addition to the conservative theological framework received in evangelical educational institutions.

The connection between black evangelicals and predominantly white institutions extended into African American involvement in parachurch organizations, such as InterVarsity Christian Fellowship, Youth for Christ and the Billy Graham Evangelistic Association. However, black evangelicals were increasingly frustrated at racism in white evangelicalism. Miller notes:

> During the early stage, many black evangelicals were frustrated with the white evangelical movement. This tension primarily sprang from what blacks perceived as

white evangelicals' indifference and lack of sympathy for the evangelistic needs of African Americans. This eventually led some black evangelicals to charge their white counterparts with a spiritual "benign neglect." Eventually the charge of neglect evolved into a stronger allegation of racism.[33]

The NBEA gave black evangelicals the opportunity to connect with one another and to develop an evangelical theology that incorporated greater sensitivity to the African American community.

The fourth thread of the NBEA came from African American evangelists whose evangelistic ministries mirrored those of white evangelicals, expressed in crusades, altar calls and the prioritizing of personal salvation. Because of the emphasis on personal evangelism, many of these evangelists received sponsorship and support from white fundamentalists and evangelicals. Ralph Bell was a black evangelist. Howard Jones, an evangelist, and Jimmy McDonald, a musician, both served with the Billy Graham Evangelistic Association. Jones would frequently appear on the radio in Graham's stead, and Graham's style of preaching was strongly imprinted on Jones' presentation. These African American evangelicals effectively incorporated white evangelical forms of evangelism.

But a group of "young Turks" in the NBEA, including Tom Skinner, Carl Ellis, Columbus Sally and others, were more holistic in their approach to evangelism. Some of the fundamentalist roots of the early NBEA would come into conflict with the social-justice emphasis of the younger black evangelicals. At the 1969 NBEA conference in Atlanta, Bentley notes, "lines were clearly drawn between those Blacks who were identified with a more socially conservative bent, and who, on account, some felt, enjoyed close relationships with the white evangelical establishment, and those Blacks who felt that more conscious efforts ought to be made to actively accept our own culture and carefully relate the Gospel claims within that context."[34]

The emergence of this social-justice emphasis and a strong black identity provided a balance to the emphasis on personal evangelism in the early years of the NBEA. "As a result," Miller writes, "for the first time in the history of the organization, the position was unequivocally expressed that white

---

[33]Miller, "African-American Evangelicalism," 265.
[34]William H. Bentley, *National Black Evangelical Association: Evolution of a Concept of Ministry* (published privately, 1979), 19-20.

methods to reach Black people had been historically proven to be inadequate."[35] There was increasing awareness of the shortcomings of white evangelicalism applied in the African American context. The NBEA, therefore, became a safe place for African American evangelicals to explore issues specific to their own community and to develop their own theological framework and evangelical identity. However, the formation of a black evangelical identity meant the diminishing support of the white evangelical community. Such diminishing support for black evangelicals is exemplified in the story of Skinner.

In many ways, Skinner's story mirrors the trajectory of the NBEA. He was a nationally recognized evangelist, his story was evangelical through and through, and he had a gripping testimony that appealed to both blacks and whites. His ministry, however, would eventually be considered outside the mainstream of the dominant culture's evangelical expressions. His initial acceptance among evangelicals was rooted in his ability to share his personal conversion story and speak about his individual salvation journey. His ability to powerfully communicate an evangelical gospel message caused many in both the white and black communities to stand up and take notice. Bentley reflects on the emergence of Skinner:

> Young and captivating, charismatic and capable, Tom expanded the mental and spiritual horizons of what Black ministry could be. His rare gifts of communication made him, even then, a figure to be reckoned with. . . . With [his first book] *Black and Free*, he became an overnight sensation and to many, "the" major voice of Black Evangelicalism.[36]

Skinner represented the best of black evangelicalism as sought by white evangelicalism. White evangelicals could spot the image of God expressed in Tom Skinner because his ministry initially mirrored the approach of white evangelicals. Eventually, he would also come to exemplify white evangelicalism's inability to deal with black evangelicalism.

Skinner was the son of a Baptist preacher in Harlem, New York. His family pushed him toward intellectual engagement with the world around him. In an interview for the Billy Graham Center Archives, Skinner revealed:

> My father . . . placed a strong emphasis on the mind. So my father urged us . . . to read very early. By the time I was twelve, thirteen years old I had read five or six of Shake-

---

[35]Hiller, "African-American Evangelicalism," 20.
[36]Bentley, *National Black Evangelical Association*, 18.

speare's plays. I had read Othello and Macbeth and Hamlet, Julius Caesar. . . . He
believed that the way black people overcome is that you just have to be educated.[37]

Skinner was a good student, "president of his high-school student body, a
member of the basketball team, president of the Shakespearean Club, and an
active member of his church's youth department."[38] At the same time, Skinner
was also the leader of the Harlem Lords, one of the most feared street gangs
in New York City.

Skinner expressed dissatisfaction with a God who was seemingly distant
from the sufferings of his community. Skinner writes, "As a teenager, I looked
around and asked my father where God was in all this? I couldn't for the life
of me see how God, if He cared for humanity at all, could allow the conditions
that existed in Harlem."[39] Skinner states that he felt "it was necessary for me
to disavow religion, Christianity. I could not reconcile the things that I was
hearing in church with what was going on in the street. The violence, the
hunger, the poverty, the oppression."[40] Skinner voiced disenchantment with
white Christianity's inadequate gospel:

> There were whites who made a lot of noise about how God was the answer to all
> our problems and how the Bible was our hope. . . . Basically, this individual had a
> half dozen Bible verses for every social problem that existed. If you went to him and
> told him that a place like Harlem existed, he would say, "Well, what those people
> up there need is a good dose of salvation." That all sounded well and good, except
> for the fact that I never saw the fellow actually in Harlem administering that "dose
> of salvation."[41]

Disappointed with the black church of his father's generation, Skinner lived a
double life: the good church kid and the violent gang leader. The night before
a big fight that could establish him as a major gang leader in New York, Skinner
was converted by an unscheduled gospel radio broadcast. The broadcast featured a preacher Skinner characterized as emotional and uneducated, but

---

[37]Tom Skinner, "Collection 430 - Tom Skinner. T1 Transcript," at the Billy Graham Center Archives, www.wheaton.edu/bgc/archives/trans/430to1.htm. Transcript completed by Wayne D.
Weber in February 1999 of an interview of Tom Skinner by Robert Shuster, June 13, 1990.

[38]Edward Gilbreath, "A Prophet Out of Harlem," *Christianity Today*, September 16, 1996, www
.christianitytoday.com/ct/1996/september16/6ta036.html.

[39]Tom Skinner, *Black and Free* (Maitland, FL: Xulon Press, 2005), 43.

[40]Skinner interview.

[41]Skinner, *Black and Free*, 43-44.

Skinner "got a spooky feeling this guy was talking right to me."[42] He experienced a personal, spiritual conversion, left the street gang and embarked on a path of becoming an evangelist.

Skinner began to preach on the streets, attracting crowds and winning converts. He scheduled a major crusade at the world-renowned Apollo Theater in Harlem, which would cement his reputation as a powerful evangelist. More than 2,200 people would respond to his preaching during the Harlem crusade. All who heard him preach, including prominent white evangelicals, recognized Skinner's oratory gifts. He also had the ability to mirror the ministry expression of white evangelists. His ability to project the expected image of an evangelical evangelist led the evangelical world to embrace him. With the backing and endorsement of many white evangelicals, Skinner's profile rose. He began making appearances on Moody Radio and speaking at evangelistic crusades around the country and in the Caribbean.

The story of a tough gang member converting to become a crusade evangelist was irresistible for many white evangelicals, but Skinner's testimony did not emerge out of a vacuum. His evangelistic efforts were in the shadow of a growing black nationalism and the civil rights movement. As Skinner's standard testimony about his life story became widespread, he began to move his message beyond the story of personal salvation and incorporate more teachings on the kingdom of God and the necessity of social concern, responsibility and action. Skinner was invited in 1969 to address Wheaton College. In a stirring talk titled "Jesus the Revolutionary," he cemented his move away from the standard evangelical testimony toward social concerns.

Skinner furthered this rhetoric at InterVarsity Christian Fellowship's 1970 Urbana Student Missions Conference. He directly challenged white evangelicalism's failure to address the social sin of slavery:

> You must keep in mind that, during this period of time, in general (there were some notable exceptions, but in general) the Evangelical, Bible-believing, fundamental, orthodox, conservative church in this country was strangely silent. In fact, there were those people who during slavery argued, "It is not our business to become involved in slavery. Those are social issues. We have been called to preach the gospel. We must deliver the Word. We must save people's souls. We must not get involved

---

[42]Ibid., 56.

in the issues of liberating people from the chains of slavery. If they accept Jesus
Christ as their Savior, by and by they will be free—over there."[43]

Skinner addressed the history of white racism from slavery to Jim Crow laws
and used examples from white evangelical churches. He also confronted an
important social-historical foundation of evangelicalism—emphasis on individual salvation and piety over and above social justice. He revealed the folly
of a hyper-individualistic gospel. Skinner confronted the apathy of white evangelicals who ignored social problems, going so far as to call them cowards. He
refused to hold back his understanding of the intersection between racial
justice, social justice and the gospel of Jesus Christ. He masterfully wove together multiple themes in raising a challenge to the status quo.

Skinner's Urbana speech, and the standing ovation he received, would
signal a significant moment in African American evangelicalism. Skinner's
sermons no longer operated exclusively in the realm of individual salvation.
At a prominent evangelical conference, Skinner had elevated the need to
engage in social justice alongside personal evangelism. Pannell notes, "Skinner's speech that night was the climax to a conference that was being refocused.
. . . This made some [InterVarsity] leaders very nervous. What would become
of 'foreign' missions if students' attention was redirected to the USA and its
urban challenges?"[44] Skinner's presentation signaled the increasing promi-
nence and the fresh prophetic voice offered by black evangelicalism. However,
Skinner also represented a voice that would make many white evangelicals
nervous.

As Skinner spoke more about the kingdom of God, he began to be perceived as having a political agenda.[45] Gilbreath recalls, "Just as Skinner's ministry was attracting more attention from whites, his outspoken views on issues
of social injustice facing the black community intensified (a fact that would
lead many Christian radio stations to drop his program due to its 'political'
content)."[46] White evangelicalism became increasingly suspicious. Skinner's
rejection by the broader white evangelical community came to a head when
he divorced his first wife in 1971. "With the rejection from much of the white

---

[43]Tom Skinner, "The U.S. Racial Crisis and World Evangelism (1970)," transcript posted at http://
urbana.org/transcript/us-racial-crisis-and-world-evangelism-1970.
[44]William Pannell, interview with the author, April 27, 2010.
[45]Ibid.
[46]Gilbreath, "A Prophet Out of Harlem."

evangelical community compounded by his divorce, Tom's life went through what can be described as a 'wilderness experience.'"[47]

Skinner would continue in ministry but in a different form, opting to focus on Christian leadership training. He would increase in influence with African American leadership in other segments of society, including serving as a chaplain for the NFL's team in Washington, DC, and working with the black congressional leadership, through which he would meet his second wife, Barbara Williams-Skinner. By the time of his untimely death in 1994, Skinner's voice in the larger evangelical community could be considered negligible.

CONCLUSION

The racialization of the image of God results in the sin of elevating human standards over God's standards. The racialization of the image of God means that white American evangelicals can assume that the superiority of white bodies, minds and theology provides the capacity to make determinative decisions about the world around white American Christians. The shifting narrative of urban versus suburban ministry reveals the assumption of the superiority of white expressions of American Christianity versus nonwhite expressions. The failure to embrace African American evangelicalism reveals the inability of the American evangelical theological imagination to embrace a nonwhite evangelical narrative. The power to determine the status and standing of others becomes the dominion of white evangelicals.

Whose perspective determines the narrative of American evangelicalism's relationship to the world? Whose image is included in American evangelicalism? The power to decide who is considered an evangelical insider is determined by people's ability to approximate whiteness, but that endowment is easily taken away. The assertion of a strong black identity or the assertion of the necessity for racial justice can lead to dismissal from the American evangelical fold. Dominant-culture evangelicalism seems willing to accept evangelicals of color as long as they fit the mold that is cast by white evangelicalism. Historical patterns of American evangelical Christianity indicate a privileging of the white narrative and expressions of ministry in the latter part of the twentieth century.

---

[47]Skinner, *Black and Free*, 183. This quotation is from an epilogue taken from a 1994 profile of Skinner in *Urban Family* magazine.

In the early decades of the twenty-first century, the demographics of American Christianity have shifted significantly. The decline of white American evangelicalism comes at the same time that nonwhite American evangelicalism is on the increase.[48] In both snapshots offered in this chapter, we have seen the discomfort experienced by white evangelicalism when encountering strong nonwhite identity and images. When challenged, dominant-culture evangelicalism reverted to the comfort of existing norms of white evangelical theology and ecclesiology. This prevents the reception of the gifts that other cultures bring. Rather than furthering the sense of otherness that often characterizes evangelical responses to nonwhite Christianity, the future of evangelicalism requires a greater sense of embrace.

Despite projections of evangelicalism's rapid movement toward a multi-ethnic future, the assumption of a white-dominated evangelicalism remains entrenched. Evangelicalism lacks nonwhite leadership in nearly all areas of influence. National pastor's conferences continue to be dominated by white evangelical leadership. Christian publishers continue to focus on white authors. Seminaries and Christian colleges struggle to hire and retain minority faculty. If evangelicalism is to be prepared for its next stage, diverse voices need to be represented.

The image of God must be recognized in all races and cultures and evidenced in denominational leadership, seminary faculty, Christian conferences and the authorship of books. The dysfunctional theological imagination must be challenged with a presentation of authoritative spiritual voices that reflect the fullness of the image of God.

---

[48]See Soong-Chan Rah, *The Next Evangelicalism* (Downers Grove, IL: InterVarsity Press, 2009).

11

WITNESSING IN FREEDOM

Resisting Commodification of the Image

Beth Felker Jones

INTRODUCTION

The nineteenth-century American poet Walt Whitman was not a self-conscious friend of Christian orthodoxy. Nevertheless, I wonder whether he got some things right in his poem "I Sing the Body Electric" precisely because they were so deeply Christian—that is, he might not have seen them at all were they not part of the lingering fumes of Christendom that are at least as American as Whitman himself. Perhaps the poet-prophet would not have permitted himself to speak these things if he knew how coherent with the gospel they were. In any case, I am attracted to Whitman's theology of the body as it speaks truth about what it means to be embodied—truth that could not be true outside the wider truth of incarnation and resurrection.

Whitman sings "the body electric" in a way that tells the truth about the psychosomatic unity of the human being. His poem tells the truth about the irreducible, enfleshed worth of each and every human being as embodied images of the One who forbids the making of idols, "whether in the form of anything that is in heaven above, or that is on the earth beneath, or that is in the water under the earth" (Ex 20:4). Those human beings are embodied images of the One who, nonetheless, expects us—in the flesh—to testify to the character and power of the Lord:

Was it doubted that those who corrupt their own bodies conceal themselves?
And if those who defile the living are as bad as they who defile the dead?

And if the body does not do fully as much as the soul?
And if the body were not the soul, what is the soul?
The love of the body of man or woman balks account, the body itself balks account,
That of the male is perfect, and that of the female is perfect.[1]

One does not need a full technical account of human constitution to recognize, as someone whose hands and feet are supposed to show the living God to the world, that "if the body were not the soul, what is the soul?"[2] This celebration of male and of female bodies echoes—and can only have been arrived at through listening to the echoes of—the first chapter of Genesis, where "God created humankind in his image, in the image of God he created them; male and female he created them" (Gen 1:27).

There is nothing here of first or last, of more or less, only of the absolute universality of the image, shared in the particularities of male flesh and female flesh and given the divine blessing of good work to do: "Be fruitful and multiply, and fill the earth and subdue it; and have dominion over the fish of the sea and over the birds of the air and over every living thing that moves upon the earth" (Gen 1:28). Whitman, too, celebrates the fruitfulness and dominion that are our work in this world. Only in a world in which we have known, even if we have also forgotten, that male and female flesh are "very good" could Whitman tremble before the mystery of the human body, see that it "balks account," and name it "perfect."

The present world, every bit as much as Whitman's, denies the irreducible dignity of each human being again and again. Dignity is denied as human beings are bought and sold as though they were not miracles who bear the divine image but commodities. In this essay, I articulate the problem of the commodification of human beings and argue that resistance to that commodification is inherent in the doctrine of the image of God. I then look briefly at market language used for human beings in Scripture and suggest that those metaphors also subvert any attempt to turn humans into commodities. The

---

[1] Walt Whitman, "I Sing the Body Electric," *The Complete Poems* (New York: Penguin, 2005), 127-36.
[2] I am most persuaded by accounts of the human being as some kind of minimal duality, especially Thomas Aquinas's (for an excellent explanation, see Eleonore Stump, *Aquinas* [New York: Routledge, 2005], chap. 6, "Forms and Bodies: The Soul"). In such accounts, though, duality is not the point: the human in the image of God is always the whole human being. For a thorough look at the most relevant biblical passages, see John W. Cooper, *Body, Soul, and Life Everlasting: Biblical Anthropology and the Monism-Dualism Debate* (Grand Rapids: Eerdmans, 2000).

next, larger section of the chapter explores an example—from sexual ethics—of Christian resistance to reducing humans to commodities.

My thesis is that the doctrine of the human being in the image of God undoes the commodification of human bodies. By living in the freedom that is ours in Christ we can testify—can bear witness—to the goodness of a God to whom all human bodies are sacred. While debates about precisely what the *imago Dei* consists in or of are difficult to resolve, I am certain that Christian affirmation of the *imago* requires bearing witness. To be made in God's image is purposeful. We are to be faithful images of the God of love, images who can be touched and seen. The *imago Dei* calls us to show and tell, and resisting the reduction of persons to commodities is one of the most important areas in which Christians need to bear witness in this world.

IMAGE-BEARERS FOR SALE

One characteristic of sinners is that we take the fact of embodiment as license to treat human beings as market goods. Theologians Willie Jennings and Shawn Copeland, among others, have shown us the deep, heretical ways in which slavery broke and continues to damage our understanding of the human being. Jennings shows how white colonialism resulted in "an inverted, distorted vision of creation that reduced theological anthropology to commodified bodies."[3] Copeland insists that we not look away from the suffering bodies of black women under slavery, and that we reflect on how "the body of Jesus of Nazareth and the bodies of black women" together lay "bare both the human capacity for inhumanity and the divine capacity for love."[4] On this subject Whitman speaks again as poet-prophet, leading us into the hell that is the slave market:

> A man's body at auction,
> (For before the war I often go to the slave-mart and watch the sale,)
> I help the auctioneer, the sloven does not half know his business.
> Gentlemen look on this wonder,
> Whatever the bids of the bidders they cannot be high enough for it,

---

[3]Willie James Jennings, *The Christian Imagination: Theology and the Origins of Race* (New Haven: Yale University Press, 2011), 58.
[4]M. Shawn Copeland, *Enfleshing Freedom: Body, Race, and Being* (Minneapolis: Fortress Press, 2009), 1.

For it the globe lay preparing quintillions of years without one animal or plant,
For it the revolving cycles truly and steadily roll'd.
In this head the all-baffling brain,
In it and below it the makings of heroes.
Examine these limbs, red, black, or white, they are cunning in tendon and nerve,
They shall be stript that you may see them.
Exquisite senses, life-lit eyes, pluck, volition,
Flakes of breast-muscle, pliant backbone and neck, flesh not flabby, good-sized
     arms and legs,
And wonders within there yet.[5]

Whitman, in a catena of fleshly particularity, makes it clear that for "a man's body" to be "at auction" is incompatible with the "wonder" of the human being. And yet again Whitman speaks about the particularity of male and female flesh, evoking the good, embodied work of fruitfulness and of dominion:

A woman's body at auction,
She too is not only herself, she is the teeming mother of mothers,
She is the bearer of them that shall grow and be mates to the mothers.
Have you ever loved the body of a woman?
Have you ever loved the body of a man?
Do you not see that these are exactly the same to all in all nations and times all
     over the earth?
If any thing is sacred the human body is sacred.[6]

Slavery is not a thing of the past. The brutal facts of race slavery in the United States continue to shape the way we see bodies in the present. We live today in a world where human beings are trafficked, a world where persons, created in the image of God, are bought and sold. Statistics that must be dug out of a shadowed world of crime are difficult to ascertain, but there is no doubt that huge numbers of image-bearers are bought and sold in the world today. A 2004 approximation suggested that "some 600,000 to 800,000 people were victims of trafficking worldwide, of which 80 percent were female, 50 percent were minors, and 70 percent were trafficked for sexual exploitation."[7]

---

[5]Whitman, "I Sing the Body Electric."
[6]Ibid.
[7]Louise Shelley, *Human Trafficking: A Global Perspective* (Cambridge: Cambridge University Press, 2010), 5.

Horrifying in their immensity, those numbers are probably far too low, and a 2006 estimate from the International Labor Organization indicates there are 12.3 million people in slavery worldwide.[8] A sinful world is a world in which human trafficking flourishes, facilitated by many factors including large numbers of migrating people, inequalities and globalization.

Those who would turn image-bearers into market goods are encouraged by "low start-costs, minimal risks, high profits, and large demand. For organized crime groups, human beings have one added advantage over drugs: they can be sold repeatedly."[9] Trafficking is fed by our failures to dignify all flesh as human flesh, all human beings as image-bearers. Gender as a risk factor in being trafficked is just one example, as the "greatest likelihood of trafficking occurs where women and girls are denied property rights, access to education, economic rights, and participation in the political process."[10]

When sinners target some people for exploitation and commodification, no people escape the logic that would turn human beings into chattel. The same logic that allows for the defiling of some human beings in the slave market allows for the defiling of all human beings in all kinds of markets. That logic would take each body, including the most privileged bodies, and treat it as a commodity to be prepared for sale to the highest bidder. In Copeland's reflections on the development of race-based slavery, she says, "Since the radical and expedient subjugation of a people to demonized difference in the fifteenth century, *all* human bodies have been caught up in a near totalizing web of body commerce, body exchange, body value."[11] While the slave market is far more horrific than the market that encourages Americans to purchase their identities by buying brand-name products,[12] both markets depend on a reduction of persons to commodities. Both markets assume that humans are not of intrinsic worth but are worth what someone else pays for them or what they can pay to create their own identities.

There are endless ways bodies can be turned into commodities. Marketers offer thongs and push-up bras, even to children, suggesting that the point of

---

[8]Ibid., 5.
[9]Ibid., 3.
[10]Ibid., 16.
[11]Copeland, *Enfleshing Freedom*, 2.
[12]Even here, though, the difference between the markets is not simple. Do slaves make the clothes that make the girl?

bodies is to create market demand for undergarments, that image-bearers need to be dressed up and sexualized in order to have worth. Pornography so saturates the Internet that stumbling upon it has become an inevitable part of a person's life cycle, and many become addicted to it. The industries of pornography and human trafficking are closely linked with each other and with prostitution. The advertising industry uses sex to sell almost everything (cars, beer, clothes, technology), making the implicit claim that bodies are for sale or require upgrading via market goods in order to demand a good price. All are marketed with the message that to buy the product is to gain access to sex. Purveyors of self-help advice encourage people to use their bodies as currency in relationships, to withhold or offer sex to get what they want.

Happily, the Christian theological tradition has plenty to say about what it means to be human, about markets for bodies and about the market more generally. As theologian Stephen Long has reminded us, "faith and economic matters are inextricably linked." Long knows, though, that to maintain that link requires "considerable" theological effort "because it works against the historical development of modern economics."[13] It also works against the lucrative nature of the slave market and the many other markets in which bodies are bought and sold. My next step is to identify, within the doctrine of the image of God, features that will help us to oppose the commodification of human beings.

THE *IMAGO* RESISTS COMMODIFICATION

The practice of marketing bodies for public consumption plays on a demonic inversion of the universality and particularity inherent in the doctrine of the *imago*. The radical inclusivity of the *imago* resists commodification, testifying that every human is fully human and ought not to be bought or sold. Against that Christian affirmation of universal worth, the insistent press of commodification warps universality in an effort to include all bodies in the market. Twisted universality insists that every body should be for sale. The doctrine of the *imago* teaches respect for particularity, treasuring the fact that fleshly difference is God's good creation and protecting and valuing the particularity of each human. Against such an appreciation

---

[13]D. Stephen Long, *Divine Economy: Theology and the Market* (New York: Routledge, 2000), 9.

of all life in particularity, the logic of commodification warps particularity and diversity and uses them as market tools by claiming that particular bodies are more valuable than others.

So much depends on the fact that all humankind is created in the image of God: that the *imago* includes both maleness and femaleness, that it is not just the king or the lords[14] who are in the *imago* but everyone. The same God who longs for all without exception to come into right relationship with him also created all without exception in the divine image. So universality is a clear link between creation and consummation, between theological anthropology and soteriology. "The Lord," Peter assures us, "is not slow about his promise, as some think of slowness, but is patient with you, not wanting any to perish, but all to come to repentance" (2 Pet 3:9). The universality of image-bearing demands the universal dignity of the human being.[15] We sinners, who would exclude some from the dignity and protection that is theirs as image-bearers, are not excluded from the gospel healing that would allow us to resist the commodification of human beings. In the words of Charles Wesley, all are invited

> to the gospel feast;
> let every soul be Jesus' guest.
> Ye need not one be left behind,
> For God hath bid all humankind.[16]

The universality of creation in the divine image is matched by the universality of the offer of salvation, and both recognize the divine desire for all human beings.

The fact that we are embodied images also demands that we celebrate the particularity of the *imago* in real, historical, diverse flesh. Though the *imago* is universally the truth about human beings, the *imago* is not instantiated in

---

[14]See chapter 1 of this book for Catherine McDowell's comparison between Israel's ancient Near Eastern neighbors, among whom it was often only the king who was seen as God's representative, and Israel, for whom every human being is created in the divine image.

[15]There seems to be a trend in recent theology of growing impatience with the suggestion that dignity and rights are not theological concepts. Sarah Coakley rightly dismisses this position as one that is possible only from a position of privilege. *God, Sexuality, and the Self: An Essay 'On the Trinity'* (Cambridge: Cambridge University Press, 2013).

[16]Charles Wesley, "Come, Sinners, to the Gospel Feast," in *The United Methodist Hymnal* (Nashville: United Methodist Publishing House, 1989), no. 616.

some generic version of the human being but in particular bodies. Dan Harmon's comedy series *Community*, for example, pokes fun at the notion of a generic human being when the show's community college creates, as its new mascot, the Greendale Human Being. The dean of the college preaches, "Our symbol needs to reflect the diversity of our school and of our species. . . . We are the Greendale human beings. . . . We are developing the perfect mascot." With "no stereotypical identifiers from any race or gender," it is an "ethnically neutral mascot." The mascot is a person wrapped in a head-to-toe, ghostly white jumpsuit, with a crude face drawn in black marker. The mascot is a disaster because to strip the human being of particulars is to strip her of her humanness. Universally, the image of God is embodied in the particularities of diverse flesh.

The nature of the *imago* as both universal and particular means that it contains built-in resistance to the commodification of human bodies. All Christians—universally and particularly—are called to witness to that resistance by rejoicing in the freedom of our bodies from the market and by rebelling wherever that liberty is denied.

THE BIBLE AND MARKET METAPHORS

Scripture teaches that human beings are persons and not market goods, and it does so through direct and indirect critique of markets for human beings. The following examples show how Scripture claims (and so subverts) market metaphors in a way that makes it clear that humans are free from the market.

Amos acts as a prophet of the *imago Dei* when he denounces those who would buy "the poor for silver and the needy for a pair of sandals" (Amos 8:6). Old Testament law challenges the idea that human beings can be bought and sold. Though slavery was the economic safety net of the ancient world, the Mosaic law nonetheless included the unique injunction that a member of the family could never fully be a slave. Israelites were prohibited from reducing another Israelite to full slave status:

> If any who are dependent on you become so impoverished that they sell themselves to you, you shall not make them serve as slaves. They shall remain with you as hired or bound laborers. They shall serve with you until the year of the jubilee. Then they and their children with them shall be free from your authority; they shall go back to their own family and return to their ancestral property. For they are my servants,

whom I brought out of the land of Egypt; they shall not be sold as slaves are sold. You shall not rule over them with harshness, but shall fear your God. (Lev 25:39-43)

As Catherine McDowell has shown earlier in this volume,[17] once we realize that the universality of the *imago* implies the universality of human kinship, this law protecting fellow Israelites from being reduced to commodities must be extended to apply to all human beings.[18]

Moving to the New Testament, we discover a connection between Jesus' resistance to money changers in the temple and the fact that Christians are temples of the Holy Spirit. The Spirit who makes our bodies a temple (1 Cor 6:19) is the same Spirit who points to the one who "entered the temple and drove out all who were selling and buying in the temple, and he overturned the tables of the money changers and the seats of those who sold doves. He said to them, 'It is written, "My house shall be called a house of prayer"; but you are making it a den of robbers'" (Mt 21:12-13). The temple status of our image-bearing bodies precludes the buying and selling of those bodies. The Jesus who would drive out those dehumanizing buyers and sellers of image-bearers is the Jesus who sent us the Spirit who indwells us, making it clear that we are not our own.

Scripture subverts the market for human beings by using market metaphors to make it clear that there can be no more buying and selling of human beings. We were "bought with a price" and are therefore to "glorify God" in our bodies (1 Cor 6:20). By making it clear that humans have already been "obtained with the blood of [God's] own Son" (Acts 20:28), Scripture takes human beings off the market entirely. In taking humans off the market, God opens up the possibility that we might become holy witnesses—sanctified, embodied representatives of the kind of freedom (including freedom from the market) that only comes from Christ. We can witness to that freedom with the confidence of those who, as Peter says, "know that you were ransomed from the futile ways inherited from your ancestors, not with perishable things like silver or gold, but with the precious blood of Christ, like that of a lamb without defect or blemish" (1 Pet 1:18-19). There are many ways that we can so witness, including through habits of buying and selling,[19] budgets that reflect

---

[17]See chapter 1.

[18]Raymond Westbrook and Bruce Wells, *Everyday Law in Biblical Israel: An Introduction* (Louisville: Westminster John Knox, 2009).

[19]For example, Made in a Free World is an organization seeking to empower consumers to buy goods

godly priorities, and resistance to racial, gender and economic injustice. The rest of this chapter develops one such example.

AN EXAMPLE FROM SEXUAL ETHICS

I want to develop an extended example of Christian resistance to the commodification of human bodies in the area of sexual ethics.[20] One embodied outworking of the basic insight that human beings are not commodities may be found in traditional Christian resistance to *porneia* (usually translated "fornication" in English Bibles) and contemporary Christian resistance to pornography. Both the biblical category *porneia* and the contemporary category "pornography" take a good created gift—sexuality—and transfer it from the context of personal relationship to the context of the market. Because human beings are image-bearers, Christian sexual ethics opposes any sex that is bought and sold. In this, Christian sexual ethics is and always has been profoundly countercultural.

Historian Kyle Harper demonstrates the countercultural nature of early Christian sexual ethics in the context of the ancient Roman Empire, an understanding that helps us see how and why Christian sexual ethics should continue to look countercultural today. Harper traces the process by which Christian sexual morality replaced—or tried to replace—the sexual morality of the Roman Empire, and his analysis reveals that Christian sexual ethics rejected the market for bodies in favor of freedom in Christ.

Every culture has a system of sexual ethics, a way of policing proscribed sexual activity and legitimizing sex the society considers licit. In ancient Rome, sexual morality supported the interests of the state. It protected the masculinity and authority of men with power. In that context, the word *porneia*—the same word the New Testament uses for sexual sin—referred to prostitution. *Porneia* referred to commercial sex and those people, men and women, whose business it was to sell it.

Roman sexual morality divided women into two categories: honorable and shameful. The bodies of wives were protected, and the bodies of prostitutes were available for anyone's use. For honorable women, sexual morality

---

made without slave labor (https://madeinafreeworld.com).
[20]The example of sexuality used here appears in different form in my book *Faithful: A Theology of Sex* (Grand Rapids: Zondervan, 2015).

meant making it clear that their husbands were the fathers of their children. So, honorable female sexual morality required girls to be virgins when they married and avoid adultery or any appearance thereof after marriage. Society policed their sexual honor. "Ancient women," Harper tells us, "lived every moment engaged in a high-stakes game of suspicious observation."[21] Husbands controlled their wives' bodies, and wives were for having babies. In a world in which no woman could think of childbirth without fear of death, it was a free woman's job to produce babies for the state. Rome needed citizens and soldiers.

For free Roman men, sexual morality was more complicated. The cultural imagination did not include chastity for them, though they were expected to engage in moderation in order to demonstrate self-control. Even so, most recognized that moderation was unlikely in the years between puberty and marriage. Male sexual morality also required adherence to rules that made it clear that the free Roman man was always in power.

The system of Roman sexual morality for free persons depended on the existence of people for whom honorable sexual status was impossible: slaves. Harper shows how "the sex industry was integral to the moral economy of the classical world."[22] Slaves were everywhere, and therefore free Roman men had constant access to sex. This was seen as a social good, which kept young men from threatening the bodies of other men's wives. Harper tells us that "commodification of sex was carried out with all the ruthless efficiency of an industrial operation, the unfree body bearing the pressures of insatiable market demand. . . . The wealthy had slaves to serve their needs. . . . Prostitution was the poor man's piece of the slave system."[23]

Christian sexual ethics challenged this world in a "coordinated assault on the extramarital sexual economy." According to Harper, this "marks one of the more consequential revolutions in the history of sex. . . . Christian sexual culture required new conceptions of moral agency."[24] An understanding of the human being as a creature with free will grew up around Christian sexual morality. Roman sexual morality was about class and gender. For the privileged,

---

[21]Kyle Harper, *From Shame to Sin: The Christian Transformation of Sexual Morality in Late Antiquity* (Cambridge, MA: Harvard University Press, 2013), 41.
[22]Ibid., 3.
[23]Ibid., 49.
[24]Ibid., 3.

morality required chastity for women and unwavering power and control for men. For slaves, Roman sexual morality—being honorable—was not an option: dishonor was their fate.

Today, to benefit consumer capitalism, bodies are turned into commodities as relentlessly as they were in Rome. Sex is for sale in obvious and subtle ways. There is a sense in which modern culture asks its citizens to be temple prostitutes, wanting bodies to be about *porneia*—and the commodification that goes with it—instead of about bearing witness to the God who has created us in the divine image and is shaping us into Christlike images of God's goodness in the world. But the promise of free sex turns out not to be free after all.

In ancient Rome, the idea that all human beings are free creatures made in the divine image and are meant for freedom in Christ was one of the strangest things about Christian sexual ethics. Christian bodies were no longer for the state or for powerful men. They did not belong to the pornography industry or the beauty industry. Bodies were for the Lord. Christians were free to witness and to love. They were free to marry or not to marry, to have babies or not to have babies, because the future of the world depends on Jesus, not on the size of the Roman army. "The body is meant not for *porneia* but for the Lord" (1 Cor 6:13). God redeems what we have forfeited. God makes the broken whole.

Christian sexual ethics recognizes marriage as the appropriate context for sexual expression because in marriage there is—or ought to be—no specter of compulsion, of bodies being bought and sold, and because marriage is a covenant—a context in which coequal image-bearers can offer their bodies to one another, not for a price, but as gift. The Song of Songs gives us a biblical portrait of this sort of context, of marriage as a place for delight in the loved one that is possible because of friendship and mutuality. In marriage, delight in the loved one's body should be free, happy and secure because in marriage the lovers no longer have to try desperately to meet an unmet need. Imagine a way of living in which people claim freedom from grasping after self-satisfaction because they are secure in God. Imagine resting in God's faithfulness in a way that relativizes human love and so sets that human love free from the economy of sin. The Song helps us to imagine that world, where the lover sings:

His speech is most sweet,
and he is altogether desirable.
This is my beloved and this is my friend,
O daughters of Jerusalem. (Song 5:16)

In God's redeeming power, Christian marriage may be a garden of delights where sex is freely given and freely received, where there is no price on bodies because Jesus Christ has already paid the price in full. Again, knowing we have been "bought with a price," we are set free to "glorify God" (1 Cor 6:20). When all is grace, we can rest in love—both human and divine. In God's redeeming power, hearts that were captive to sin are loosed from their chains. In God's redeeming power, our very bodies become temples of God the Holy Spirit (1 Cor 6:19), and God gifts us with the power to resist exploitation. God gives us the power to relinquish the kind of sex that would use the other for our own purposes and to delight in the spouse who is both beloved and friend.[25]

Early Christianity, in rebelling against Roman sexual morality, was bold enough to imagine that all have—in Christ—the freedom to bear witness to who God is. In Rome, only some people get protection and honor; in the kingdom, everybody's body is honored. In Rome, bodies are for power or pleasure or the state or the market; in the kingdom, bodies are for the Lord. In Rome, sexual morality sets forth very different rules for men and women; in the kingdom, we are universally called to be chaste. In Rome, those marked as sexually shameful had no route to honorability; in the kingdom, there is forgiveness and healing and grace and freedom. In Rome, humans are either slave or free; in the kingdom, all are free. Because sexuality is a sign of God's grace, it can never be commodified. It can never be wrenched out of the framework of free, mutual, consensual relationship and placed on the market floor.

This is at least part of the meaning of the one-flesh union of Genesis. Jesus returns to Genesis, and to God's good creative intentions for humans, when some Pharisees come to test him, asking, "Is it lawful for a man to divorce his wife?" (Mk 10:2). Behind their question was a debate about the interpretation of a passage in Deuteronomy: "Suppose a man enters into marriage with a

---

[25]Christian sexual ethics does not, of course, require marriage. We are also set free, in Christ, to be faithful in singleness. Such faithful Christian singleness is another way of witnessing, through sexual ethics, to the freedom of image-bearers. See my *Faithful*, especially chapter 5, "Radical Faithfulness," and chapter 7, "Thriving."

woman, but she does not please him because he finds something objectionable about her, and so he writes her a certificate of divorce, puts it in her hand, and sends her out of his house; she then leaves his house" (Deut 24:1). The debate centered on what constituted legitimate grounds for divorce. What was the "something objectionable" about his wife that would make a husband's desire for divorce reasonable? The rabbinic school of Hillel argued that Deuteronomy legitimates divorce if anything about a wife displeased her husband. The school of Shammai taught that "something objectionable" could only mean sexual immorality, and regarded divorce for other reasons as illicit. So when the Pharisees brought their question to Jesus, they wanted to know if he stood with the permissive camp or the rigorist camp.

Jesus explained the passage in Deuteronomy not as legitimating divorce, but as a concession to human "hardness of heart" (Mk 10:5). Then he asked his hearers to think about God's good intentions for marriage: "From the beginning of creation, 'God made them male and female.' 'For this reason a man shall leave his father and mother and be joined to his wife, and the two shall become one flesh.' So they are no longer two, but one flesh. Therefore what God has joined together, let no one separate" (Mk 10:6-9). He told his disciples, "Whoever divorces his wife and marries another commits adultery against her; and if she divorces her husband and marries another, she commits adultery" (Mk 10:11-12).

This is revolutionary. People assumed adultery was a crime against a man's property: his woman. Men were not thought capable of adultery. Women's bodies were property, and as such they alone could be stolen or damaged by others. Jesus—by making it clear that *men*, too, can be adulterers—challenges the whole market economy that would buy and sell bodies, especially women's bodies. Adultery is not a property crime. Adultery is a violation of God's intentions for humanity as image-bearers.

Christian sexual ethics are not just for women. They expect holiness, purity and chastity from men, too. While Christianity was born in a world of stunning "indifference toward male chastity,"[26] Jesus expected chastity of all of us. Jesus radically equalizes the man and the woman in the one-flesh union. Both are persons in the mutual, consensual, covenantal freedom of that union. Either may violate it. Neither body is a piece of goods to be traded. Both bodies—

---

[26]Jones, *Faithful*, 52.

united—should testify, in their union, to the faithfulness of God. When we embody our witness to the truth that bodies are not commodities, we bear witness to the freedom that is in Christ and to the faithfulness Jesus shows to the Father and to us.

Under the condition of sin, many—maybe most—people and cultures have treated female bodies as commodities, as property, as chattel. But God's good revelation challenges the status quo again and again. The biblical concept of the *imago Dei* insists that all humans are fully human and created in the image of God. Scripture dignifies singleness and marriage. Both Christian singleness and Christian marriage refuse sex that is bought or sold. In chaste singleness, Christians commit sexual identity to God alone. In chaste marriage, sex is about mutual, personal, consensual, covenantal relationship.

We witness against the commodification of human beings when we teach the gospel of grace. Human relationships, including sexual ones (especially sexual ones, in that sex involves such complete and vulnerable mutual self-giving), ought to be testaments to grace. Sexual love cannot depend on the partner meeting this or that condition. Sexual love cannot be purchased or coerced. If sex is to reflect something about the unconditional love the Creator has for us, if sex is to reflect something about the free grace of relationship with God, then it, too, needs to happen in freedom. The marriage bed—a place of equality, mutuality, delight, covenant love and consent—is the context for that kind of freedom. And so, in Christian sexual ethics we see a powerful witness to the God who frees us from the market for bodies, who loves every particular body with a universal love.

CONCLUSION: WITNESSING IN FREEDOM

To be a bearer of the image of Christ our Lord is to be free from the logic of the market and to have opened up the possibility that our lives might mean something good and beautiful by testifying truly to who God is. We become those who can "glorify God" in our bodies (1 Cor 6:20). John Donne wrote:

> To'our bodies turn we then, that so
> > Weak men on love reveal'd may look;
> Love's mysteries in souls do grow,
> > But yet the body is his book.[27]

---

[27]John Donne, *The Complete English Poems* (London: Penguin, 1977), 55.

The body, Donne sings, is love's book. The faithful body can be a revelation of the God who is love. The faithful body tells a story of God whose love is steadfast, of God who desires his people, of God who reaches out to us, asking that we reach back in a real relationship of true mutuality. When we embody freedom from the logic of the market, we speak to a world in need of the God who is love.

Paul is clear that we, in Christ, are "washed" and "sanctified" (1 Cor 6:11). The meaning of our bodies rests in our relationship with the Father through Jesus in the Spirit. We are "members of Christ" (1 Cor 6:15) and "temple[s] of the Holy Spirit" (1 Cor 6:19). These are cosmic, theological claims. The promise of future resurrection means God gives us the grace, now, for our bodies to mean what they are supposed to mean.

God gives grace for Jesus to be made visible in our flesh. Our flesh is for mission, for witness, for giving glory to the God who saves. Christians are called to embody our freedom from the market and to witness to Christ by living out the truth that Christ has set us free. The fallen world wants to craft the body into something to be consumed. Christianity insists instead that the body is meant to be a witness, and image-bearers are creatures who have the freedom to witness in faithfulness. We are free from the logic of the market, free from the reign of sin and even from fear of death, and freed to tell the truth, with our bodies, about what Christ is like.

Theologian John Behr, after calling Jesus "the first true human being in history,"[28] speaks of the way that—in being set free from fear of death by the promise of resurrection—we are free even to die, to be witnesses—martyrs— testifying to what Christ has done. "In and through Christ," says Behr, "we now have the possibility of freely using the givenness of our mortality to be reborn, by choice, so coming to be in a life without end. Only now does freedom—not necessity—become the basis for a truly human existence in Christ."[29] Again:

> In order to be a true human being in the image of God, who is Christ the true human being, we must be born into a new existence in Christ by a birth effected through our voluntary use of our mortality—as an act of sacrifice through

---

[28]John Behr, *Becoming Human: Meditations on Christian Anthropology in Word and Image* (Crestwood, NY: St. Vladimir's Seminary Press, 2013), 35.
[29]Ibid., 53.

baptism—thereby freely choosing to exist as a human being and grounding that being and existence in an act of freedom, so living the same life of love that God himself is.[30]

I will give Whitman the last word in this essay, as his words continue to point to the givenness of bodies and the living of embodied life together as a denial of the false promises of the flesh market:

> O my body! I dare not desert the likes of you in other men and women, nor the likes of the parts of you,
>
> I believe the likes of you are to stand or fall with the likes of the soul (and that they are the soul).[31]

[30]Ibid., 65.
[31]Whitman, "I Sing the Body Electric."

12

THE STORM OF IMAGES

The Image of God in Global Faith

Philip Jenkins

Every image is a revelation and representation of something hidden. For instance, man has not a clear knowledge of what is invisible, the spirit being veiled to the body, nor of future things, nor of things apart and distant, because he is circumscribed by place and time. The image was devised for greater knowledge, and for the manifestation and popularizing of secret things, as a pure benefit and help to spiritual health, so that by showing things and making them known, we may arrive at the hidden ones, desire and emulate what is good, shun and hate what is evil.

ST. JOHN OF DAMASCUS, *APOLOGIA OF ST. JOHN DAMASCENE AGAINST THOSE WHO DECRY HOLY IMAGES*

INTRODUCTION

Dare I begin by pointing to a paradox in the Great Commission itself? Jesus told his followers to preach the gospel to all nations, and implicit in that gospel is the message that human beings are formed in God's image. Yet, every Christian who bears that message carries a sense of what that image is that might well not be the same as that of the listener. This is especially true when the gospel is carried from one culture to another on the other side of the world. How shall we preach the Lord's image in a strange land?

The story of this encounter is as old as Christianity itself, but the issues involved are acute in our day. Since the mid-twentieth century, Christianity's center of gravity has moved decisively southward away from its former heartlands in Europe and North America. By 2050 or so, in numerical terms, the faith will be concentrated in Africa, Asia and Latin America. That shift would be important enough if it were merely geographical, but of course it is not. The newer faces of Christianity are developing in regions with very different cultural patterns, not rooted in familiar Euro-American assumptions about faith.[1]

These newer churches have very different, even revolutionary, concepts of the image of God. These new images are likely to have a positive political and cultural impact, transforming social arrangements that have proved stubbornly resistant to other kinds of intervention. Having said that, we should on occasion be cautious about how newer churches imagine God, just as we should be cautious with their Northern-world counterparts. Sometimes those images can be seductively deceptive. Distinguishing between images and idols, between accommodation and syncretism, can be a daunting task.

FOUR STORIES OF BORDER CROSSING

Although this global dimension is transforming concepts of the image of God, such a process of transformation is anything but new. Through Christian history, concepts of the image have changed over time, and only partly through the logic of Christian theologians and critical scholars. Christians have always found themselves on the frontiers of other faiths, whether literally or figuratively. Encounters on those borderlands reshape faith, and this reshaped faith makes its way back to the church's core. If we do not immediately recognize examples of such a drift from the margins of faith to the center, it is because the ideas are now so mainstream that it is incredible to think they would ever have been viewed as odd or deviant. Innovations from the fringe become normal.

To illustrate this theme, I will tell four unrelated stories—those of the Nestorian stone, iconoclasm, the *filioque* and adoptionism—that affected very

---

[1]For further discussion on Christianity's global shift, see Allan Heaton Anderson, "The Dynamics of Global Pentecostalism: Origins, Motivation and Future," in *Spirit of God: Christian Renewal in the Community of Faith*, ed. Jeffrey W. Barbeau and Beth Felker Jones (Downers Grove, IL: InterVarsity Press, 2015), 110-27.

different parts of the Christian church in the late eighth century. Theoretically, one very well-traveled person might have participated in all four of these events and their attendant debates.

The Nestorian stone. For much of the Early Middle Ages, the Church of the East sent missionaries across Central and Eastern Asia. As a result of these activities, the learned scholars of that church interacted with adherents of different faiths, including Buddhists, Manichaeans, Jews and Muslims. They adjusted their message as a means to disseminate the faith among new peoples, but those influences could not fail to change those Christians themselves. Lamin Sanneh has famously remarked that the original language of Christianity is translation.[2] Perhaps the original dialect of Christian theology is border crossing.

From a vast theological literature, we might look at one evocative symbol: the memorial stone on which the heads of the church in China recorded the history of their congregations in 781. The inscription began with a summary of salvation history that was so Chinese in form that its discoverers believed they were dealing with a Taoist or Buddhist text:

> Behold the unchangeably true and invisible, who existed through all eternity without origin; the far-seeing perfect intelligence, whose mysterious existence is everlasting; operating on primordial substance he created the universe, being more excellent than all holy intelligences, inasmuch as he is the source of all that is honorable. This is our eternal true lord God, triune and mysterious in substance. . . . Having perfected all inferior objects, he then made the first man; upon him he bestowed an excellent disposition, giving him in charge the government of all created beings; man, acting out the original principles of his nature, was pure and unostentatious; his unsullied and expansive mind was free from the least inordinate desire; until Satan introduced the seeds of falsehood, to deteriorate his purity of principle; the opening thus commenced in his virtue gradually enlarged, and by this crevice in his nature was obscured and rendered vicious.[3]

The fact that I am using a century-old translation may make that language sound more stereotypically Chinese than it deserves to be, but throughout it

---

[2]Lamin Sanneh, *Whose Religion Is Christianity? The Gospel Beyond the West* (Grand Rapids: Eerdmans, 2003).

[3]The text of the monument is easily available, but it is conveniently accessible via the East Asian History Sourcebook at www.nestorian.org/east_asian_history_sourcebook-_nestorian_tablet_.html.

makes free use of native terms and idioms. Across Asia, the church used, as its distinctive symbol, the lotus-cross.

Iconoclasm. Besides Asian religions, Christians interacted with Islam, with its particular views of the divine nature and of God's relationship with the world. From the seventh century, Muslim forces ruled most of the historic Christian heartland in the Middle East. As easily as we forget it in the West, through most of Christian history the normal political situation for a sizable share of the world's Christians has been as part of a subjugated minority, or even majority, population.

Christian interaction with Islamic thought also had an influence on Christian theology, and especially on the concept of the image, the Greek icon. Seeking to reject Islamic charges that Christians indulged in idolatry, the Roman Empire and its church condemned human-made images, and this iconoclastic movement prevailed from the 720s to the 780s. Countless paintings and figurative works were destroyed throughout the empire in what has variously been termed the Icon-Struggle (*eikonomachia*) or, more intriguingly, the Byzantine Reformation. Such visual works were only safe for Christians living under the more tolerant rule of the Islamic caliphs. In 754, an iconoclastic council met at Hiereia outside Constantinople and stated precisely how the image of God could and could not be represented:

> We found that the unlawful art of painting living creatures blasphemes the fundamental doctrine of our salvation—namely, the Incarnation of Christ, and contradicted the six holy synods. . . . If anyone shall endeavor to represent the forms of the saints in lifeless pictures with material colors which are of no value (for this notion is vain and introduced by the devil), and does not rather represent their virtues as living images in himself, etc. . . . let him be anathema.[4]

Human beings alone were to serve as the divine image, the true icon.

But John of Damascus continued to assert the case for images. He could do this because he was based under a Muslim regime that did not care about internal Christian struggles. His work *On Holy Images* remains one of the great Christian explorations of art, and a justification for that art:

---

[4]"The Definition of the Holy, Great, and Ecumenical Seventh Synod," in *The Seven Ecumenical Councils*, ed. P. Schaff and H. Wace, trans. H. R. Percival, vol. 14 of Nicene and Post-Nicene Fathers, 2nd Series (Grand Rapids: Eerdmans, 1955), 543-44.

Of old, God the incorporeal and uncircumscribed was never depicted. Now, however, when God is seen clothed in flesh, and conversing with men, I make an image of the God whom I see. I do not worship matter, I worship the God of matter, who became matter for my sake, and deigned to inhabit matter, who worked out my salvation through matter. I will not cease from honoring that matter which works my salvation. I venerate it, though not as God. How could God be born out of lifeless things? . . . I honor all matter besides, and venerate it. Through it, filled, as it were, with a divine power and grace my salvation has come to me. Was not the thrice happy and thrice blessed wood of the Cross matter? Was not the sacred and holy mountain of Calvary matter? What of the life-giving rock, the Holy Sepulchre, the source of our resurrection: was it not matter? Is not the most holy book of the Gospels matter? Is not the blessed table matter which gives us the Bread of Life? Are not the gold and silver matter, out of which crosses and altar-plate and chalices are made? And before all these things, is not the body and blood of our Lord matter? Either do away with the veneration and worship due to all these things, or submit to the tradition of the Church in the worship of images, honoring God and His friends, and following in this the grace of the Holy Spirit.[5]

It was John who made famous the critical distinction between worship (*latreia*)—reserved for God alone—and mere veneration (*proskynēsis*).

Icon veneration gained ascendancy again in the 780s. This was the era in which Christians in China were framing their theology in suitably Chinese terms. These Christians believed that the rejection of material imagery was heretical in itself, and as they reasserted their beliefs, they made icons a fundamental component of Orthodox thought and belief. The Second Council of Nicaea reasserted the legitimacy of icons in 787. A second wave of iconoclasm occurred in the first half of the ninth century, but orthodoxy soon reasserted itself.

Filioque. Those violent Eastern debates had their impact in the West, not least in persuading the Frankish kings that the East was scarcely to be trusted in matters of orthodoxy. That distrust of the East contributed to ideas of Western independence and ultimately of empire. Meanwhile, those Western churches reframed their own notions of the divine image as they confronted their own non-Christian adversaries and new converts.

To take one example, a majority of Christians around the world regularly recite a version of the Nicene Creed that proclaims belief "in the Holy Spirit,

---

[5]John of Damascus, *On Holy Images*, trans. Mary H. Allies (London: Thomas Baker, 1898), 10-17.

the Lord and Giver of Life, who proceeds from the Father *and the Son.*" The phrase "and the Son" (Latin *filioque*) is not part of the original text and is condemned by the Eastern Orthodox churches. The *filioque* originated in the distant borderlands of Christianity as it existed in the sixth and seventh centuries, as Catholics in Spain and Gaul confronted issues unfamiliar to the mainstream church of the day, which was centered in Constantinople. As they encountered Arians, who rejected the equality of Father and Son, local Catholics wanted to assert the dignity of Christ. They did so by taking what seems like a breathtakingly bold step: they altered the quasi-sacred text of the creed in order to reflect local needs and realities.[6]

By the eighth century, the *filioque* had spread across Western Europe, and Charlemagne and his heirs popularized it as part of their campaign to spread Christianity throughout the Germanic world. It was only in the eleventh century, though, that this border practice was accepted by the papacy. By that time, the *filioque* had become a proud symbol of the emerging Western church and an assertion of its distinctiveness from the ever more distant—and, arguably, heretical—church of the Eastern empire.

Adoptionism. A fourth example of how theology adjusted to cope with surrounding realities arose in Spain. At the end of the eighth century, Spain was a predominantly Christian country in terms of population, but most of the territory had been under Muslim rule for some three generations. By that point, Christians must have realized that the Islamic presence was no passing occupation, nor were the occupiers mere barbarians. The Umayyad Emirate of Córdoba dates from 756, and 786 marked the beginning of the legendary Grand Mosque in that city. Spain at this time was the scene of intense three-sided debates between Christians, Jews and Muslims. Christians found themselves increasingly on the defensive, especially over such distinctive claims as the triune nature of God and the incarnation of the Son.

In the last quarter of the century, Spain evolved what has been termed their adoptionist Christology. Despite the name, this was much more nuanced than the adoptionism of antiquity, which held that Christ's divine nature descended on the man Jesus and left him at the crucifixion. The pioneer of adoptionist Christology in Spain was Elipandus, who held the

---

[6]There is an excellent summary of the *filioque* debate in the *Catholic Encyclopedia*, at www.newadvent .org/cathen/06073a.htm.

sensitive position of bishop in Muslim-controlled Toledo. He taught that, at least in his human nature, Christ was the adoptive Son of God. The roots of this idea remain controversial, and perhaps it draws somewhat on older Nestorian thought, but in any case the theory had a special appeal for Christian thinkers confronting Muslim theologians. Their context made it attractive not to have to maintain the strictest Chalcedonian doctrines regarding the incarnation.

In practice, Spanish adoptionism seemed to diminish Christ's role as precise image of God in both flesh and spirit. By the 790s, Carolingian councils were condemning the doctrine as heresy, and the Council of Frankfurt in 794 effectively ended the movement, at least outside Spain. We must wonder whether imperial authorities would have responded so furiously to what seems a technical deviation from orthodoxy if they were not concerned about far more sweeping concessions to Islamic pressures.

LOCAL AND UNIVERSAL

These cases show the power of local circumstances and constraints in forming belief, most evidently in the case of the *filioque*. A vigorous emerging church formulates its beliefs, and even its basic theology, according to immediate local needs and pressures rather than waiting for the approval of venerable but distant mentors. What the "mainstream" church thinks is not terribly important for these churches, and "mainstream" is a designation that changes anyway. Over time, those innovations begin to seem so obvious that most people are unaware that things were ever different.

Every Christian society has been influenced by secular realities to some extent in shaping its sense of the divine image. The Western and European church was no more guilty of this than any other. To take one potent example, modern Western interpretations of the atonement—both Catholic and Protestant—owe much to the medieval writings of Anselm of Canterbury.[7] For Anselm, human sins were like grievous offenses committed against a great lord, debts that required a ransom or restitution of great price. In Christianity, this took the form of the death of God's Son. Although Eastern Orthodox

---

[7]Adapted from my book *The Next Christendom: The Coming of Global Christianity* (New York: Oxford University Press, 2011), 7. Anselm proposed his satisfaction theory of the atonement in his dialogue *Cur Deus Homo?*, trans. Sidney Norton Deane (Chicago: Open Court, 1903).

theologians rejected this theory as overly legalistic, it made excellent sense to a Western society that was deeply sensitive to questions of honor, fealty, seigniorial rights and acknowledging the proper claims of lordship. The biblical Lord became a feudal lord. European Christians reinterpreted the faith through their own concepts of social and gender relations, and then imagined that their culturally specific synthesis was the only correct version of Christian truth.

Today, that feudal interpretation might seem like an overly generous or even embarrassing concession to secular realities. But it was perhaps as appropriate for the time as the compromises that modern thinkers make, usually without recognizing they are doing so. If we know the cultural setting and the partners and rivals with whom the faith is in dialogue, then we can form a sense of how the image of God is perceived and, in turn, how that image is believed to be manifested in humanity. Tell me the needs, and I will tell you the theology.

IMAGES WORLDWIDE

In the modern West, at least over the past century, much theological debate has been shaped by dialogue with skepticism and rationalism. More recently, though, the dramatic shift toward the global South has opened many new questions, including some having to do with older debates that Western thinkers had thought long settled or irrelevant. Today we again see churches struggling to come to terms with the needs and pressures of a non-Christian society. In these modern instances, though, the outside society is not shaped by Christian or near-Christian influences and often draws from wholly different religious systems.

I first encountered the contemporary debate over Western and non-Western theologies from a somewhat odd source: the writings of Charles Williams. Williams was a brilliant writer on many topics, and some of his best work concerns images. For example, he famously described rival ways to God as the affirmation and denial of images.[8] This rather cloistered Anglican also wrote one of the best early explorations of reinterpreting theology in light of non-Western cultures.

---

[8]Charles Williams, *The Place of the Lion* (1931; repr., Oxford: Benedictions Classics, 2008).

In his 1945 play *The House of the Octopus,* Williams used a non-European setting to suggest how familiar dogmas might be reimagined in other cultures.[9] The play is set on a Pacific island during an invasion by the Satanic empire of P'o-l'u. When alien forces occupy the island, they demand the submission of the native people, who have recently become Christian converts. Terrified, one young woman, Alayu, denies her Christian faith and agrees to serve instead as "the lowest slave of P'ol'u," but even that apostasy does not save her life. This is where the theological issue becomes acute. The Western missionary priest, Anthony, is convinced that Alayu's last-minute denial of Christ has damned her eternally. The local people, however, understand that salvation has to be communal as well as individual:

> We in these isles
> Live in our people—no man's life his own—
> From birth and initiation. When our salvation
> Came to us, it showed us no new mode—
> Sir, dare you say so—of living to ourselves.
> The Church is not many but the life of many
> In ways of relation.[10]

That last assertion sounds profoundly African and contemporary. Wiser than Anthony, the island people know that death itself is a permeable barrier, and so is the seemingly rigid structure of time. As a native deacon asks, could not Alayu's original baptism have swallowed up her later sin?

> If God is outside Time, is it so certain
> That we know which moments of time count with him,
> And how?[11]

Alayu is saved *after* her death, through the support of her people and the intervention of the Holy Spirit. Formerly an apostate, the dead Alayu becomes a saint interceding for the living, and in turn redeems the missionary priest. It is a startling idea. Not only is this apostate girl in the image of God, but that likeness extends to the ability to transcend time.

---

[9]Charles Williams, *The House of the Octopus: A Play in Three Acts,* in *Collected Plays by Charles Williams,* ed. John Health-Stubbs (1945; repr., London: Oxford University Press, 1963). The rest of this section has been adapted from Philip Jenkins, "Charles Williams, Playwright," *Books & Culture* 19, no. 3 (2013): 22-24.

[10]Ibid.

[11]Ibid.

Although Williams was claiming no special knowledge of newer churches and missions, recent developments have given his work a contemporary feel. The ideas he was exploring in 1945 have become influential in rising churches of the global South, especially the emphasis on the power of ancestors and the communal nature of belief. In such settings, the ancient doctrine of the communion of saints, the chain binding living and dead, acquires a whole new relevance, and offers a new set of challenges for churches that thought these issues long since settled.

IMAGES OF THE WEST

We would not dare speak of Western Christianity as uniform, and we should certainly not do so for Southern faith. In each case, the broad geographical region comprehends a multiplicity of cultures, histories, denominations and faith traditions. Sicilian Catholics are not Scottish Calvinists any more than Brazilian Pentecostals are Congolese Catholics. In economic terms alone, China and South Korea differ radically from Ethiopia or Rwanda.

Having said that, newer churches do have certain common features that justify treating them together, not least the new character of the faith, at least as a mass popular movement. Christian faith is commonly a second- or third-generation phenomenon, which means that older images of divinity and authority remain firmly in the mental background. In most cases, Christianity also arrives bearing heavy foreign and specifically Western associations. Even in countries with ancient Christian roots—as in Latin America or Ethiopia—the forms of faith that have gained traction with rapidity generally follow American styles of belief and worship. God appears bearing a foreign image.

Throughout the history of mission, a stage always arises when native Christians arise to proclaim that God is authentically one of them. When mission is intimately associated with empire, such a declaration often has nationalistic and seditious overtones, and violence commonly results. That was, for instance, the case in black Africa from the late nineteenth century onward. Yet, that recognition, that appropriation, is a *sine qua non* for the spread of faith as a grassroots phenomenon. If African believers, for example, do not necessarily conceive of God as black, then at least they do not imagine him as a white colonialist. As one Catholic archbishop has remarked, "Our Namibian African people have accepted Christ. But this Christ walks too much among them in a European garment."[12] Inculturation must be carried deeper than just music, drums and clapping of hands.

Over the past half century, a vast theological literature has rooted the divine image in the cultures of the global South. Scholars like Kwame Bediako, John Mbiti and Byang Kato have sought to place the Bible and the Christian message in African or Asian traditions, to permit believers to understand God's word on their own terms.[13] However impressive this intellectual achievement, though, it is small in comparison to the enormous popular effort of translation and inculturation, the people's own work of bringing God's image home. And God's image here generally does not imply visual forms. While it is true that artists across Asia and Africa have portrayed Jesus and his disciples in native, local forms, with appropriate physical features and clothing, those depictions rarely achieve a mass audience. In the Protestant tradition particularly, it is through *words*, whether read or sung, that believers form their concept of the divine. When God spoke through Luther's German or King James's English, it was all too easy to imagine him in suitably European guise. It was during the mid-twentieth century, as imagery of the divine was being localized and nativized, that traditions of religious music and hymn writing began their astonishing upsurge across the global South. Across Africa especially, God-in-Christ spoke and sang in local languages.

Also during these years, Catholics began an enthusiastic and perhaps over-optimistic attempt to localize God's image through liturgical reform.[14] An ancient church maxim is *lex orandi, lex credendi*: the law of prayer is the law of belief; how we worship shows what we believe. Almost heroically, they tried to revise the liturgy to borrow traditional African customs and language, to reinforce the message that God's image was as much at home in Africa as in France or England. Where these efforts went wrong was in assuming that Africans would remain in their traditional cultural settings, rather than moving in vast numbers to new cities, where native languages gave way to English,

---

[12]Bishop Bonifatius Hauxiku of Namibia, quoted in Alan Cowell, "Vatican Ponders Church's Role in Africa," *New York Times*, May 1, 1994, www.nytimes.com/1994/05/01/world/vatican-ponders -church-s-role-in-africa.html.

[13]For example, Kwame Bediako, *Theology and Identity* (Oxford: Regnum Books, 1992); John S. Mbiti, *Bible and Theology in African Christianity* (Oxford: Oxford University Press, 1987); Byang Kato, *African Cultural Revolution and the Christian Faith* (Jos, Nigeria: Challenge Publications, 1976).

[14]Jenkins, *Next Christendom*, 140-44.

French and Portuguese. But although those liturgies now look dated and even artificial, the goals they sought have been widely achieved.

GOD IS IN THIS PLACE

The image of God in a person necessarily implies the image of God in a place. Nativizing means localizing. For Christians throughout history, the Holy Land was no mere piece of Levantine real estate but a spiritual terrain as real as the soil under one's feet. Seventeenth-century Scots Presbyterians spoke of their nation as stretching "from Dan to Beersheba." In his prophetic visions, William Blake saw in London an imagined Hebrew geography:

> The fields from Islington to Marybone,
> To Primrose Hill and Saint John's Wood:
> Were builded over with pillars of gold,
> And there Jerusalem's pillars stood.[15]

The song "Jerusalem," which decisively locates Christ's presence on English soil, has long been England's unofficial national anthem. A few years after Blake wrote, Joseph Smith gazed over the hills of upstate New York and saw the clashing kingdoms and armies of displaced Hebrew populations.[16]

Modern Christians, too, seek ancient parallels to their situations. In South and East Asia, theologians correctly note that the gospel originated in an— admittedly distant—corner of the same continent, and they seek distinctively Asian elements in the faith. Using an unfashionable ethnic classification, Korean Wonsuk Ma writes, "Asians should remember that the revealed words were given to Orientals (Hebrews for the Old Testament, and primarily Jews for the New Testament). Since God uses human thought mechanisms, His revelation assumes a close affinity to Oriental worldviews."[17] The task for theologians in the modern world is to strip away the Western accretions to recover a gospel in its natural social setting. Put another way, we are, in our specific culture and cultures, made in God's image.

---

[15]William Blake, "Jerusalem," in *The Poetical Works of William Blake,* ed. John Sampson (Oxford: Clarendon Press, 1905), 353. See my "Continental Drift: Lemuria and Other Lost Edens," *Books & Culture,* May/June 2005.

[16]Richard L. Bushman, *Joseph Smith and the Beginnings of Mormonism* (Champaign: University of Illinois Press, 1984).

[17]Wonsuk Mar, quoted in my *The New Faces of Christianity: Believing the Bible in the Global South* (New York: Oxford University Press, 2006), 48.

Few moderns try to plant their roots in Hebrew soil as enthusiastically as Africans. Vernacular prayers and liturgies come to be associated with new holy places, with shrines or martyrdom sites drawing on local traditions. The independent churches of southern Africa have been very active in spiritualizing the landscape through vast ritual gatherings and pilgrimages. One of the great shrines is Ekuphakameni, in South Africa, the "high and elevated place" chosen by prophet Isaiah Shembe. The site has acquired all the cultural resonance of the biblical Zion, and it features in the hymns of the group's Nazarite Baptist Church:

> I remember Ekuphakameni
> Where the springs are
> Springs of living water
> Lasting for ever.[18]

Even though the language is biblical, its associations are purely African. Ekuphakameni may, in time, become as great a Christian shrine as Lourdes or Walsingham.

THE IMAGE OF WOMAN

It is tempting, but misleading, to describe Christianity in the global South in Protestant or Pentecostal terms alone. In fact, the Roman Catholic Church led the way in globalization from the sixteenth century onward, and that church is by far the largest Christian presence on the African continent. The world's three largest Christian nations are the heavily Catholic Brazil, Mexico and the Philippines.

I stress this because of the rather different ways in which Catholics form their images of the divine, especially of feminine forms of divinity. Catholics protest at any suggestion that the Virgin Mary is portrayed as a deity or goddess, citing the ancient division between the worship due to God and the veneration appropriate for creatures, including the Virgin and saints. In practice, though, that distinction breaks down; it would take a subtle anthropologist to determine that the Virgin as imagined in Mexico or Cuba or the Philippines is not a divine being who receives full worship. Discussion of Christian images of divinity, and of humanity being formed in the divine

---

[18]Bengt Sundkler, *Zulu Zulu and Some Swazi Zionists* (Oxford: Oxford University Press, 1976), 198.

image, must take account of this ancient and widely established precedent. For centuries, Catholics have spoken of the faithful as spiritual children of the Virgin as much as creatures formed in the divine image.

If we grant that point, then Catholic popular faith deserves credit for taking the lead in inculturation. In Latin America and the Philippines, native peoples began from the sixteenth century to imagine the Virgin in local or native guise, commonly with dark non-European skin tones. Mexico's Virgin of Guadalupe and Cuba's Virgin of Caridad del Cobre are two examples. It is possible to take such depictions to indicate that Catholicism had only a tenuous hold on the native and African peoples, who carried on their ancient religions under a thin disguise. This may have been the case at first, but the cult of the Virgin in particular helped native people accept the full panoply of Catholic belief and ritual and also served to Christianize the slave populations. Ethnically as much as spiritually, she is *their* Virgin. Just as Guadalupe is usually seen in the company of the Indian Juan Diego, so images of La Caridad show her appearing to rescue black and mestizo sailors. In Ecuador, the equivalent of Guadalupe is the Virgin of El Quinche, who is so popular because her skin color is that of the local mestizos. Honduras is home to Our Lady of Suyapa, a tiny but enormously influential figure of the Virgin in dark wood, who is La Morenita—the Little Dark One. In Indian Guatemala and southern Mexico, the Black Christ of Esquipulas is another figure whose color repudiated white claims to racial dominion.

This process is not confined to Latin America. Older traditions shaped the rich devotional life of the Philippines in the celebration of the Santo Niño and the dark-skinned Jesus venerated as the Black Nazarene. Asian Catholics are equally inspired by the Virgin, who dominates the religious thought of the Philippines no less than that of Mexico. The Virgin has offered rescue and refuge during the times of persecution and massacre that have so often befallen the communities of China, Korea and Vietnam. Here, too, accounts of apparitions are central to popular piety; if Mexico has Guadalupe, Vietnam has its shrine at La Vang. In Asia, too, the Virgin has assumed the attributes of older female divinities, especially the beloved figure of the Buddhist Guanyin. At the South Indian shrine of Vailankanni, the Lourdes of the East, Mary's image as Mother of Good Health makes her a congenial sister to the great female deities of Hinduism.

IMAGE OF SPIRIT

God is imagined differently according to the needs of his followers. Relatively comfortable Europeans or North Americans imagined a God who could fulfill their spiritual needs, defined in limited terms and demarcated rigidly from the material realm. In this perception, God is too often a last refuge, a "God of the gaps."

That image is quite different from the all-encompassing concept of the divine that once prevailed in early modern times, and that is today the standard in much of the global South. In societies where the state mechanism is strictly limited and where economic structures seem of little use or relevance to ordinary people, the gaps where God is found expand to fill much of life. That is nowhere truer, perhaps, than in matters of healing, which define the concept of God for so many modern-day believers. In trinitarian terms, God is perceived as the all-permeating Holy Spirit, who brings health and wholeness to mind, body and spirit.

Steeped as they were in Jewish tradition, Jesus's first followers portrayed him as the great high priest. Modern Africans, in contrast, find more power and relevance in the vision of Jesus as great ancestor, an idea that also resonates in East Asia. This Jesus exercises for all people the same care and love that the ancestor of a specific tribe would for his or her descendants. Integrating the idea of ancestors into the liturgy has been a primary goal of newer African Catholic rites. In contemporary eucharistic prayers, God the Father is firmly placed in this ancestral context:

> O Father, Great Ancestor, we lack adequate words to thank you. . . . O Great Ancestor, who lives on the brilliant mountains . . . Our Father, father of our ancestors, we are gathered to praise you and to thank you with our sacrifice.[19]

Independent churches also stress Jesus' role as prophet and healer, as Great Physician. Although this approach is not so familiar in the modern West, this is one of many areas in which the independents are very much in tune with the Mediterranean Christianity of the earliest centuries. The more God is needed, the more powerful and dominant is his image, as a necessity of daily life.

---

[19]Jenkins, *Next Christendom*, 164.

IMAGES OF HOPE

Christians today thus preach a vision of human beings as the image of God through various means. To quote John Calvin, "We are not to look to what men in themselves deserve, but to attend to the image of God which exists in all, and to which we owe all honor and love."[20] The radicalism of that concept is difficult to convey to a society that has for centuries had some familiarity with the ideas of human equality derived from that notion. Nor, of course, have Christian societies ever pursued those implications to their logical conclusion. In modern times, though, that Christian theme has confronted societies with very different anthropologies, societies where large sections of the population are excluded from full humanity by various stigmas, commonly ascribed to ancestral evils or hereditary curses. The new faith brings a sense of human worth that is far more basic than concepts of political democracy.

As one example, we may look at India, where some two hundred million people, one-sixth of the population, are excluded from full human status: the untouchables, the so-called Dalits. This example reminds us of the many millions of others whose humanity is impaired by low caste or by tribal status. In modern times, Christianity has had a special appeal for such groups, who find in the faith a revolutionary new notion of human dignity. Theologian Sathianathan Clarke tells a story that indicates the aura that surrounds the Bible in the Indian context for this reason. He reports teaching sessions in southern India for Dalit activists. He writes that, to make a point,

> I delicately tossed the Bible on the ground in front of me saying that there was nothing intrinsic to the materiality of the Christian Scripture that made it holy and venerable. Two reactions ensued. First, the activist closest to me picked it up and moved it away from me. He later confessed that he was afraid that I might kick the Bible with my foot by mistake, which would have been a big insult to the whole Christian religion. [Many] also shared their fear that I was going to do something dreadful with the Bible. They asserted that for them the principles for universal human rights came from the Bible.[21]

---

[20]John Calvin, *Institutes of the Christian Religion*, trans. Henry Beveridge (Peabody, MA: Hendrickson, 2008), 453.

[21]Sathianathan Clarke, "Viewing the Bible Through the Eyes and Ears of Subalterns in India," quoted in my *New Faces of Christianity*, 36.

Even beyond India, it is among the very poor that the churches have won some of their greatest recent victories. In Latin America, Pentecostalism has appealed particularly to the poorest, including Brazil's black population and the Maya Indians of Central America. The traditionally disfranchised find, in the churches, a real potential for popular organization. That is above all true of women, without whom global South Christianity makes no sense whatever. In practical terms, churches provide a social network that would otherwise be lacking and help teach members the skills they need to survive in a rapidly developing society. As David Martin famously argued,[22] it is also in these churches that new Christians, suddenly aware of their fully human status, acquire for the first time the tongues of fire with which they can speak out publicly in a society that hitherto neither saw nor heard them.

THE STORM OF IMAGES

I have spoken optimistically of the impact of these understandings of the image of God in emerging Christian societies. In fairness, I should also note some of the dangers and distractions in new images. John Calvin famously warned that "man's mind is like a store of idolatry and superstition; so much so that if a man believes his own mind it is certain that he will forsake God and forge some idol in his own brain."[23] We are all expert idol-makers.

The worst idols are perhaps those of aggression and repression, when believers project their own most retrograde social values onto the divine, making God a terrifying being indeed. Some Christians have found justification for such idol-making in the Old Testament, cherry-picking the most threatening passages and reading them out of context. During the Rwandan genocide of 1994, preachers regularly cited the Old Testament's condemnations of Canaanites and (especially) Amalekites, with horrific effect.

The solution to such distortions lies in history. The best contribution that older churches can make to rising communities is in sharing their accumulated experiences and understandings. They can share their gallery of images of the divine, assessing those that have posed dangers and those that have proved most fruitful. Before beginning such an enterprise, those world-weary

---

[22]David Martin, *Pentecostalism: The World Their Parish* (Malden, MA: Blackwell, 2002).
[23]John Calvin, *Sermons on the Epistle to the Ephesians* (Carlisle, PA: Banner of Truth Trust, 1973), 179-80.

Euro-American churches need first to rediscover their own histories and understand those images. They need, above all, to appreciate which are honest
attempts to view the face of God and which are mere projections.

Let me conclude by applying a Dutch and Calvinist word, *Beeldenstorm*—
the storm of images—to our current situation. Mainstream historians often
understate the role of iconoclasm and image-breaking that was widespread in
Europe throughout the sixteenth century.[24] For anyone living at the time,
including educated elites, iconoclasm was not just an incidental breakdown
of law and order; it was the core of the whole movement, the necessary other
side of the coin to the growth of literacy. Those visual and symbolic representations of the Christian story had to decrease in order for the literate world of
the published Bible to increase. In cities such as Basel or Geneva, widespread
iconoclastic riots destroyed virtually all the material tokens of traditional
Catholic worship and devotion in the cathedral and the city's leading churches.
Even these German and Swiss manifestations were dwarfed by the devastating
Storm of Images (*Beeldenstorm*) that swept over the Netherlands in 1566. In
terms of the lived experience of people at the time, image-breaking was *the* key
component of the Reformation. In the rioting and mayhem, a millennium-old
religious order was visibly and comprehensively smashed.[25]

Is that not a central theme of Christian history? In every century, new
images are erected and then smashed, sometimes wantonly, sometimes as part
of what we can only call creative destruction. Christians surround themselves
with images of God and will continue to do so. But they will always live in ages
of transformation, of ever-new storms of images.

---

[24]The rest of this paragraph is taken from Philip Jenkins, "The Breaking of Images," *The Anxious Bench*
(blog), Patheos, July 14, 2014, www.patheos.com/blogs/anxiousbench/2014/07/the-breaking-of
-images.

[25]Carlos M. N. Eire, *War Against the Idols* (Cambridge: Cambridge University Press, 1989); Lee
Palmer Wanderl, *Voracious Idols and Violent Hands* (New York: Cambridge University Press,
1995); James Noyes, *The Politics of Iconoclasm* (London: I. B. Tauris, 2013).

Epilogue

Jeffrey W. Barbeau and Beth Felker Jones

Canon, culture, vision, witness. The image of God commands the attention of Christians in every age. To bear the image of God is to be marked as one of God's own. Thomas Merton, meditating on his own remarkable journey of faith, pondered the idea of image-bearing: "When a [person] is conceived, when a human nature comes into being as an individual, concrete, subsisting thing, a life, a person," he claimed, "then God's image is minted into the world."[1]

The Image of God in an Image Driven Age encourages continued reflection on the *imago Dei* in a time when narcissism reigns and new patterns of living are desperately needed. In a world where murders and mass shootings confound the public and bring grief to families, where environmental degradation stems from a misuse of power, where wealth and income inequality bolster class distinctions and imperil future generations, where complex questions of embodiment and sexuality continue to bewilder the churches no less than the public and where the toxic venom of racism paralyzes institutions no less than individuals, profound reflection, contemplative prayer and open conversations about human beings in the world are desperately needed. Churches, tempted to neglect action for confession alone, must lead the way forward through application of the Scriptures, active engagement with culture, the embodiment of ancient practices in everyday life and faithful witness to the communities in which we live, work and worship.

Through the recovery of freedom in Christ, "the image of the invisible God" (Col 1:15), individuals and communities may be returned to the divinely

---

[1]Thomas Merton, quoted in "Introduction," by Robert Giroux, in *The Seven Storey Mountain: An Autobiography of Faith*, 50th anniversary edition (Orlando: Harcourt, 1998), xiv.

intended path of growth in likeness to God. Setting aside the temptation to dominate, isolate or exclude, Christians can lead the nations through prophetic witness to the true nature of all creation. Love, once more, can fill "the whole expansion" of our souls.[2]

> O let me ne'er forget
> that though the wrong seems oft so strong,
> God is the ruler yet....
> The Lord is King; let the heavens ring!
> God reigns; let the earth be glad![3]

[2]John Wesley, "The Image of God," in *Works*, vol. 4, *Sermons* IV, ed. Albert C. Outler (Nashville: Abingdon, 1987), 294.
[3]Maltbie D. Babcock, "This Is My Father's World," in *The United Methodist Hymnal* (Nashville: United Methodist Publishing House, 1989), 144.

Contributors

Daniela C. Augustine is assistant professor of theological ethics at Lee University. Her latest book is *Pentecost, Hospitality and Transfiguration: Toward a Spirit-Inspired Vision of Social Transformation* (CPT, 2012).

Jeffrey W. Barbeau is associate professor of theology at Wheaton College. He is the author of *Sara Coleridge: Her Life and Thought* (Palgrave Macmillan, 2014) and *Coleridge, the Bible, and Religion* (Palgrave Macmillan, 2008). He has also edited, with Beth Felker Jones, *Spirit of God: Christian Renewal in the Community of Faith* (IVP Academic, 2015).

Jill Peláez Baumgaertner is professor of English and dean of humanities and theological studies at Wheaton College. Her poetry includes *What Cannot Be Fixed* (Cascade, 2014) and an edited volume on the image of God, *Imago Dei: Poems from Christianity and Literature* (Abilene Christian University Press, 2013).

Craig L. Blomberg is distinguished professor of New Testament at Denver Seminary. His many books include *Can We Still Believe the Bible? An Evangelical Engagement with Contemporary Questions* (Brazos Press, 2014) and *Christians in an Age of Wealth: A Biblical Theology of Stewardship* (Zondervan, 2013).

William A. Dyrness is dean emeritus and professor of theology and culture at Fuller Theological Seminary. Among his recent books are *Senses of Devotion: Interfaith Aesthetics in Buddhist and Muslim Communities* (Cascade, 2013) and *Poetic Theology: God and the Poetics of Everyday Life* (Eerdmans, 2011).

Brett Foster (1973–2015) was associate professor of English at Wheaton College. His collections of poetry include *Fall Run Road* (Finishing Line Press, 2012) and *The Garbage Eater* (Triquarterly Books/Northwestern University Press, 2011).

Timothy R. Gaines and **Shawna Songer Gaines** were recently co-lead pastors of Bakersfield First Church of the Nazarene, and Tim is now assistant professor of theology at Trevecca Nazarene University. Together they are the authors of *A Seat at the Table: A Generation Reimagining Its Place in the Church* (Beacon Hill, 2014) and *Kings and Presidents: Politics and the Kingdom of God* (Beacon Hill, 2015).

Philip Jenkins is distinguished professor of history at Baylor University. He is the author of many books, including *The Next Christendom: The Rise of Global Christianity* (third edition; Oxford University Press, 2011) and *The Great and Holy War: How World War I Became a Religious Crusade* (HarperOne, 2014).

Beth Felker Jones is associate professor of theology at Wheaton College. She is the author of several books, including *Practicing Christian Doctrine: An Introduction to Thinking and Living Theologically* (Baker, 2014) and *Faithful: A Theology of Sex* (Zondervan, 2015). She has also edited, with Jeffrey W. Barbeau, *Spirit of God: Christian Renewal in the Community of Faith* (IVP Academic, 2015).

Christina Bieber Lake is Clyde S. Kilby Professor of English at Wheaton College. She authored the prizewinning *Prophets of the Posthuman: American Literature, Biotechnology, and the Ethics of Personhood* (University of Notre Dame Press, 2013) and *The Incarnational Art of Flannery O'Connor* (Mercer University Press, 2005).

Catherine McDowell is assistant professor of Old Testament at Gordon-Conwell Theological Seminary Charlotte. She is the author of *The Image of God in the Garden of Eden* (Eisenbrauns, 2015).

Ian A. McFarland is Regius Professor of Divinity at the University of Cambridge. He is most recently the author of *From Nothing: A Theology of Creation* (Westminster John Knox, 2014) and *In Adam's Fall: A Meditation on the Christian Doctrine of Original Sin* (Wiley-Blackwell, 2010).

Matthew J. Milliner is assistant professor of art history at Wheaton College. He has published widely in scholarly journals such as *Theology Today* as well as popular print and online venues. He blogs at millinerd.com.

Joonhee Park is associate professor of art and communication at Wheaton College. He is an active filmmaker and media artist, and the films he produced for the Wheaton Theology Conference behind this volume are available online.

Soong-Chan Rah is Milton B. Engebretson Professor of Church Growth and Evangelism at North Park Theological Seminary. He has written books including *The Next Evangelicalism: Releasing the Church from Western Cultural Captivity* (InterVarsity Press, 2009) and *Many Colors: Cultural Intelligence for a Changing Church* (Moody, 2010).

Janet Soskice is professor of philosophical theology at the University of Cambridge and a fellow of Jesus College. Her written works include *The Kindness of God* (Oxford University Press, 2007) and *Sisters of Sinai: How Two Lady Adventurers Discovered the Lost Gospels* (Chatto/Knopf, 2009).

NAME AND SUBJECT INDEX

SCRIPTURE INDEX